P9-CBP-769

DISPATCHES FROM THE PACIFIC CENTURY

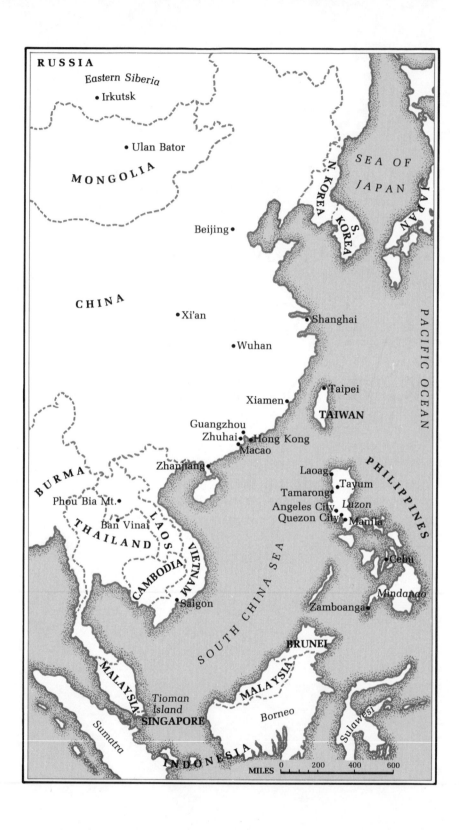

RUSSIA

Eastern Siberia

• Irkutsk

• Ulan Bator

MONGOLIA

N. KOREA

S. KOREA

SEA OF JAPAN

JAPAN

CHINA

Beijing •

• Xi'an

• Wuhan

Shanghai

PACIFIC OCEAN

Xiamen •

• Taipei

TAIWAN

Guangzhou

Zhuhai •

Hong Kong

Macao

Zhanjiang •

Laoag •

PHILIPPINES

BURMA

Tamarong •

• Tayum

Phou Bia Mt. •

Angeles City •

Luzon

Ban Vinai

Quezon City •

• Manila

THAILAND

LAOS

VIETNAM

• Cebu

CAMBODIA

• Saigon

SOUTH CHINA SEA

Mindanao

Zamboanga •

BRUNEI

MALAYSIA

MALAYSIA

Tioman Island

Borneo

Sulawesi

Sumatra

SINGAPORE

INDONESIA

MILES   0   200   400   600

DISPATCHES

FROM THE

PACIFIC

CENTURY

Frank Viviano

ADDISON-WESLEY PUBLISHING COMPANY

Reading, Massachusetts   Menlo Park, California   New York
Don Mills, Ontario   Wokingham, England   Amsterdam   Bonn
Sydney   Singapore   Tokyo   Madrid   San Juan
Paris   Seoul   Milan   Mexico City   Taipei

Library of Congress Cataloging-in-Publication Data

Viviano, Frank.
    Dispatches from the Pacific century / Frank Viviano.
       p.   cm.
    Includes index.
    ISBN 0-201-63290-X
    1. East Asia—Politics and government.   2. Asia, Southeastern—
Politics and government—1945-   I. Title.
DS518.1.V47   1993
959—dc20   92-34348
                                                  CIP

Jacket design by Diana Coe
Text design by Barbara Cohen Aronica
Set in 11-point Berkeley Old Style by Jackson Typesetting, Inc., Jackson, Michigan

1 2 3 4 5 6 7 8 9-MA-96959493
First printing, April 1993

For my grandfather, Frank P. Viviano,
who left Sicily at the age of twelve
to precede me down this road
and has always been my guide.

And for Sharon Silva,
who has shared so much of the journey.

CONTENTS

PROLOGUE: ADRIFT IN THE PACIFIC CENTURY   xi

PART ONE: THE SIGNAL

On the South China Sea   3
The Signal   7
Ferrymen's Rules   29
Cigarette Subdivision   38
The Drums of Ban Vinai   54

PART TWO: CITY OF THE MAIN CHANCE

City of the Main Chance   71
Election Week   80
The System   92
The Bones of Saint Francis   103
Sons   114
Democracy Spring   126

PART THREE: DUST IN THE WIND

June 1989   147
Mongolian Lambada   166
The Speech   181
The Governor   189
Fever in Siberia   200
After the Revolution   211
Dust in the Wind   228

EPILOGUE: THE LAST OF THE HMONG   244

ACKNOWLEDGMENTS   251

PROLOGUE:
ADRIFT IN THE
PACIFIC CENTURY

Pacific News Service was the smallest wire service in America, a shoestring operation with four desks and a shifting cast of eccentric stringers. But Sandy Close, the editor, had spent a decade in Asia and her news instincts on the Far East were the best in the business.

Sandy knew that the world she had covered as a reporter, counting bombers over the Plain of Jars and watching China from across the sealed border in Hong Kong, was vanishing. Neither she nor anyone else knew what might replace it. The phrase "Pacific Century" hadn't entered the jargon yet. There was just Sandy's certainty that everything was up for grabs—that a powerful story was waiting to be written.

On a Monday morning in April 1979, she asked me to go to Asia. I had been a freelancer in Europe and Latin America, a medical writer in Michigan and a magazine editor in San Francisco. But I had never been west of California before, not even to Hawaii, and less than a year had passed since I'd begun working as a part-time copy editor and writer for the news service. It was a big chance and a bigger risk.

When I pointed that out, Sandy just said she had a hunch. "Maybe I'm wrong, maybe you'll be back in a week," she said. "Asia possesses people or it repels them. Either you'll be at this desk again before spring—or you'll find what I think you'll find, and you'll never want to come back."

That was about all there was to the assignment: a hunch and a check for a couple thousand dollars to get under way. I used $500 to buy the ticket in Chinatown, at a cut-rate travel agency that booked suspiciously cheap trips to the Far East. The plane turned out to be a shuttle that carried Indochinese refugees to the West Coast; it had flown back to the Orient empty until the Chinatown agency cracked a deal with the airline. There were 450 seats packed into the passenger cabin, about half again as many as normal. Signs posted on the bulkheads in Vietnamese, Mandarin, Lao, and Khmer explained the purpose of the air sickness bags. We made five stops before reaching Singapore on a torrid equatorial morning, thirty-six cramped hours after departure from San Francisco International.

The return ticket was good until February 1980. It expired the day I applied for my first Chinese visa in Hong Kong. A dozen years and roughly a million miles later, I was still on the road.

Everywhere on that journey, from the Sulu Sea to the Russian Far East, from the last throes of the Cultural Revolution in China to the collapse of communism in Mongolia, I found a mirror: a world that teemed with an immense cast of fellow wanderers. A world of people adrift, caught somewhere between the waning past and a vague future, between city and country, between cultures East and West.

There were two stories, always, in the dawn of the Pacific Century. One was the quantified balance sheet of high technology, capital flows, gross national products, and Japanese-American rivalry. It was the Pacific viewed from the outside, where all vectors soared and confidence seemed universal. The Pacific of the economic boom. The Pacific of trade figures and growth rates.

The second story could be seen only from the inside, where the currents of change were anything but certain and the characteristic experience was an absence of moorings.

In the deluge of business literature spawned by the boom, it often seemed the Pacific Century held no human beings—that it was a depopulated laboratory of economic progress, as lifeless and clinical as a computer manual. But from the inside, it was an epic drama of human strengths and foibles, sometimes deeply tragic and other times marvelously comic.

The Pacific Century was the *bui doi*—"dust in the wind"—orphaned Southeast Asian teenagers who roamed an archipelago of cheap California motels, surviving on car heists and gas station stickups. It was Zhuhai, the Chinese Las Vegas, a honky-tonk resort town on the Pearl Delta for the newly affluent of the People's Republic. It was Mike Chen the jockstrap king, the world's largest producer of athletic supporters, whose meteoric rise from Taiwanese cabbage farmer to head of a global business empire raised moral dilemmas he never bargained on.

The Pacific Century was a suburb of Manila where the streets were named for American cigarette brands, the architecture was Los Angeles baroque, and the electricity, water, and gas were purloined from the municipal utilities system through an ingenious network of illegal shunts and taps. It was Irkutsk, Siberia, in the summer the Soviet Union fell apart, jammed with fast-buck artists from a dozen nations and reeling with consumer fever.

The Pacific Century was the Hmong, a Stone Age tribe from the Golden Triangle, who fought their way through a four-year military siege in Laos and across a mysterious American continent to a promised land in California. It was Father Victor López, a Manila priest struggling to keep afloat in the violent political riptides of the Philippines. It was Liang Baihua, a daughter of Shanghai's clandestine underground, on her last morning in China.

The Pacific I came to know, in a dozen years on its roads and sea-lanes, was far more than a business arena. It was a universe in cataclysmic transition, where former Red Guards became Beijing commodities traders, new cities exploded into existence in a matter of months, and the familiar, almost everywhere, was yielding to a road without maps.

This drama is related in three broad acts. The tales in Part One concern the powerful signals—the tom-tom beat of modernism—that emanated from newly industrialized East Asian cities in the mid-1970s and early 1980s to ignite the Pacific upheaval.

These years marked the final passage of the war in Indochina, played out in an immense wave of refugees that swamped Southeast Asia. But they also marked a beginning, a headlong plunge into the unknown. China repudiated the Cultural Revolution and took its first tentative steps into the global economy. Singapore shook off the last vestiges of British colonialism, in the process leaving the British standard of living in the dust. The old Asia, rooted in traditions that have scarcely changed in fifteen hundred years, was coming apart.

Everywhere there was motion, flux, a swarm of new ideas and new people to explain them. In a part of the world that had embraced a collective sense of society and culture since long before Mao Zedong, individuals were emerging, proclaiming themselves, separating from the mass.

Part Two is the moment of the yea-sayers: the crumbling of the walls between China and Hong Kong, China and Taiwan; the breathtaking events on Manila's Epifanio de los Santos Avenue in 1986 that unseated Ferdinand Marcos and made a president of a self-described housewife; the drunken euphoria of a sudden prosperity that seemed to sweep aside everything in its path in the second half of the 1980s.

It was a moment of profound confidence for small societies, a moment in which Taiwan, with less than twenty million people, could become a ranking industrial power and the city of Hong Kong set out to buy the People's Republic of China. It was the moment of the gambler, the day of the main chance. Deals were being made everywhere. The pontificators said the future was no longer being molded on the Atlantic seaboard but in the Pacific, where a new conglomerate culture, neither Western nor Eastern, was bursting into view.

In Part Three, which opens with the events that brought China to the brink of civil war in 1989, ambiguity descends on the stage. A price was to be paid for too much change, too fast. The 1990s have been about the violence of second thoughts.

Yet the signals of upheaval are still radiating at a dizzying rate, sending their ripples farther into the remote corners of East Asia than anyone imagined possible when the first days of the Pacific Century dawned: to the distant frontiers of China, to Russian Siberia and the high plains of Mongolia.

Entire nations have been uprooted in this revolution, their people moved thousands of miles and resettled. Centuries have been leaped in months. Governments have crumbled. Ideologies have evaporated. Part Three is about dislocation—about the meaning of exile—as much as it is about the meaning of change.

Dispatches from the Pacific Century is one American reporter's account of a tumultuous journey: the life of a wandering observer whose home is an endless succession of hotels, ships, and passenger trains, on the voyage that carried Asia from the preindustrial past to the eve of the twenty-first century.

Paris
August 14, 1992

DISPATCHES FROM THE PACIFIC CENTURY

PART ONE

The
Signal

ON THE SOUTH CHINA SEA

Two hours out of Hong Kong in the police launch, we sighted the boat, pitching around the windward corner of an uninhabited island. As we closed the distance at full throttle, a jumble of blurred shapes and colors aft of the single mast came into focus. People crammed every square foot of the deck, squatting on their haunches shoulder to shoulder. I made a rough count as the launch slowed to draw alongside: fifty men, thirty women, twenty children.

The vessel was wooden and shallow-keeled, about sixty feet long—a coastal fishing sloop, not at all suitable for crossing the South China Sea in the typhoon-plagued autumn of 1979. There were no rails, no cabin, just the open deck and a small wheelhouse near the stern. It seemed impossible that so many people could fit on board.

A gaunt, bare-chested man jumped atop the hatch of the tiny wheelhouse, waving his arms and yelling over the swells in fractured Cantonese. His slacks were torn below one hip into ribbons of khaki that slapped and furled around a spindle of a leg.

"I am the captain," he shouted twice. "We are three weeks on sea. Three weeks."

He was visibly relieved when we said we'd take him in tow. The boat looked ready to break apart; it wouldn't have lasted more than another few days. The police crew secured a line to the bow, then dropped a rope ladder over the side. I joined the boarding party, three Hong Kong Maritime Patrol officers and a Vietnamese interpreter.

The refugee captain was extremely talkative, almost manic, now that the ordeal was over. He laughed at inappropriate moments in the police interview. Later, Inspector Gin told me he was afraid the man had gone mad, that he would lose control completely and they would have to put handcuffs on him. But he calmed down, except for the strange laughter.

They were from the north of Vietnam, the captain said, and had set sail from Haiphong on an overcast night after bribing the port sentries. There had been all of the usual problems: pirates, food, the weather. Five people were lost overboard when the boat ran into heavy seas east of Hainan Island.

"No possibility of finding them. China. No possibility."

He laughed when he said this, and also when he spoke of the Thai pirates, who had raped a few of the younger women while everyone watched, and quickly turned up a few gold coins and bracelets that had been shoved under loose deck planks when their speedboat broke the western horizon. The boat people expected that. But at least the Thais had left without killing anybody. Inspector Gin told me it was often worse when the refugees had no gold at all. Sometimes the pirates would sink a boat out of spite for wasting their time.

Gold didn't come easily to these voyagers. They were part of the second wave of boat people, poor farmers and fishermen. They didn't have much gold because they didn't have much of anything. The war against the Americans, preceded by the war against the French and followed by the war against the Khmer Rouge, had bankrupted the Vietnamese economy, destroyed the fields, poisoned the rivers.

The first wave had been mostly ethnic Chinese from the south, from Cholon, the big Chinatown of Saigon. They'd had money hidden away, American dollars and South African Kruggerrands and jewelry, since the city fell to the North Vietnamese army in 1975. So when relations with China soured and it wasn't safe to be Chinese in Vietnam anymore, they were prepared. Some of the early ones carried enough gold to open grocery stores and restaurants in San Francisco and Orange County and in the Thirteenth Arrondissement Chinatown of Paris.

But the pirates got wind of this from their own immigrant relatives in California and France, and soon virtually every small vessel that made a midnight departure from a Vietnamese harbor was met by heavily armed Thai speedboats an hour or two after it cleared Vietnam's territorial waters.

We weren't far from Hong Kong now, although the city was still hidden by the mountainous green bulk of Lantau Island. I went out on deck, leaving Inspector Gin to his interrogation of the captain.

The boat moved forward with a jerking motion as the line to the police launch slacked and tightened in the swell.

On the first boats you could always find somebody who spoke English: a secretary from one of the American typing pools in Saigon, or maybe a South Vietnamese officer who'd done liaison with Army Intelligence in the Parrot's Beak or the central highlands. But on these northern boats, Vietnamese was usually the only language, and the police interpreter was busy in the wheelhouse. There wasn't much I could do but smile reassuringly and make hand gestures, trying to establish some kind of connection.

We had "hello," "okay," and the thumbs-up sign in common.

When I said "American" the people who heard me laughed a bit like the captain had, as though it was a terribly funny joke. Just a few years before, B-52s had been dropping napalm on them. It was certain from their ages that when the bombers passed overhead most of the men on this vessel had been North Vietnamese regulars, padding down the Ho Chi Minh Trail on their way to ambush U.S. marines.

I edged back against the wheelhouse and aimed my camera at them. A cheer went up.

"Hello. Okay."

More laughter.

They were in a very thumbs-up mood. When I had the photographs developed in Kowloon, you'd have thought I'd taken snapshots at a holiday outing, except for the dilapidation of the boat and the shredded clothing. Everybody smiled. Two young men in their late teens mugged for the camera, adopting the pose of a couple of affable tough guys. Mothers held their babies up in the air, wanting them to be in my pictures. They thought they'd made it.

The mood was contagious, and despite myself I started grinning mindlessly. But there was a catch in my throat all the while, because I knew what these people faced in a few hours. They were headed for the camp at Sham Shui Po, where they would be stowed away in warehouses that had been divided into thousands of thirty-square-foot cubicles, one for every four people, until somebody, somewhere, agreed to sponsor them. Only the lucky ones—very few among these northerners—had relatives in America or Europe who would sign for them.

Two days earlier I had spent a morning at Sham Shui Po. A short, agitated man of sixty or so, dressed in the saffron robes of a Buddhist monk, had grabbed me by the arm as I was walking through one of the warehouses. The Hong Kong government press officer glanced warily at the policeman who accompanied us but didn't intervene.

The monk was very bitter. He'd been in the camp for four years. No one wanted him. The Americans said they had information proving he had participated in demonstrations against the government of South Vietnamese president Ngo Dinh Diem in the early 1960s. The whole world knew that the CIA had gotten rid of Diem, the monk said. Washington had arranged for him to be assassinated. How could the Americans hold it against him that he too had been against Diem? I hadn't known what to say.

I was thinking about the monk, and about the prospects of the men on this boat who were of an age to have shouldered a gun in the war, when the crowd abruptly fell hushed. Absolutely silent. Everyone was staring past me, beyond the wheelhouse, at the northern horizon.

We had just left the channel buoys at Cheung Chau Island in our wake. Suddenly, Hong Kong rose before us in vertiginous splendor, a dazzling forest of skyscrapers climbing the island ridges and blanketing the Kowloon Peninsula in concrete, glass, and polished steel. The harbor swarmed with the freighters of five continents, hundreds of ships jockeying frantically for position in the busiest anchorage on earth.

Nothing these people had ever seen or heard could have prepared them for this sight. They were literally dumbfounded.

The police launch slowed at the harbor entrance, then angled toward the Sham Shui Po wharf. The wooden boat was shoved against the pilings, where it would be tied up until a tug could be freed to tow it to the scrap yard. Eight policemen herded the refugees into a holding area surrounded by barbed wire, where they would wait to be trucked to the camp.

They were still gathered there in shocked silence, staring across the harbor, when I flagged a taxi and returned to my hotel.

SINGAPORE PACES EAST ASIAN BOOM

SINGAPORE (August 9, 1980) — In a speech marking his nation's 15th independence celebrations, Prime Minister Lee Kuan Yew announced that Singapore's economy grew at a record annual rate of 14.4 percent over the first six months of 1980.

This is the fourth consecutive year of double-digit growth for the prosperous Southeast Asian city-state. The sizzling economy has seen Singaporean wages, which are set by the government, reach an average of nearly $3,000 per year, second only to Japan in Asia.

Lee said the wage hike next year would be 20 percent if the growth rate continued at its present pace.

Singapore's boom has been echoed in nearby Malaysia, where the economic growth rate hit 7.2 percent in 1979. Overall, the East Asian economies have dramatically outpaced the rest of the world in recent years, spurring talk of a powerful new trade bloc.

"For the past few centuries, the focus of all that mattered has been the Atlantic region," said Graham Wilde, editor of the Hong Kong–based *Asian Banking*. "But what we're seeing in these numbers is the dawn of an age that will belong to Asia and the Pacific."

THE SIGNAL

Mersing was an unlikely gateway to paradise. Yellowed newspaper pages blew down its streets in the monsoon wind. The harbor was nothing more than a muddy channel scooped out of a river mouth eighty miles north of Singapore on the east coast of Malaysia, with a clutter of wooden fishing vessels nosed into its banks. Most of the boats had the long hand-planed hulls that Joseph Conrad noted a century ago on the shores of the South China Sea; the riverfront couldn't have looked very different when he passed through gathering the material that he would one day refashion as *Lord Jim*. The skies hung low with ponderous gray clouds, draining color from the scene and making me wonder whether this was the moment to embark for an island fifty miles out to sea.

"Nonsense," Nuri said. "Is no time like the present."

Nuri Rahman was (among other things) a transportation agent of sorts—a tout, more precisely—who sold passages up the river, down the Malay Peninsula, and over the South China Sea to the Borneo coast. He had walked up within minutes of my arrival at the riverbank and introduced himself.

"Please sir, what is your liking. I can arrange all."

He had a business card, which he presented with a theatrical flourish when I told him where I was headed. On one side it identified him as NURI RAHMAN, TRAVEL COORDINATOR. On the other it read

> NURI RAHMAN, PROPRIETOR
> NURI'S VACATION COTTAGES
> PULAU TIOMAN
> MERSING, MALAYSIA

The island was his birthplace, he said. "If you want to stay in Tioman, it is done. Nuri can arrange all."

He was a puffy, bandy-legged man somewhere on the far side of fifty, but I had a difficult time keeping up with him as he scrambled along the muddy riverbank asking the proprietors of Mersing's fleet if there were any departures imminent for Tioman. Finally, after about an hour, he jumped aboard a small open boat bobbing uncertainly in the waning tide and motioned for me to join him. There wasn't any time to think, much less barter. If the boat was to clear the Mersing sandbar, we'd have to put off immediately, before the channel grew too shallow.

"Over here, make comfortable," Nuri said, pointing at a pile of cargo haphazardly jumbled on the deck. "Captain say leaving now, now, now."

I settled as best I could into a stack of canvas bags packed hard with flour, and handed over twenty *ringgit*—about $8—to my shipping agent and soon-to-be hotelier. It covered the cost of the journey and the first night's accommodations.

"Just say 'Nuri send,'" he instructed, and jumped out of the vessel with a parting wave. "Everybody in Tioman know Nuri. No problem, no problem."

My passage was on a nameless mango boat that plied the Tioman trade twice weekly, powered by an ancient Evinrude outboard motor.

It carried out loads of pantry staples, canned vegetables, corned beef, butane cylinders, and radio batteries and returned with sacks of the juicy yellow fruit that was Tioman's only source of income.

The toothless old captain and his crew of one, a ten-year-old boy, addressed me in Bahasa, the language of Malaysia. I exhausted my Bahasa vocabulary after the usual exchanges celebrating the cloudy morning, praising each other's country, and enumerating our respective achievements in fathering children. The captain won handily, four sons and three daughters to my none. The crew was his nineteenth grandchild. I congratulated him, then we fell into a mutual silence that prevailed for the remainder of the voyage.

It was a near thing clearing the sandspits that encircled the river mouth in a great frothy arc of surf. The mango boat was flung almost entirely out of the water a few times, coming back down into the waves with such crashing force that I thought my spine would crack against the waterproof tarp the boy had stretched over the bags of flour while we were still in the river.

When the heavens parted, as the captain had evidently known they would, gargantuan buckets of rain sloshed around the heaving deck and came close to washing me overboard. I skated off the tarp on my backside, turned a 180° twist as we crested a wave, and banged up headfirst against the scuppers. The captain saved the day, seizing my left leg with a bony hand as I rocketed past the tiller on my return trip. He had the grip of a New York stevedore twice his size, and left purple bruises on my ankle that were still faintly visible after three months had passed.

Fifteen minutes after the rains began, according to equatorial form, the sky had cleared and we were steaming dry. But the waves let up only modestly, even after the sandbar was far in our wake, and the next six hours were a bouncing, stomach-wrenching ordeal. I shuddered at the thought of sailing back to the peninsula the same way.

The captain too found the seas rougher than his liking. He couldn't risk tying his boat up at Tioman's single precarious wharf, which jutted into a broad bay that received the full brunt of north-west swells like these; he'd have to spend the night anchored in the protection of the island's lee. With any luck, the morning would be calmer. But first he intended to put me ashore.

I learned all this after the fact, when the island itself suddenly popped out of a fogbank that sat directly before us, and the captain pointed the boat's nose straight into what looked like the flank of a very big mountain. It climbed out of the sea in a sheer green wall of jungle vines and seabird nests. He gestured to the south, where the jetty was, and made a rapid up-and-down motion with his hand that told the story.

"We stay. You go," he said in a stripped-down Bahasa he hoped I'd understand.

But just where was it that I was going?

We closed with the mountain, which now filled the entire foreground of our line of sight and hung over us, immense and menacing. Although I couldn't understand why, it somehow looked familiar, like the vestiges of a half-forgotten dream.

I was peering up at its craggy brow, which was wreathed in a sheet of mist, when the boat started bucking even harder. We'd reached a reef line, a coral cliff that was as flat as the side of a building on its seaward face and was marked by an ominous band of breaking waves. The captain, who was one talented helmsman, had edged the bow right up against it and was now signaling for me to disembark. Quickly. I stepped onto the reef, reached for my duffel bag, and lofted it to my shoulder.

The mango boat was already puttering back into the safety of the deep when I looked around to say goodbye. The old man nodded once over his tiller and the boy yelled *"Salamat jalan"*—"Have a good walk." Then I crossed the reef and gingerly put a foot into the dead-calm lagoon that separated me from the shore by a few hundred yards. The water was as tepid as a bath and only four feet deep. It would have been an easy wade if the bottom hadn't been covered with sea urchins.

Nuri was on the beach, waiting, when I crawled up on my hands and knees. My feet were a tangle of black urchin spines and bloody, lacerated flesh. After the first few horrifying steps on the lagoon bottom, I'd rolled over on my back and paddled toward the shore with one flailing arm, while executing furious leg-kicks and trying to hold the duffel bag atop my stomach with the other arm. The strategy nearly drowned me and was miserably unsuccessful in keeping the bag dry.

"Aha! Surprise! Welcome to Nuri's Vacation Cottages," he said, trying not to stare at my feet.

I pulled out the spines while my host toted the waterlogged bag up to a small wooden shack beyond the top of the beach, then limped after him. It would be a week before I was able to put on a pair of shoes.

Nuri explained that he had come out to the island two hours earlier, in a passenger launch that left Mersing for the island once a day. He planned to return on it at five.

"If you wait until noon, you can take also. But you in hurry."

The existence of this launch hadn't been mentioned in our search for transport. I took a deep breath and swore at him under it.

"Anyway," he added, "tourists like mango boat."

He showed me around the shack, which appeared to be the totality of Nuri's Vacation Cottages. It sat at the head of an otherwise deserted cove that opened to the lagoon, alongside a small creek over which a primitive rope bridge swung. The building itself was a bleached wooden structure that enclosed a single small room. It was almost entirely filled by its sole piece of furniture—a straw mattress raised above the plank floor on a platform. A mosquito net was providentially suspended above the bed; the creek was certain to be thick with insects when night fell.

Out back, under a lean-to, Nuri had equipped a modest kitchen: There was a frying pan, a butane burner, a stockpot, basic cutlery, and most remarkable of all, a full set of the same flowered Melmac plastic dishes that my mother once won in a Detroit supermarket raffle in 1959. In front a simple porch offered a spectacular vista of coconut-fringed beach, lagoon, and open sea beyond.

The mountain shot up into the sky about half a mile to the rear of the cottage. At this distance, in the lengthening shadows of early evening, it had taken on the texture of velvet and a rich emerald hue. The peak was scalloped into two shaggy wings across its western exposure, which made it appear to be embracing the cove. Mist still swirled around the crown.

"Nice spot, Nuri," I said.

"Yes, Bali Hai," he answered.

He meant it literally. Tioman, I later learned, was the island where the Bali Hai sequences in the film version of James Michener's *South Pacific* had been shot in 1958. The remains of the sets and camera towers had long since vanished, crumbled from the onslaught of tropical mildew and equatorial storms, and the only trace of the episode that remained was a vague memory among islanders of a moment when Tioman had, however briefly, been a direct appendage of Hollywood—and a souvenir Nuri had framed and hung on the cottage wall: a print of an A-frame Swiss chalet in an Alpine meadow left behind by some homesick cast member or camera grip. For Nuri, it was a picture of the future. Tioman's future. His future.

The idea wasn't as crazy as it first seemed. In fact, it had a touch of genius to it. What preoccupied him in the print was the chalet, its perfect simplicity. For twenty years he had been staring at it, and for twenty years the same notion had come to him, over and over.

"Is something I can make. Anybody can make," he said.

He was right, of course. The A-frame was the epitome of accessible architecture, just two vertical plywood surfaces joined at the top to form a roof and sides, with plywood facing hammered in to complete the other two sides. By contrast, the shack on the cove was hopelessly complicated, a jigsaw puzzle of corner joints, porch columns, and roof beams that required a trained carpenter to execute.

But *anybody* could build an A-frame, and Nuri aimed to do just that. He planned to build A-frames all over Tioman, all over the island that Hollywood itself had officially labeled a genuine, marketable paradise during Tioman's brief taste of fame. The business card was the herald: NURI RAHMAN, PROPRIETOR. NURI'S VACATION COTTAGES. That was the vision: He would A-frame Bali Hai.

The shack, which had been here for years, generated seed money. The five or six dollars Nuri made from each guest after he paid the mango boat captain went straight into the bank, into the A-frame fund. The bank account alone made Nuri someone special on Tioman, someone, as he had put it, whom everyone knew. He was the island's only, and automatically its foremost, native capitalist.

There aren't many places on earth where life is still lived as it was before the invention of money. Tioman, when I limped ashore there, was one of those places. Jean-Jacques Rousseau, that celebrant of the endearingly savage, would have considered it heaven; Adam Smith, with his capital preoccupations, would have taken it for a barbarous hell. In the idle self-indulgence of my days there, I was decidedly inclined toward the Rousseau view (albeit only because a sum of money, however small, had made it possible for me to enjoy the illusion).

When the sun reached a certain point above the cottage and shone onto my bed through a hole in the roof, I'd get up, put on a snorkel mask, hobble down to the lagoon on those tender feet, and dive right in. Each day started with a slow float out to the reef, peering down through the utterly transparent water at the sea urchins—ebony starbursts of needle-thin spine, as beautiful as they were diabolical—and the occasional giant clam gaping up at me from the sand. At the far end of the lagoon were waving beds of anemone in every conceivable color and flotillas of striped angel fish darting through the turrets of purple and yellow coral castles. Every now and then a leopard shark would make a lazy, inoffensive pass at me, more in curious courtship than hunger.

Some days I did this for five or six hours, finally emerging from the lagoon with my skin shriveled from water absorption and my eyes bloodshot from gawking. When night fell, the immense silence was broken only by the sound of waves lapping on the reef and the foraging of huge land crabs, some of them a foot or more across at the carapace, that invaded my garbage in search of tasty scraps and pointed their fat claws at me in unsubtle warning if I dared interrupt. Under my mosquito net I slept naked as a baby, cooled by the lagoon's breezes and blissfully safe from the intermittent squadrons of nocturnal insects that longed for my skin.

Local business on the island, dating back into the unrecorded past, was conducted in two huts attached to a couple of the traditional stilted Malay houses where most Tioman people still lived. The huts, which were never staffed for more than an hour a day and sometimes went unoccupied for days on end, traded the captain's canned goods, butane, and cigarettes for the mangoes he hauled back to Mersing.

But you couldn't call such bartering capitalism, not in any sense that would have pleased Adam Smith. The mangoes grew wild on

Tioman; no one seemed to claim them as private property. When I asked Nuri's nephew how I could buy butane, since ringgit never changed hands at the huts, he was dumbfounded by the question.

"Just pick mango," he said, looking at me as though I was an idiot.

The same nephew, a teenager named Ali, would paddle an outrigger a few yards past the reef line each afternoon and bring me back a fish for supper. If I was napping when he arrived, he would cook it himself. The only thing he would accept in exchange was a daily thirty-minute lesson in English. Even teenagers broke the mold on Tioman.

It was paradise. It was Bali Hai.

Two things happened, in the 1970s, that slowly edged Nuri Rahman away from the idyll, away from Jean-Jacques Rousseau, and toward the machinations of Adam Smith. The first and most important was Singapore.

From the salon of a Pacific & Orient steamer, the city of Singapore must have been a comforting sight to Edwardian British civil servants fresh out of Oxford and Cambridge, after the rolling decks and numbing vistas of Sumatran swamp afforded by the seven-hundred-mile passage down the Strait of Malacca. It mattered less what the company clerks and rubber plantation foremen in second class might feel. As for the steerage, where Tamil cane workers and Straits Chinese coolies faced a last bout of seasickness in the teeth of the Northeast Monsoon, opinions there counted not at all.

Set on a lowland island one degree above the equator, Singapore alternately bakes and steams from 85° temperatures and abrupt, enormous downpours like the one that nearly sent me overboard off Mersing; it has been known to rain as much as nineteen inches in a single twenty-four-hour period. But the comforting part, to English colonial officials in the early years of this century, was that it looked for all the world like Greenwich. As the P & O edged into Empire Dock, European newcomers could see the contours of their expatriation mapped out in a familiar institutional topography: the Anglican spire of St. Andrew's Cathedral rising above the Cricket Club veranda to punctuate a primly British skyline that stretched from Cavendish Bridge and Parliament House to the Raffles Hotel.

Seven decades later I paid my own first visit to Singapore, landing at Paya Labar Airport on a flight from New Delhi. It was raining, as advertised, at a volume that seemed more appropriate to a tidal wave. Negotiating the ten yards from the terminal to the taxi stand produced the same result as diving fully clad into a swimming pool. Between the walls of water marching forward outside the cab and the rivers running off my soaked head and clothes, I could barely make out the roadside.

Then, as suddenly as it had doubtless arrived, the torrent departed, the clouds vanished in the direction of Java, and my taxi was hurtling along a boulevard framed by sunstruck rows of jacaranda, coconut palm, and balconied high-rise apartment buildings. Off in the distance, forests of cranes grew denser and denser as they converged on the downtown vestiges of Edwardian Singapore, where a commercial complex larger than Rockefeller Center was rising from the harbor shore.

Empire Dock, Cavendish Bridge, St. Andrew's, Raffles, Parliament House, the Cricket Club: They were all still there, drying out in the blazing sun as the taxi turned toward my hotel on the right bank of the Singapore River. But they were now little more than quaint counterpoints in a landscape that stunned the newcomer even more thoroughly than it had once comforted imperial bureaucrats.

Before me stretched what looked like a vast tropical golf course, planted strategically with ranks of thirty-story towers and wreathed in an astonishing necklace of flowered gardens and parks. But more astonishing yet was the fact that here, in the sweltering climes of Malthusian, equatorial Asia, was a city without visible evidence of poverty. No slums. No unemployment to speak of. No hungry children shining shoes in the streets. It was, to all appearances, the dream that had both mesmerized and eluded the giants of the postwar independence movements—the future that was never realized by Nasser, Kenyatta, Nehru, or Ho Chi Minh.

More to the point, it had been forged not by European expatriates—they had virtually abandoned Singapore in the dismal 1950s, left its wharves to rot when it seemed ready to become another Cairo

or Calcutta—but by the progeny of those very coolies and cane workers who once filled the steerage holds on the Malacca Strait.

It was a miracle, Singapore, an Asian-made miracle. It was also
the most despised city in the Far East.

The miracle—and the spite—were to a remarkable degree the work
of one man. Virtually every facet of the modern Republic of Singapore
was molded to the personal blueprint of Lee Kuan Yew, the redoubt-
able and single-minded politician who had been its only prime
minister since independence. Like the colonial world he was born
to in 1923, Lee was an encyclopedia of cultural contradictions: a
Chinese who spoke no Chinese, raised in an Asian city that was
founded and run by Europeans and even designed to their architectural tastes. Thanks to a grandfather who had arrived in Singapore
as a coolie and followed his trading instincts to a fortune, he had
gone to Cambridge for legal training in the 1940s and finished
first in his class. Virtually nobody in Singapore or Britain even
knew his Chinese name then; he was Harry Lee, a sharp young
attorney who might have made a fortune of his own in the city of
London.

Instead Lee returned to Asia and, with a systematic intensity that
was to become his trademark, set about to eliminate Singapore's—
and his own—contradictions. Harry Lee mastered Malay, Mandarin,
and two other Chinese dialects, emerging as Lee Kuan Yew, a brilliant
political firebrand and union organizer who browbeat Whitehall into
freeing the island from its imperial stranglehold and went on to win
its first election in a landslide. Lee took the vote as a personal mandate, not only to govern Singapore but also to make his People's
Action Party—the "PAP"—its indispensable embodiment, a political
machine that operated with ruthless efficiency. As a new Singapore
rose over the roofs and steeples of the colonial past, new apartments
were built and allotted by PAP housing commissions. New jobs were
generated by PAP employment policies that attracted manufacturing
investment from dozens of multinational corporations. New Singaporeans were diapered and educated by PAP day-care centers and
PAP-endowed schools.

More than 75 percent of the population was, like Lee, Chinese:

certainly enough to govern with in a racially defined party, the Southeast Asian norm. But Lee wanted more than that; 75 percent of the electorate wasn't enough for his ambitions, and unlike his peers in nearby Malaysia and Indonesia, he recognized that Southeast Asia was a tinderbox of racial hostilities that separate political parties could only inflame. So the PAP saw to it that Malay and Indian candidates ran alongside their Chinese colleagues in every election, and Lee appointed Malay and Indian ministers to high posts in his cabinet. And he didn't hesitate, when racial issues began to shadow Singapore's membership in the Malaysian federation in 1965, to pull out and go it alone, declaring independence for a minuscule city-state one-fourth the size of Rhode Island with scarcely two million citizens.

By 1968, the twelve opposition parties were so daunted by the power and popularity of the PAP that they were left absolutely voiceless in the Singaporean Parliament; in the next six elections, including the campaign that was under way when I arrived at Paya Labar Airport in 1980, Lee's organization won every seat in the seventy-nine-member body.

Ruthlessness had something to do with it, to be sure. There wasn't much room for the opposition to breathe, politically, in a country where virtually all institutions were intimately identified with the ruling party and its steamroller leader. But it was not the pocket-stuffing ruthlessness that Sukarno exhibited in Indonesia, or that Ferdinand Marcos was adopting in the Philippines; it was a ruthlessness so unsullied with nepotism or graft that its only measure was visible progress: the miracle.

In the four years prior to my first visit to Singapore, the country's exports had more than doubled. The gross national product had increased by more than 50 percent and foreign investment by nearly 80 percent, paying for the skyscraper forest of apartments and office buildings on the waterfront. This wasn't supposed to happen in nonwhite Third World cities perched on the equator, where fatal lassitude was the rule. It defied the odds.

But Lee Kuan Yew and his party had no patience with anyone who didn't take the kind of long view that could foresee plunking a Rockefeller Center on landfill in what had been a malaria-infested swamp. The PAP under Lee was like Lee himself: all brush-cut practicality when it came to the business of governing, and so determined to succeed, to make Singapore a success, that the slightest whiff of political corruption or rancorous opposition was anathema. The PAP forged a policy and then implemented it, period. There was no fat on the party's bones. In the image of its fitness-crazed leader, who addressed Parliament in tennis shoes and regarded cigarette smokers as national traitors, the PAP was all sinew.

No weakness was tolerated, no dithering allowed. The return on this toughness was Lee Kuan Yew's Singapore—whose foreign critics, in Lee's frequently expressed opinion, could go to hell.

Success always breeds spite, but there was a peculiarly bitter quality to the anger that Singapore aroused in foreigners. It was the smugness of the place. Books could be filled with other explanations, but it all came down to the smugness, because the other reasons never quite explained the sheer hatred that Singapore engendered among many Europeans and Americans.

They damned it for building too many new buildings, for destroying so much of its past. They damned the no-nonsense, authoritarian government, which peremptorily squashed even the smallest perceived threat to social peace. They damned Singapore for being boring, sterile, bland. It wasn't that any of the charges was wholly (or in the case of the PAP's authoritarianism, even partly) inaccurate. But the critics were usually the same people who dearly loved Hong Kong, where the wrecking ball had been far more merciless in its scorn for the past. They were crazy about Rangoon and Shanghai, whose anachronistic charms rendered daily life miserable. They called Singapore boring, I sometimes suspected, precisely because it lacked the forlorn child prostitutes of Manila and Bangkok, the desperately seedy back alleys of Jakarta, the easy dope scores of Chiang Mai and Kathmandu.

Those cities were the "real" Asia, the critics said. Singapore wasn't.

What they meant was that Singapore had violated all of the polarities of the West's Asian fantasies. It had refused to remain either sleepy or teeming, chaotic or quaint. And worse yet, when it changed, it did so with blunt scorn for the fantasists. It refused to honor the unwritten agreement that there should be just two Asias: a "timeless," quintessentially Oriental countryside and a modern, quintessentially Occidental urban world, whether its idiom was borrowed from Moscow (as in China) or New York (as in Hong Kong).

Singapore was neither of these Asias. It was its own creation— or more properly, Lee Kuan Yew's.

Singaporeans, especially Singaporeans like Professor M., didn't do much to ease the hostility that Lee and his tiny republic provoked. She didn't care what the outside world thought. When she agreed, often reluctantly, to discuss her country's affairs with foreigners, it was with a tense, unpleasant smile that said she knew you were too dunderheaded to understand.

It was typical of the PAP to have eventually signed her up, part of its genius to view a potential dissident as a potential recruit. A few years before, Professor M. had expressed public reservations about the party's methods; she was taken by many to be one of the more promising younger voices in the opposition. She was extremely bright, articulate, a prolific writer. In her way, she recalled the young Lee Kuan Yew.

Almost always, the Professor M.'s of Singapore were given a choice by Lee and his party. They could bring their brains and their complaints into the PAP—"join the team," as Lee put it—or they could slide into the opposition. Next, if recent history was any guide, they would either become politically irrelevant, like the rest of the opposition, or cross the line separating opposition from dissidence and promptly find themselves in jail.

Professor M. joined the team.

I wangled an interview with her once, in her office on the west end of the island. It was between terms and there weren't many students around. I arrived twenty minutes early and ate a quick bowl of prawn noodles in the nearly deserted university cafeteria—maybe too quick, since I had to fight back the effects of indigestion throughout our conversation. Not that a belch would have mattered. There was already that half-smirk of condescension on Professor M.'s face when I sat down in her office. The stamp of the uncouth barbarian was on me.

We discussed the changes, the economy, the new habits that a double-digit growth rate had wrought. I wanted to know about her own life. Had prosperity changed it?

The children, she said, had piano lessons. There were two daughters under twelve; she didn't mention a husband. Her car was a Mercedes, though not from Germany—it was a basic, more modestly priced model, assembled in Southeast Asia expressly for the new Asian bourgeoisie. She saw herself as a member of that new professional class, and it was important, vitally important, that the government—the PAP—understand that people like her were the future.

"We are the ones who will matter, not the hawkers."

I was taken aback by this sudden pronouncement. The subject of hawkers had touched a raw nerve. I'd brought them up because for me the hawkers—the city's traditional market stall proprietors— *were* Singapore. The small-time merchants who rose at 5:00 A.M. to clean vegetables and fire up their woks in the hangars behind housing estates or, later in the day, in empty parking lots on Orchard Road. To my mind, the hawkers were the true heirs of those turn-of-the-century coolies whose business acumen provided the foundation for modern Singapore. I had thought to interest Professor M. in the notion that Singapore's success was built on the hard work and ambition of people who peddled prawn noodles and curry from outdoor stalls, or ran small shops in the commercial centers. In the old days, they had been the backbone of the PAP.

The idea didn't capture her fancy.

"Yes, they were important once. But they are a drain now. They get far too many breaks, on taxes and licensing and everything else. They can hide a lot of the money they make, you know. It's easy at their level."

What seemed to bother her most was their cars.

"There are lots and lots of them. You look in the car parks near their stalls, you'll see—they have new automobiles. Real Mercedes sometimes. German ones."

Professor M. was wearing an impeccably white silk blouse that morning. How did she avoid sweating into it when she left her car for the walk to the office? My own shirt was streaked with perspira-

tion stains from the same walk. I remember having a distinct image
of her, in that blouse, pulling up at a traffic light in her Asian-made
Mercedes next to a real one from Germany, with a snaggle-toothed
hawker at the wheel. She was quite angry.

But I have to confess, that I loved the hawkers and their Singapore
for what Professor M. would have sneered at as all the wrong reasons—silly, sentimental reasons that made me more like the Americans and Europeans who damned Singapore than I wanted to admit.

I stayed at the Majestic in those days, out on Bukit Pasoh Road.
This was before I had the clips that translated into expense accounts
and hotels like the Shangri-la or the Mandarin. The Majestic was very
cheap. Its rooms were rank with the smell of mildew, and fronted
by tiny balconies where you could hang underdrawers to dry after
washing them in the sink. Guests took showers outdoors, in a cage-
like affair behind the main building. There was a Sikh doorman who
fidgeted nervously with his beard and the loose end of his turban;
doddering Chinese "room boys," men in their seventies or older,
lounged all day in their skivvies on cots in the hallways and fetched
cigarettes or tea for a few cents.

I'd get up in the morning and head over to Temple Street, where
there were hawkers of Malay curries, Indian *chapatis*, and Cantonese
rice porridge. Hundreds of other stalls lined the blocks that surrounded the big Kreta Ayer housing estate on New Bridge Road,
some of them no more than a few feet of counter backed by a
cookstove and a grinning owner-cook-bottlewasher who was genuinely delighted that a *lo faan,* an old ghost of a foreigner, had picked
his porridge out of the pack.

Customers sat at the common tables that ranged along the
streets, and someone, usually the teenage son or daughter of the
hawker, putting in a couple of hours' work before school, would
bring over the food, and someone else would walk by with cups of
dark black coffee in the Southeast Asian manner, poured over a
dollop of thick sweetened condensed milk. The hawkers yelled out
the claims for their dishes in a cacophony of Chinese dialects, Indian
Tamil, and Malay Bahasa—that was why they were called "hawk-

ers"—and the place was redolent with the rich aromas of food as well as the smell of human sweat that was so mysteriously absent from Professor M.'s blouse.

Journalism, like most writing, is in its subtext a form of autobiography. For me, the hawker streets around Kreta Ayer were the Western Farmer's Market in Detroit, where my grandfather had a produce store until the end of the 1950s. I'd go there on Saturdays during the school year and three or four times a week in the summer. My grandfather saw to it that I had my own modest hawker's business, pushing a cart of lemons through the streets, yelling out my price. The Western Market wasn't Asian. Its Sicilian fruit vendors worked alongside German and Polish farmers, Jewish egg and cheese wholesalers, Lebanese grocers, black long-distance truck drivers delivering melons and berries from the Deep South. But it was of a piece with these Far Eastern streets on the edge of the equator, full of noise and that honest stench of hard work and decaying fruit.

Everywhere I traveled in Asia I listened for echoes of that lost world of my youth, which had long since been paved over by an expressway and replaced by supermarket chains and odorless cellophane. I heard these echoes in what was left of old Singapore, and I felt at home in their rhythms.

Kuo Wongkuo heard them too. W.K., as his business associates called him, was Hokkien Chinese, the descendant of illiterate wayfarers from Fujian Province, and the Hokkien don't let go of the basics without a struggle. They have that inexplicable Chinese talent for business, the sharp intelligence that leads to professions and money, big money. But they aren't good at putting on airs. They have a tendency to be a bit too loud, too indiscreet, for certain company. Even the Hokkien dialect is loud, full of outrageously excessive tonal shifts that lend color to a market stall argument but disrupt the affected politeness of corporate negotiations.

W. K., who was a friend of a friend, had been raised in Malaysia, a few miles from Mersing, and immigrated to Singapore when the Lee Kuan Yew miracle was just getting under way. He did very well as an investor, racking up mountains of cash, and had broken into the true big time recently, acquiring a significant interest in one of the heavyweight international construction firms. W.K. was known far and wide as a man who didn't do anything small. Reno and Vegas casinos would fly him in at their expense to gamble, sweetening the pot with free skiing jaunts in the Sierras for his wife and kids. But beneath the jet-set surface he was that Hokkien kid from Malaysia who had made it in the city by his raw wit, and not cut from the mold that produced Professor M. or the corporate culture that was taking root in the fertile soil of Singapore's prosperity.

Still, he tried to fit in. When I showed up at his office, just under the penthouse in one of the grandest new high rises on Shenton Way, the Wall Street of Singapore, he had his corporate symbols seated next to him: the lawyer and the accountant. They were supposed to guide the interview, in the corporate way. But after introducing the two of them with the same telltale, can-you-believe-it flourish that accompanied his allusions to stock holdings and debentures in the Kuo portfolio, he completely ignored them and said whatever came into his mind. So it was a useful two hours for my purposes, much more useful and illuminating than the time I'd spent skirting issues with Professor M.

At the end, at noon, W.K. said simply, "Let's get something good to eat, huh?" and we set off into the streets with his right-hand man, Mr. Goh, a Hokkien in his fifties with a quick and boisterous laugh who seemed painfully out of place at the conference table. The lawyer and the accountant remained behind.

Goh drove. "Good" didn't mean a restaurant to these two; we went to a hawker's joint. W.K., who insisted on treating—he was immensely pleased when I told him it violated journalistic ethics—filled the table with plates of *satay,* grilled meat in chili sauce, and fat curried shrimp and a whole Hainan chicken raised the old way, with the chicken fed on sesame seeds. We didn't talk business anymore. I told him about Professor M. and about my grandfather, about the market, and why I liked the hawker stalls.

"Then you'd better enjoy this," he said, biting into his mutton *satay*.

I thought he was about to agree with me, but he was more realistic than that. His own career choices, after all, had brought him corporate towers and executive jets, not a hot stove in a postage stamp–cooking stall.

"You'd better enjoy this, my friend, because very soon it will be gone forever. Whatever you may think of her, the professor is right. This is the past. The doomed past."

He spit a bone onto the floor and sent Goh to get another Tiger beer.

When Singapore was only a hawker's world, when it was a decaying, half-abandoned port town in the years immediately after the British withdrawal, it didn't have much influence on the rest of the South China Sea littoral. But as its new identity took shape under Lee Kuan Yew's firm guiding hand in the 1960s and 1970s, as Singapore prospered and modernized at a breakneck pace, it became harder and harder to ignore.

Singapore sent out signals, messages, in that incomprehensible but devastatingly powerful way that wealth and ambition do everywhere.

The signals rolled past the Johore Strait into the Malay Peninsula and continued north into Thailand. They streamed south over the Riau Archipelago into Java and west across the Malacca Strait to the oil towns of Sumatra. The signals were a tom-tom beat that pounded out a hymn to "money, money, money" and all of the possessions it could buy. The signals made people in the villages of Malaysia and the Philippines and even Borneo want things they didn't have, sometimes for the first time in their lives. Things like the radios that were being built in Singaporean assembly lines by 1965. Then the televisions, by 1970. And the polo shirts and jeans that were being imported from France and America by 1975 for the shelves of Singapore's department stores.

Eventually the signals reached Mersing, reached the ears of Nuri Rahman, who had always had more ambition than his neighbors and had moved across the fifty miles of South China Sea between the peninsula and Tioman to become a transportation tout. The signal would make him, with his vision of an A-framed Bali Hai, the island's preeminent native capitalist.

But it was already too late for Nuri to be Tioman's first experience of capitalism; the signal had already taken care of that. A Malaysian hotel group owned by ethnic Chinese in Kuala Lumpur had recognized the marketability of paradise even before Nuri did and bought a couple hundred acres of the island south of the jetty. The resort the group opened there was a kind of Malaysian equivalent of Club Med. It's air-conditioning system was supplied with power from its own generators. It was serviced by its own fleet of launches and seaplanes and staffed by people from the peninsula and from Singapore, which was the source of most of its guests.

The resort was fenced off from the rest of the island and its people. The island's sole road for motor vehicles went a scant mile from the guarded resort gate to the jetty and no farther. But its luxuries were the visible product of that signal from Singapore, which would inevitably have their effect.

After Lee Kuan Yew's boom in Singapore, a second thing happened that aroused the proto-capitalism in people like Nuri Rahman. Another kind of signal rippled through the Malay Archipelago, this time from Dr. Mahathir Mohamed, who became prime minister of Malaysia in 1981 but was already its most important political figure half a decade earlier.

In the early 1970s Mahathir had written a book, *The Malay Dilemma,* that sounded a clarion call for his people to put their Rousseau idyll behind them forever and embrace the gospel of Adam Smith—to add a Malay chapter to the new Asian *Wealth of Nations* that was being written on the South China Sea, not just by Singapore, but also by Hong Kong and Taiwan.

The book was unabashedly, unflinchingly racist. It called not only for home-grown Malaysian capitalism; that already existed. The dilemma to which the title referred was that Malaysian capitalism was almost entirely the province of Chinese Malaysians like the ones who had built the Tioman resort. No matter that ethnic Chinese had lived on the Malay Peninsula and in Malaysian Borneo for generations, or that they accounted for almost 40 percent of the nation's population; they were neither Malays nor Muslims. They weren't, in the Bahasa phrase that Mahathir's politicking made into a household word, *bumiputra,* "sons of the soil."

The subtext was that the Malaysian Chinese didn't belong in Malaysia. That their success wasn't really Malaysian success. That it was a form of theft from the real owners—a racial theft.

There was no question that when Mahathir wrote his book an imbalance characterized the Malaysian economy, an imbalance that had its fundamental source in the colonial era. In the first half of the nineteenth century, when British rule took hold in what was then called Malaya, hereditary Malay sultans were the autocratic masters of local governance. London found it more convenient to share power with the sultans than to take it away from them. That meant, by necessity, respecting the Malays' traditions, which placed enormous importance on maintaining a formal, rigid social order. Getting along with the sultans excluded, by and large, the wholesale recruitment of Malays as sweat laborers in the mines and rubber and palm oil plantations the British established. A plantation overseer would have been yet another master for the Malay villagers to answer to, and the sultans preferred to keep the job for themselves. The Malays, who had never built cities of their own, were deemed unsuitable too as workers for the ports and the urban trading centers the British built up in the Straits Settlements of Penang and Singapore. So Indian laborers were imported for the plantations, and Chinese laborers—the coolie ancestors of Lee Kuan Yew and W. K. Kuo and the owners of the Tioman resort—were imported for the tin mines of the Malay Peninsula and the wharves of Singapore and Penang.

The Malays were left in their picturesque stilted houses and rustic *kampong* villages, sleeping the long traditional sleep that was still evident on Tioman and in many other parts of Malaysia years after the end of colonialism. They slept while the Chinese and to a lesser extent the Indians of Malaysia became engineers and businessmen and capitalists, a new urban elite installed in skyscraper apartments that made Kuala Lumpur, the Malaysian capital, look ever more like Singapore.

In 1970, Chinese Malaysians controlled 36 percent of the national economy. The Malays controlled 4 percent. Foreign corporations held most of the rest. Hence the rise of Mahathir Mohammed, who said, in effect, that it was time for the slumber to end—that it was time for the Malays to take Malaysia back from outsiders, not just actual foreigners but also the native-born Malaysian Chinese. It was that simple, that blunt. Corporate share would be taken away from Malaysians who happened to be yellow and given to Malaysians who were brown. The strategy was enshrined in a document called "The New Economic Policy," which forcibly tilted Malaysian law and institutions to the interests of the 48 percent of the population that was certifiably *bumiputra*. The vast majority of jobs in the government bureaucracy were henceforth to be awarded to Malays. At least 80 percent of the slots in Malaysian universities were reserved for Malays. Special low-cost government loans were made available to Malays only.

The enticing signal from Singapore, the desire to generate the capital necessary to buy into the future, lit the fire of ambition. That was one element in the changes that came to Southeast Asia, even to remote little islands like Tioman, in the late 1970s and early 1980s. The second was a terrible, dangerous envy, a heightened racial consciousness that brought deadly riots to Malaysia as early as 1969 and had already plummeted Indonesia into an apocalyptic inferno in 1965 that ended with the slaughter of more than five hundred thousand ethnic Chinese on Java and Bali. Now it was enshrined as government policy in Kuala Lumpur.

Even at its mildest, the *bumiputra* syndrome produced irritation with its never-ending, nagging reminders that the Malaysian Chinese were supposed to think of themselves as barely tolerated guests.

A February morning, in a rubber-trading town one hour north of the Johore Strait: My Chinese hosts were about to begin preparing the complex dinner that marks the arrival of the lunar New Year. Two American friends were there, along with various adult children who had come home from as far away as London and Sydney. Suddenly the water failed in the town's Chinese district. No one answered the phone at the water department. No one explained what had happened. The year before, there had been a sudden ban on the importation of oranges—the symbol of prosperity that was the traditional decoration and dessert for the Chinese New Year feast. Another year the dragon dance had at the eleventh hour been deemed "too provocative."

Little reminders, every year.

The eldest son of my host was missing an ear. He had lost it in 1969, in the riots that killed hundreds in Kuala Lumpur. The new policies, he believed, made it certain that worse was to come. "It's a sure thing," he said.

His mother was angry with him for saying this and left the room.

Nuri's A-frames? I never went back to Tioman again. But I sent friends, and little by little the tale of the island's business revolution slumped into a desultory muddle.

Each friend returned to say that the one cabin I had found on the cove now had an A-frame nearby—then another, and another and another. By the end of the 1980s there were scores of them lined up along the shore of Tioman, from the gates of the resort to the point north of my cove where the mountain marched into the South China Sea, making it impossible to extend construction any farther.

Nuri had had a good idea, no doubt about it, and many people picked up on it. In Nuri's case, the idea genuinely had something of Adam Smith's invisible hand to it; he had seen a market, and on the strength of his own initiative, he had dreamed of tapping it. But most of the latecomers relied on the visible hand of Dr. Mahathir—on cheap government loans that were extended to virtually any *bumiputra* who called himself a businessman.

Eventually the reports darkened. People returned with stories of fierce wrangling between rival A-frame owners; there were too many of the damn things. The supply was too big for the market—and worse, the market was declining because the oversupply put Tioman's attraction, that Bali Hai beauty, at fatal risk. None of this made any difference at the resort, which remained sealed off from the rest of Tioman; business roared right along inside the fence. Outside, in the A-frame jungle, it made all the difference in the world.

I stopped sending friends to Tioman. Too many had come back complaining that I'd sold them a false bill of goods: It was anything but Bali Hai. I don't know what became of Nuri.

CHINA'S NEW TOP COMMUNIST
PUSHES OPENING TO WEST

BEIJING (October 10, 1981) — Hu Yaobang, a leading advocate of economic reform, was named chairman of the Communist Party of China today.

Hu, the son of a poor peasant family in the central Chinese province of Hunan, replaces Hua Guofeng, the hand-picked successor of the late Chairman Mao Zedong. The move is seen by China watchers as a bold step toward the adoption of free-market economic practices by Chinese paramount leader Deng Xiaoping.

Last year, Deng engineered the appointment of another economic liberal, Zhao Ziyang, as prime minister.

The new party secretary is widely regarded as the most pro-Western leader in the Chinese politburo. He has been outspoken in his support for expanded foreign investment in China.

In a related development earlier this month, the Chinese government formally legalized the establishment of private businesses in the country, 15 years after Mao's radical Cultural Revolution banned such enterprises from China.

FERRYMEN'S RULES

The ferry was a terrible disappointment to the French, bordering on an affront. Zhanjiang was their show: They'd signed one of the first foreign drilling contracts here, talked up the nearby Nanhai oil fields to the Americans, the British, the Australians, the Japanese. Worse, it had been their town—their little Hong Kong—before 1949, when the city at the strategic intersection of the Gulf of Tonkin and the South China Sea was known as Fort Bayard, and its surrounding ocean of cane fields poured sugar into the coffee of l'Indochine.

But that was another time and Fort Bayard was another place, just faintly recalled three decades after Liberation in a tightly shuttered miniature neo-Gothic cathedral, fast asleep on a downtown street, amidst a string of once-grand *maisons particulières* that now served as office warrens for party bureaucrats. On occasion, visiting foreigners might encounter an elderly man on the waterfront sporting a moth-eaten beret, and elicit an amiable nod or a mumbled "*Bonjour messieurs-dames.*" But these moments were the last, fading souvenirs of Fort Bayard. It was Zhanjiang now—"Deep River City"—and thoroughly Chinese.

Except, that is, for the new village across the bay, where the foreign petroleum engineers, geologists, and technical advisers lived in an astoundingly precise reproduction of a Western suburb. Hardly anyone outside southern Guangdong Province knew about this village. It was a kind of state secret of Beijing's, an elaborate experiment about which expatriate Occidentals were contractually pledged to maintain a discreet silence. Far more was being probed here than the Nanhai oil fields. After its decision to open the investment door in the early 1980s, the party had decided to make Zhanjiang a laboratory in joint venture living, a quiet test of the reformers' premise that you could invite the *gweilo*—the "foreign devils"—back to China without giving the nation away.

The Nanhai planners devised an ingenious strategy to achieve this end: Welcome the foreigners (and their investments) warmly. And allow them—indeed, require them—to remain as foreign as possible. There would be no going native at Zhanjiang.

Structural engineers, masons, electricians, plumbers: to a man, they were brought down from Hong Kong in the winter of 1982. Outfitted with architects' blueprints purchased abroad, they set to work on the flat expanse of a small peninsula that jutted into the sea across the long, wide bay from Deep River City. Six months later the job was complete and the construction army returned en masse to Hong Kong.

It left behind a compact version of the world the expats had known back home in Dallas, north Sydney, and the affluent reaches of the Parisian *banlieue,* a perfect copy that was far more painstaking in its details than the Western-style suburbs that were mushrooming elsewhere around the South China Sea in these years. There were red-tiled Spanish hacienda townhouses, each boasting a small enclosed backyard where swings and monkey bars were supplied for the expatriate children of expatriate families. There was a private community club, equipped with a bar and a swimming pool and a discotheque. There were two hotels in the unmistakable Holiday Inn mold, with two restaurants serving *boeuf à la bourguignonne* (the beef imported from Wyoming), grilled lamb chops (the lamb imported from Queensland), and spaghetti Bolognese. There was even a supermarket where you could buy a decent Bordeaux or lager, Kleenex and Tampax, Knorr instant soup and Old El Paso brand tortillas.

All this existed in a state of nearly complete, if splendid, isolation. The east shore of the bay had no airport landing strip, no railhead, no long-distance bus terminal. Every link with the rest of China, not to mention the outside world, was in Zhanjiang proper. There were two ways to get there: a 120-kilometer, four-hour drive around the bay, or the ferry.

Ostensibly the ferry observed a schedule. Ostensibly its crossings consumed no more than twenty minutes. Ostensibly it was a link between what Zhanjiang had been and what it might, if all went well, become. In reality, the ferry was a barrier, for what nobody had reckoned on, not even the cautious planners in Beijing, was that the ferry crew had a memory. Not of old Fort Bayard, but of post-Liberation, pre-reform Zhanjiang, of a China that was walled into a cozy hermitage of its own design.

Something the West didn't understand, couldn't understand, was that life in this China was congenial in its peculiar way for those who were not from intellectual or professional families in the big cities. The inhabitants of a place like Zhanjiang, the ferrymen and the dock workers and the bureaucrats who supplanted the *colons* in their ocher villas, didn't get sent to the countryside for reeducation by the People.

They were already in the countryside. They *were* the People.

The Red Guards didn't bother with them. And they gradually drifted, in the years after the French turned the city over to Mao, into the same slumber that enveloped the deserted cathedral. China, for most Chinese, wasn't violence and paranoia during the 1960s and 1970s; it was a prolonged, drowsy daydream. People worked when the urge moved them, which often meant not at all. And in a city as remote as Zhanjiang, they clung to the shelter of Mao's hermitage long after Canton was remaking itself as a go-go clone of Hong Kong, and Shanghai was reinstituting the stock market, and Beijing was tearing down the Manchu courtyards behind Changan Avenue to erect thirty-story apartment towers.

*   *   *

The ferry came and went whenever its crew felt like it, according to whims that were much less predictable than the winter typhoons that swept across the Guangdong cane fields from the South China Sea.

Some days there would be five or six crossings, and the forty-foot vessel would make a respectable showing. Several dozen trucks would voyage back and forth from the peninsula; the round trip from the Nanhai village to the airport would take one hour instead of eight. Other days there would be one crossing or none, and lines of waiting vehicles would stretch for kilometers, abandoned by drivers who knew better than to ask the question that preoccupied Occidentals—"Why?"—and simply settled into a roadside noodle house to play cards and drink cheap Shandong brandy.

The ferry crew, half a dozen indifferently dressed men and two women, all in their fifties or older, would also play cards—usually pinochle, another French holdover—passing the day in the boathouse over endless cups of tea, flicking the ashes of an endless chain of cigarettes onto the floor. If you asked why the ferry wasn't leaving, they'd smile wordlessly, or point to the azure tropical sky and say, in thick local dialect, "Maybe a typhoon's coming."

When the crossings resumed, chaos ensued. Because none of the ferry crewmen regarded traffic control as part of the job, the truckers were left to their own devices. And they, like Nature, abhorred a vacuum. On both sides of the bay, trucks filled both lanes leading to the docks, their noses pointed expectantly toward the water. When the ferry nudged into the shore with its first load of vehicles after a half-day layoff or more, it provoked consternation instead of progress. No truck could disembark from the ferry because the putative exit lane was a solid mass of other trucks waiting to embark on the same vessel.

The only resolution was a tedious, nerve-wracking process of almost unmeasurable forward motion, inch by inch, amidst a generally rigid posturing that bore great similarity to Chinese business negotiations.

The ferry situation drove the French especially crazy, and became the central, overwhelming obsession of the man I'll call Yves.

Every bit as much as the communist faithful who had rioted

or slept in response to Mao's erratic urgings a decade earlier, Yves was a believer. He believed in France; not the nation, but the idea (as he saw it) that distinguished France from its European neighbors. Calm, careful, unassailable logic: That was what separated France from the feverish emotional hysteria of Italy and the frigid intellectual hysteria of Germany. As for the British, their decline was now so advanced and their confusion so complete that no one could even remember what they stood for. Britain was nineteenth-century Europe.

France was the twenty-first century.

"Which country has the fastest, most advanced trains in the world?" Yves would ask in a favorite rhetorical exercise that invariably surfaced somewhere in his first conversation with newcomers to the Nanhai village. "What is the only place in the world in which every citizen is provided on request with a home computer terminal?" The answer to both questions, of course, was France, mother of the *Train à Grande Vitesse* and the *minitel*, among other wonders.

At the end of the quiz Yves would smile gently and raise his shoulders in a nonchalant shrug, as if to put the newcomer at ease. France, after all, was not Germany or Italy. There was no closeted hysteria, hot or cold, lurking behind these accomplishments, no danger that some dark, hidden megalomania would be suddenly unveiled. Indeed, they were the antithesis of darkness: the bright, shining offspring of calm, careful, unassailable logic—the grand legacy of a French civilization, Yves insisted, that was not the same thing as French nationalism.

"Otherwise," he would say, in his closing remarks, "why would we share the TGV with the Swiss and the Germans? Why would we sell *minitels* to the English?"

It was a fine ideology for a computer engineer like Yves, a worldview well suited to a profession that makes a religion of logical analysis and divides the globe along patent lines rather than national boundaries—but also, as it happens, traces its mathematical origins to a French savant, René Descartes.

In a China that was striving to create, as Deng Xiaoping put it, "a market economy, but with Chinese characteristics," Yves viewed himself as a committed internationalist, but with French characteristics.

*   *   *

On a grayish morning in April, Yves convened an emergency meeting of his fellow engineers and administrators from the global petro-conglomerates of America, Britain, and Australia—internationalists all, but with American, British, and Australian characteristics.

There was no need to invite the Japanese. Long before, Tokyo's oil executives had sensed the direction of the wind (or more accurately, its utter lethargy) and somehow won the right to take up residence in a Japanese-financed hotel that was conveniently situated on the mainland side of the bay. It was sheer speculation, but many Western oilmen thought there was a connection between the hotel arrangement and the sudden appearance of a stable of Toyota mini-vans at party headquarters in Zhanjiang.

With French backing, Yves explained, a subsidiary experiment was about to be undertaken in the spirit of the Nanhai joint-venture accords. "Our view," he said, "is that the ferry management is lacking motivation. Very simply, they have no reason to cross the bay."

It was a theory much on the minds of those assembled, as it was in the deliberations of every foreign firm with an early foothold in the new China. How do you motivate people when there is no way to reward the efficient or punish the laggard? Foreign firms had no right to hire or fire; that was the monopoly of the state work units that provided labor. It was exercised uniquely in one direction: hiring—often a matter of harvesting the crop of siblings, children, cousins, nieces, and nephews of the local party leadership. The work units also paid salaries according to an inflexible remuneration scale that had nothing to do with productivity and even less with the amount charged the firm. It was not unusual for a Western manufac-turer to pay a work unit $150 a month for an employee, of which $20 might find its way into the worker's own pocket.

Providence alone could explain, in these circumstances, why some employees worked harder than others. And even Providence was at a loss in explaining why someone might be inclined to work hard on a state ferry that not only was slumbering in a generation-old daze but also paid roughly half as much as a job in a joint venture.

"What is the only motivation we can offer?" Yves asked, in a variation on his Franco-Socratic dialogue. "What is the only thing that can inject logic into this matter?"

Everyone knew the answer: "Money."

"Yes!" Yves responded. "And tonight I can tell you that, after some formidable difficulties, we have persuaded the authorities to let us employ this tool. At our own expense, *bien sûr*."

It was an enormous coup. That had been the hard part, immensely hard, getting the permission. The easy part was the system itself. Systems come easily to the kind of people who met with Yves that night; they live by systems and die by them. It took less than an hour to hammer down the details.

Quite simply, the crew members would be paid a bonus for every crossing. The more they worked, the more they made. If they wanted to play cards, well, that was their choice. But no one, least of all Yves, expected that pinochle had much of a future on Zhanjiang Bay.

The engineers of the Nanhai village went home to their haciendas with the self-assurance of generals who know the final battle is about to be joined and believe the enemy is hopelessly trapped.

On one point there is no question. By the end of the two days the bonus system prevailed, the Zhanjiang ferry had made the largest number of crossings toted up in any forty-eight-hour period in its checkered history.

There were, as Yves had predicted so confidently, no card games in the boathouse. The crew worked with a fury that astonished, observing the precise letter of the new arrangement in what all parties now agree was an unqualified catastrophe.

The very logic of the situation, the carefully considered and unassailable logic of Yves's own devising, placed a premium on quantity. It was the number of crossings that mattered. By noon on the first day, the ferry had been transformed, awakened, galvanized into a water-borne calculator, ticking off landings one after another with such phenomenal regularity that stupefied crowds gathered at the dock to watch.

What the crowds saw, in effect, was an elaborate parody. For no sooner would the ferry touch the eastern shore than it would reverse its engines and carom off toward the west, waiting nary a minute for a vehicle to board for the return trip. Records tumbled in the crossing category as record lines of trucks built toward the horizons, while observers from Zhanjiang swung their heads back and forth from east to west, following the ferry's trajectory like an audience at one of the Ping-Pong matches that had served as a Chinese diplomatic instrument in the last eccentric days of Chairman Mao.

The crossing count rose. The bonus payments ticked away. The lines grew. At 5:00 P.M. on the second day, just shy of a record-shattering four passages in one hour, the crew reversed engines with such speed that a frantic trucker—one of the few who even tried to board the manic vessel—pitched his rig straight into the bay.

The truck sank with a loud gurgle to mid-window, then settled into the mud directly in front of the loading ramp. It was the end of the experiment.

There's a postscript to this tale. A few years after the episode of the Ping-Pong ferry, Yves and his colleagues were gone. The offshore South China Sea oil fields did not prove viable, and the conglomerates absorbed considerable losses on the Nanhai joint venture. They carried home what they could, which wasn't much.

I've often thought about the village they once called home. Is the ferry running at all now? Is anyone living in the hacienda townhouses? Every once in a while I imagine the tennis courts and the poolside club baking away in futility under the pitiless Guangdong sun. Nobody from the West has a reason to go to the village anymore. Hardly anyone knows it's there. Its supermarket and monkey bars must seem eloquent archeological relics, like the forgotten ruins that inspired Shelley to pen his poem "Ozymandias": "Look on, ye mighty, and despair."

One day I asked a China scholar, a well-known historian at Berkeley, what he knew about Zhanjiang. It had a painful history, he told me, "the history of a place that was synonymous with failure." Long before the French arrived, he explained, Deep Water City had been a final way station in imperial China, the last port on the mainland en route to Hainan Island, where disgraced officials in the mandarinate were sent to live out the rest of their days in the most distant, primitive outpost of the Middle Kingdom. "For the Chinese," the historian said, shaking his head sadly, "Zhanjiang was the bank of the River Styx."

HUGE CROWD AT AQUINO FUNERAL

MANILA (August 31, 1983) — More than one million mourners lined the streets of Manila today as the funeral procession of former Senator Benigno "Ninoy" Aquino wound through the city.

Aquino, the leading opponent of Philippine president Ferdinand Marcos, was assassinated on the tarmac of Manila International Airport ten days ago. He had just returned from three years of exile in the United States.

Philippine authorities say the murder was committed by a lone gunman, Rolando Galman Dawang, who was shot dead by soldiers on the airport runway. But many Filipinos believe government officials were behind the assassination of Aquino.

Buildings along the funeral route to Santo Domingo Church in suburban Quezon City were covered with banners calling for the resignation of Marcos. Local observers called it the most open display of public discontent with the regime in a decade.

In a funeral sermon that hinted at a government role in the killing, Roman Catholic prelate Jaime Cardinal Sin spoke of widespread "tyranny and oppression" in the country. Cardinal Sin is among several prominent figures who have refused to sit on a government commission established to investigate the murder.

Corazon Aquino, the former senator's widow, also declined to participate on the commission, saying that a government investigation would be "meaningless until we have democracy."

CIGARETTE SUBDIVISION

Because of Auntie, Father Victor López spent several nights a week at the house in the cigarette subdivision, on Kool Street near Marlboro. It was one of the newer developments along the Don Mariano Marcos Highway in Quezon City, the brainchild of a Metro Manila developer who was evidently infatuated with smoking. Other streets were named Camel, Chesterfield, Salem, Newport, Kent; "cigarette subdivision" wasn't the development's formal name, but there was no avoiding its use. The plots had been sold to individual contractors after the streets were surveyed, and Father Vic's brother Tony bought one.

He'd built a typical American ranch-style house there, adding a few Ibero-Filipino touches like polished granite floors and an outdoor kitchen. The house fit in perfectly. The surrounding blocks were rife with middle-class Filipinos who had emigrated to the States and then returned a decade or two later to Manila, where the proceeds from the sale of a home in California could set a family up in comfort for many years. They'd filled the cigarette subdivision with tributes to the eclectic residential landscapes of Los Angeles and San Mateo County: The streets were a jumble of miniature Tuscan palaces, bilevels and trilevels, Cape Cods and colonials.

It could easily have been south San Francisco or Anaheim were it not for the tropical foliage that ran riot over the yards, and the fact that the developer had run out of money and was unable to pave the streets, wire the subdivision for telephone service, or bring in city water. For a fee, a barbershop on the Don Mariano Marcos Highway took calls, sending messages to the homeowners via a troop of kids from a shantytown. Behind each house, pumps sucked what they could from a crazy quilt of underground wells—or more often, from a complicated network of illegal shunts and taps that hijacked water from a nearby municipal conduit.

The house on Kool Street wasn't for Tony, who had a bungalow of his own in San Fernando, Pampanga, not far from Angeles City and the Americans' Clark Air Base, where he made his living as a builder and consumer goods wholesaler. Nor was it for Father Vic, who lived in the rectory maintained by his order in the city center. The idea behind the ranch home, Tony told me, was to lure their mother, Aurelia, their sister Melinda, and their brother Danny from San Francisco. "If they can live exactly the same here as in California, why not?"

It half worked, or more accurately, half of one-third. Mrs. López, who had retired from her job at a semiconductor plant in San Jose, came roughly every eighteen months and stayed for six months. The house would have been vacant for a year at a time if the two López sons hadn't leaned on Auntie to move down from the family's village in the northern mountains. Although they'd provided her with a color television set, cassette deck, and houseboy, Auntie—the only name anyone seemed to know her by—hated the subdivision. Her village home had packed dirt instead of granite floors and a thatched roof that rustled all night with the gyrations of insomniac sparrow bats. But she had scores of relatives around her (almost everyone in the village was a cousin), who stopped by at all hours to gossip or share a meal of fried salt fish and garlic rice. On Kool Street she was alone most of the time, except for the resolutely taciturn houseboy, Marlon, and on the nights when Father Vic took the long jitney ride out to keep her company.

Father Vic was a wiry man in his late forties with a sharp nose and darting, deep-set eyes. He chain-smoked Kents on Kool Street and was prone to long, unpredictable bouts of black thoughts. In the midst of a party, sometimes in the midst of one of his own stories, he would suddenly lapse into a meditative silence and stare into the distance at nothing in particular. He worried about lots of things. There was the house on Kool and his scattered family. He was in charge of the budget for his order, a Catholic missionary group based in Europe. And he somehow found time to run a church-owned factory that manufactured statues of Jesus and His saints. Plenty to mull. But mostly he mulled over the Philippines, which in his own lifetime had moved from the visible forefront of progress in Asia to its obscure margins.

"What is it about us?" he'd say, agonizing aloud on excursions into the Luzon countryside, when he'd accompany me to the occasional interview. "Why can't we get off the dime? It's more than Marcos. I'm afraid it's something in our character, and if we can't shake it, we'll never get out of the bind we're in."

Constant mulling had left Father Vic afflicted with a wide array of nervous tics, small flinches and exasperated sighs. His preoccupation wasn't quite despair; he was too much the priest for that. But it came perilously close whenever he was reminded of the Filipino bind. He flinched when he walked past the rear window of the Kool Street house and heard the pump come on, even though he'd heard it a thousand times. It wasn't the insistent hum of the pump itself; it was what it symbolized—that jerry-built maze of illegal pipes and taps where a simple water main ought to be. He sighed, in short involuntary gasps, when shipments of wood for the religious statues turned out to be worm-eaten, for no reason other than that somebody had forgotten to spray the lumber with the insecticide sitting next to it on the loading dock.

There were moments now and then when it seemed Father Vic

couldn't take it much longer, that he'd break. But he held on, sighing and flinching and lapsing into his long silences, somehow offsetting his deep demoralization with an extraordinary reservoir of patience.

It was a strange in-between time for Manila, a time when the bind seemed especially strangling. Ninoy Aquino had been in his grave for nearly a year, and the marches on the Malacanang Palace had multiplied again and again in number and size. Six months earlier there had been hope that a new era was about to dawn, that things would finally turn around. But lately, despite the marches, a sense of resignation was taking root, a sardonic acceptance of what seemed inevitable: Ferdinand Marcos would escape the ghost of Ninoy Aquino just as he had escaped every other dilemma he'd created for himself in a thirty-year career of unparalleled flimflammery and national decline.

As late as the 1960s Manila had been the boomtown, the icon of Southeast Asian stability. Then it was the overcrowded, decaying postcolonial cities of Taipei, Hong Kong, and Singapore that looked to become the Calcuttas of the Far East. But that was a distant, incredible memory now. The Philippines had become a global laughingstock over the two decades of Marcos's presidency as boodle and bumbling on a massive scale reduced what was once Southeast Asia's most sophisticated economy to a tragicomic farce. Meanwhile, the nation's nearest regional neighbors were skyrocketing ahead into the computer age. Borne forward on a floodtide of foreign investment and high technology, Hong Kong, Taipei, and Singapore were getting rich.

Filipinos were painfully aware of the contrasts. All around them on the periphery of the South China Sea they saw money, mass consumption, and zooming living standards by the 1980s: the dawn of the Pacific Century. At home, in the crumbling *barranguays* of metro Manila and in rural villages that remained locked in another century, they saw only failure.

The self-indictment was made more acute by the constant stream of emigrant traffic across the Pacific, which kept Filipino expectations in close step with California fads. Philippine Airlines, the national carrier, even offered a special "*balikbayan* shipping service"—the term loosely translates as "homeward-bound"—that flew enormous boxes stuffed with American products from the Filipino suburbs of Los

Angeles and San Francisco to Manila and Quezon City. *Balikbayan* boxes from Danny and Melinda were delivered to the house in the cigarette village virtually every month I was in town, crammed with Converse tennis shoes and Papermate ballpoint pens, Fruit-of-the-Loom underwear and Ban roll-on deodorant, Sunbeam electric blenders and Hewlett-Packard pocket calculators. "Just look at these things," Father Vic would say as Auntie and Marlon went through the latest shipment. "Why can't we produce them ourselves? They aren't even made in America anymore. They're from out here—from Taiwan and Hong Kong."

It was the canned pineapple that really got to him: Several cases of it had been sent over the years from California and neatly stacked in the Kool Street garage. The pineapple itself was from the Philippines, from down south on Mindanao Island; it was sold fresh in the market two blocks away on the Don Mariano Marcos Highway. But no one in Manila wanted to eat it that way; Filipinos knew that Americans ate Philippine pineapple from American cans, and if they could afford it, so would they.

"Pineapple!" Father Vic would say, piling the cans up on the living room floor. "What's wrong with us? They're making computers in Taiwan and we're buying our own canned pineapple from America. Why can't we get off the dime?"

They couldn't get off the dime, and they knew it. That was an essential part of the Philippines' tragedy: What paralyzed people like Father Vic was that they knew too much. They knew the price of their national inertia. "We're the bums of the Pacific basin," he would mutter now and again.

He meant it as a kind of joke. But he flinched every time he said it.

I never saw Victor López more miserable than the day we went to Bangued, the capital city of the province of Abra where he had been born. Road conditions were reasonably good up the long coastal drive north on National Route 3. But ten minutes after we headed east into Abra, the official Petron Oil *Philippines Road Atlas* deteriorated into a cartographer's fantasy. The thick red line that was optimistically marked National Route 6 on the map proved to be a rutted dirt track, inexplicably broken by two-hundred-yard patches of blacktop at the approaches to Bangued and several smaller towns. A single six-mile stretch between the coast and Bangued took ninety minutes in the missionary order's Toyota. During the seasonal monsoon, mud limited the passage to oxcarts.

The patches of asphalt here and there—that was the really odd part. "Every year for the last decade," Father Vic explained, his voice tight, "government contractors have received monies to complete this road. And every year a small piece of pavement is laid down, without any foundation work, at the entrance and exit of another town. Afterward, somebody takes nice Polaroid pictures of the 'finished' road. That's the evidence that the work has been done, just in case a legislator brings the matter up.

"In fact"—Father Vic had a habit of starting sentences with the phrase "in fact," perhaps because facts were so rare in Philippine political dialogue that they had to be identified—"in fact, the monies that are supposed to go into the road go right back to Manila, straight into the pocket of a crony in that same legislature."

Cronyism. The clawing network of greased palms without which nothing at all ever got done in the Philippines, and with which everything was done badly. It was inescapable. Father Vic couldn't escape it, even though he was what the press came to call an "activist priest"—an advocate of the theology of liberation, which called for direct political action, as well as prayers, to relieve the plight of the oppressed. He was a deeply committed man, faithful to his convictions at enormous personal risk. But still, he had to go along with the customs of cronyism, to be a witting, angry accomplice.

Everyone did, because the alternative was to do without. Like the illegal pumps and shunts under the backyards of the cigarette subdivision, greased official palms were the only way to move things, or people, through the Philippine pipeline. Liberation priests, businesspeople, journalists: Whatever our intentions, we were all enmeshed in the system.

Arriving at the airport on my first visit to Manila, preceded by a letter of introduction from relatives of Father Vic's, I was met in the customs zone by two men in shirtsleeves who spotted me at the baggage claim and addressed me by name.

"Mr. Frank Viviano? Please: We'll take care of that."

My bags were whisked off the belt and past the customs officers without examination. I was waved straight through the gate
behind them, fanning the air with my passport. Nobody bothered
to look at it.

Father Vic was outside in the Toyota, waiting. The men, he later
explained, were his order's "airport expediters"; they were professional palm-greasers, hired to plant the appropriate bribes in the
transportation bureaucracy so that priests, friends, and relatives
weren't, as Father Vic put it, "unnecessarily delayed" at the passport
check.

"In fact, you might have been there three hours, four hours,
who knows? This is the way our country works . . . the 'Filipino
way.' "

His sentence edged around a raspy cough, then audibly trailed
off.

The Filipino way: The phrase had been a matter of pride once,
a summing up of the easygoing manner and native intelligence of the
Filipino people, the qualities that still made them among the world's
best doctors, nurses, and administrators—once they emigrated, as
most of the López family had, to California or other points abroad.
But at home, under Marcos, the Filipino way had been twisted out
of shape. It was a catchphrase for national shame now, applicable to
virtually every snafu. It explained the rutted track to the capital of
Abra. It explained why the sidewalks of Ermita, which was billed as
the "tourist center" of Manila (and in reality was a red light district
stalked by boozy Germans and Australians), were an obstacle course
of broken concrete shards jutting up at odd angles. It explained the
absence of city water and telephone service in the cigarette subdivision: The developer had foolishly overspent on bribes.

The Filipino way. It explained why people like Father Vic were
near despair, consumed with repressed anger—or taking up the gun.

People often got lost looking for Art Figueroa's house, because his
street wasn't on any map and his neighborhood had two names.
Officially it was Santa Ana, a *barranguay* of Taytay in Rizal Province,
a broad flat stretch of Luzon Island where greater Manila sprawled
toward the Philippine Sea in a confused mosaic of shanty towns.

Unofficially and more commonly it was called Dupax, after a popular Filipino cowboy-and-Indian comic strip.

"It's just like the wild frontier out here," Art would say by way of explanation. "We're the pioneers."

Unlike the cigarette subdivision—a testament to a plan gone awry—nobody had planned Art's *barranguay* at all, which was why its streets followed the random logic of afterthoughts. Dupax just happened: Too many babies were born downtown in Tondo and Santa Cruz, where the Manileño poor have traditionally lived. Too many young people left the distant provincial villages of the Bicol Valley and Ilocos for the city, and they soon had too many babies of their own.

The babies were the accidents that made Dupax happen, that made hundreds of Dupaxes—a wild guess, since no one was counting—happen all over southern Luzon in the Marcos years. Manila has the world's highest urban birthrate, nearly twice as high as Mexico City's and four times as high as Hong Kong's; it is the most densely populated city on earth, with four times as many people per square mile as New York and half again as many as Shanghai.

In an effort to escape this crush, a few families migrated across the Pasig and Marikina rivers to Rizal in the late 1960s, and they drew a flood of others after them. Cardboard shacks went up, in no particular sequence, until field after field was covered. The streets were the muddy, haphazard spaces in between. Eventually wood and cinder blocks replaced some of the cardboard walls, and enough sheet metal was accumulated, family by family, to replace the roofs made of cardboard and plastic sheeting.

By the mid-1970s Dupax was more or less complete. It had happened.

The next event that mattered, aside from the nightly pistol shots that could mean anything from a spontaneous celebration to a premature widowhood, took place in 1978, when Art and Father Vic began giving the annual Christmas party at which Art sings "Jalisco." The song, of course, is Mexican, and it has been a long time since the Spanish galleons that linked Manila to Acapulco stopped sailing. But "Jalisco" is a Philippine favorite nonetheless, sung always in Spanish, and Art had polished it on countless bar-hopping excursions with his pal Salvador "Doy" De Alcuaz. It was Doy, the manager of the missionary order's bookshop, who belted out the obligatory "Yee-haaaa" that separates a memorable "Jalisco" from an ordinary one.

It fell on young ears. When children reached their teens in places like Dupax, they were reckoned adults. A very few might find jobs in Manila, as Art had. More slid into a deadly waiting game broken by short periods as casual laborers, and punctuated too often by a bullet or a knife. Most deserted the *barranguay* to build shantytown hovels of their own even farther from the city center. Many wound up in the mountains, shouldering guns—some for the guerrillas of the communist New People's Army, some for the Philippine military.

Hundreds of thousands of others headed for California, usually illegally. "In fact," Father Vic said as our car climbed over the hill that separated the Marikina Valley from Manila proper, "Filipinos are the number one export of the Philippines."

It was another of his despondent punchlines, but no one who traveled in Asia would dispute it. At any given moment in the early 1980s, there were two million Filipinos abroad on temporary work permits; a thousand left the country each day in search of overseas jobs.

In Hong Kong, thirty thousand Filipinas were employed as household servants. Almost as many had made their way to Rome, Madrid, Singapore, and Bahrain. Young Filipino men were constantly in transit through Bangkok, on their way to construction sites in Kuwait and Saudi Arabia. The twenty-five-year-old man who shined my shoes in the departure lounge at Manila International Airport had a master's degree in microbiology; he was waiting, he said, to hear from a New York doctor who had promised to look into a job for him at Bellevue Hospital.

Father Vic's mother, sister, and brother in the United States also had graduate degrees. Danny had studied philosophy at San Tomás University, the Georgetown of Asia, and Melinda had a master's in math from the University of the Philippines, the finest public institution in the country. Now Danny worked as a supermarket stock boy in San Francisco and Melinda was a bank teller near San Jose; their mother had exchanged a teaching career in Abra for an assembly line in the Silicon Valley.

In 1983, the year Benigno Aquino returned to challenge Marcos and wound up dead on the airport tarmac, no American consulate handled more immigration requests than the U.S. mission in Manila. No immigrant population in America was growing faster than that of Filipinos, who counted a million or more—like the number of shantytowns on Luzon, the figures can only be guessed at—in California alone. No place on earth was losing its young adults at a rate that approached that in the Philippines.

These were the facts of Filipino life in the Marcos years; they would still be the facts of Filipino life a decade later.

Dupax, then, was largely a city of children, and Father Vic's Christmas party was its unofficial census. A month in advance Art, his wife, and their own three children launched a house-to-house tour of the *barranguay,* writing down the name of every kid they found. Meanwhile Doy and his coworkers shook down their customers and friends. The chief shaker was Father Vic. By the night of the party I attended in 1985 he had somehow come up with forty thousand pesos, about $2,000—enough to give five bucks to everyone on Art's list. That was a lot of money in the Philippines, where the per capita income that year ran about $15 a week.

Excitement had been building since Art made his first census stop that Christmas season, reaching unbearable dimensions on the humid night we slogged and bounced down Dupax's tortured streets in the Toyota wagon. Cars were scarce here, and by the time we pulled up in front of Art's, children blanketed the vehicle, clinging to the door handles, lying on the hood, scrambling over the rear bumper onto the roof.

Light bulbs were strung between the Figueroa home and four others, powered by a smoky diesel generator. A stage had been erected. Hundreds of Dupaxistas milled about it, or stood in line at Art's for a plate of vinegar-braised chicken *adobo* and rice. Up at the microphone a guitarist and a succession of neighborhood crooners warmed the audience up with a medley of Filipino ballads and uncannily mimicked selections from the greatest hits of Simon and Garfunkel.

It was nine o'clock before Father Vic began reading from Art's list, making sure to get the nicknames right. The children pushed their way forward through the crowd to their envelopes: Ricky and

Rosie Almanacer, "Dr. J" Figueras and Kareem Abdul López (basketball is a passion in the cardboard suburbs of Manila), Peping Merienda, Missy Valdez. Four hundred kids were presented with their pesos, plus a T-shirt that read HAPPINESS IS SHARING, designed by Art, who was a graphic artist, and donated to the party by a López cousin, a T-shirt manufacturer.

But nobody left, not a single kid, until the time arrived when the guitarist looked at Art, and Art nodded at Doy. For the next few minutes, as "Jalisco" soared sweetly over the sheet metal roofs of Dupax, everyone forgot, however briefly, about the cronyism and the cardboard houses. They forgot, for a moment, about the Filipino way. They forgot about choosing between immigration and the gun.

There were guns everywhere in Zamboanga, guns of every conceivable description: Big Magnum enforcers and diminutive Smith & Wesson .22-caliber revolvers. Soviet-made AK-47 Kalashnikov automatics and Chinese imitations. Lightweight machine pistols from Singapore and Israel. American M-16s, recently stolen or bought from the Philippine military, and vintage Browning carbines that had been used against the imperial Japanese army four decades before.

At midday in this self-styled "City of Flowers" 550 miles south of Manila on the island of Mindanao, people carried pistols openly down the street, cradled in their arms, stuck in their belts, nestled in holsters. After dark, shots crackled through the humid night, making a sound unnervingly similar to the "pop" of mosquitoes on the blue insecticide lamp that hung in the corridor outside my room at the Lantaka Hotel.

Two miles or so outside the municipal boundaries, travelers left the jurisdiction of the Philippine Constabulary entirely and found guerrillas of the Moro National Liberation Front, or sometimes the communist New People's Army (its members known popularly as NPAs), nonchalantly directing traffic with Uzis slung over their shoulders. Back in the city center signs were posted in hotel lobbies and at the doors of banks and hamburger joints: CUSTOMERS ARE KINDLY REQUESTED TO CHECK GUNS BEFORE ENTERING. Young women doled out chits for the weapons, shelved them in small booths, and returned them when clients had finished with lunch or business.

I had come south on holiday. The political tension and fetid smell of urban decay in Manila were getting to me, and the Philippines National Tourist Office brochures made Zambo sound like paradise. One picture especially stuck in my mind: a sleek ferry threading its way into the city harbor between picturesque *vintas,* Sulu outriggers under full sail and laden with sea shells.

The sleek ferry, which I boarded in Iloilo on the island of Panay after a Philippines Air flight halfway to Mindanao, was the *Don Eusebio,* pride of the Sulpicio Lines fleet. At anchor offshore, before she sidled into the wharf for loading, the ship looked every bit as appealing as it had in the brochure photograph. Up close and loaded, she was a floating nightmare.

The *Don Eusebio* was about 350 feet long, a substantial vessel, triple decked. A plate on a forward bulkhead indicated that she'd been launched in Norway under a different name in the 1950s for the Stavenger service. The ship's original plan, a blueprint of which was posted in a warped frame outside the bursar's cubicle, included such niceties as a first-class restaurant and lounge, a second-class cafeteria, shops, a children's playroom, and a bar. There was a large section of four- and six-berth second-class cabins on the middle deck and a smaller number of two- and four-berth first-class suites on the top deck. The lower deck, below the water line, was for cargo.

All of that had been dispensed with. Except for the first-class suites, whose solid iron walls were too difficult to remove, every inch of the ship had been opened up and covered with wooden cots, from bow to stern and from beam to beam. A sea of cots, crossed by two lanes of walking space no more than a foot wide, had inundated the cargo deck. Cots were jammed into the walkways outside the middle deck and over the entire expanse of what had been the restaurants and cafeteria. The second-class cabins were recalled only by a line of rivets in the floor, barely visible between yet more cots, that had once held the separating partitions in place. Every cot was taken by Mindanao-born Filipinos returning home for Christmas from the shantytowns of Manila; extended families of three or four adults and their children sprawled across them, rendered inert by the effects of the tropical sun on the iron bulkheads. They were human sardines, roasting in a 350-foot can. According to the blueprint, there had been air-conditioning throughout the vessel when it was launched in Norway.

The air-conditioning still worked, in racheting fits and starts, in the first-class cabin I had booked with two friends—or thought I had. A pair of bunks had been wedged into what was originally meant to be a cabin for two, but that wasn't the problem. The problem was that there were already ten people in the cabin, which was how I met Private First Class Leo Merced.

Leo had a ticket and an arrangement. The ticket was for a single berth. The arrangement, worked out with a ship's steward who found a thousand-peso note in his pocket, was to pretend that the ticket was for the entire number one compartment and not simply for bed 1-A. Neither Leo nor the steward reckoned that anyone would object too strenuously. After all, the nine pals who crowded into Leo's pad to play cards and drink warm San Miguel beer on the slow boat to Zamboanga were army officers, Leo's bosses, and every one of them was supplied with an M-16. What their reasoning didn't take into account was my failure to notice the guns jammed under the bunks, or the three hours of pushing and shoving that my own bona fide tickets had cost in the Sulpicio Lines office on the Iloilo docks. I'd had to pay a bribe too; I wasn't about to settle for a cot in the hold.

The imbroglio brought out the Sicilian in me. I ranted, I threatened, I swore. I called the national honor of the Philippine nation into question. I invoked Holy Mother Church and the United States government. I ran off to get the steward, dragged him back to the compartment, and told him to shut up when he made a feeble attempt to back Leo's claim.

Only afterward did I notice the M-16s and the traumatized expressions on my Filipino friends' faces. People got blown away regularly in the Philippines for far less insulting behavior than mine. People disappeared when they rubbed the army the wrong way. Especially the army on Mindanao, which was engaged in a ruthless war against both the Moros and the NPA that saw more than its share of inventive tortures, decapitations, and unspeakable sexual mutilations. But instead of disappearing or losing my head (or worse), I got the cabin. Maybe it was the element of sheer surprise, the astonishment that anyone could be so stupid.

The officers got the cots, leaving their bags on Leo's single bunk. As soon as they were out of sight, he began laughing uncontrollably and held out his hand to shake mine.

"Man," he said, "that was really something else. Wow. Something else."

It was the kind of thing you only get away with once.

Darkness fell after a brief, fiery tropical dusk, as we slipped past Negros Island into the Sulu Sea. I would like to have watched the sunset, but even if it had been possible to ford the ocean of cots outside the first-class deck, there was no access to the ship's rail. The stewards had chain-locked all the bulkhead doors to keep the cot-class passengers out. The chains also had the effect of sealing us in. I had a sharp, stomach-wrenching reminder of those chains a few years later, when one of the *Don Eusebio's* sister ships went down off Mindoro, taking more than three thousand passengers with her.

Everybody in the cabin was bushed, exhausted in the aftermath of my hysteria. We ate a few bananas, washing them down with San Migs that Leo's officers had forgotten, then killed the overhead lamps.

The day's second grand performance began immediately, with an infernal racket in the ship's metal air ducts that sounded like an army on the march at quick step: the patter of a thousand feet, punctuated intermittently by high-pitched squeaks. Looking down from the top bunk, I saw a banana jerk its way toward the bulkhead, surrounded by bulbous shapes that materialized into a swarm of rats as my eyes adjusted to the dim moonlight. Within minutes the room was alive with them. They were the most brazen rodents I'd ever seen, scurrying nonchalantly over the bags and bunks in search of food, diverted only slightly from their appointed rounds by my friends' frantic kicking and yelling.

About two feet above my head an entire detachment was tightrope-walking a water pipe, their tails wrapping and unwrapping around the conduit. I prayed that they would keep their balance. For his part, Leo snored on, perched in the haphazard clutter of his officers' suitcases and boxes as though he was tucked into a feather bed.

He woke slowly, rubbing his eyes, after we turned the lamps back on and the rats made for the exits, dragging chunks of banana and bags of hard candy behind them. Rats hate fluorescent light. I'd confirmed that principle in hotel rooms all over Southeast Asia, although never so dramatically. Leo was pretty blasé about the invasion, which gave us some idea of what his camp on Mindanao must have been like, but he was a friendly guy and amenable to a night's conversation if we weren't in the mood to sleep.

PFC Merced was a Tagalog from southern Luzon, a handsome kid with a million dollar smile, on his way back from a month's leave. He was a tank gunner, and he loved the military. The army and his family—his father was dead, and at twenty-three he was responsible for his mother, a brother, and two sisters—were the magnetic poles of Leo's life. If he could stick it out on tough duty like Mindanao, where he'd already spent four years, there was a slim chance he'd be promoted to a noncommissioned officer's rank and make enough money to pay for at least one sibling to go to college. His great dream for himself was to be sent to California for special training, like some of the regimental officers I'd kicked out of the cabin.

"You were really something else," he said again.

I winced.

If anything could test Leo's determination, it was Mindanao, the nastiest arena in a civil war that had simmered or raged, on and off, for nearly three decades. It was now very much on and raging. Leo talked about it. At first the talk was like any soldier's, a mixture of the technical and the macho: how many NPAs his unit had killed, the strengths and weaknesses of certain weapons, the unpredictable tactics of the Moros. But the tenor of the conversation changed, grew less strident, as the night aged and the *Don Eusebio* drew closer to Zamboanga. And then Leo told his story, the one he would always remember from this posting. The story that had gotten him thinking.

"We were in Agusan del Sur, in the eastern part of the island. It was about eight months ago. There had been a lot of fighting, and I will tell you honestly that we were nervous. Some guys had been shot up pretty bad right in the town. It wasn't a good idea to wear a uniform there."

One day, Leo went on, he'd changed into a pair of Levi's and a T-shirt and gone to town alone, to buy some things. To take a breather. And he met a girl.

"She was really beautiful, you know—nineteen years old, the same age as my older sister. We talked and talked. She was so smart! When she asked me to have dinner with her friends, I never thought twice about the answer.

"About five o'clock we met at the marketplace and started walking out into the countryside, where she said her friends would meet us. It wasn't until we got inside the house and I saw the Kalashnikovs leaned up against a wall that I realized I was flirting with an NPA. But I had no choice about that dinner—there was no way I could leave."

So he stayed. And as the night wore on and they drank San Migs and swapped tales about Manila, about growing up in the streets and about the schools they'd gone to and the nuns who'd taught them, and about who would win the title in the States this year— would it be the Lakers again, or maybe the Celts were coming back?—Leo forgot who he was with. They were just other kids, like him. He forgot that he was there, on Mindanao, to kill them. And they were there to kill him.

"We were all Filipinos, that's what I kept thinking. It was crazy. Why were we supposed to kill each other?"

He downed a San Mig and set the bottle gently on the compartment floor.

"She looked so much like my sister."

The *Don Eusebio* crunched into the Zamboanga wharf at noon, four hours behind schedule. There were no *vintas* in the harbor. Private First Class Leo Merced and his officers boarded an army transport for the east coast of Mindanao. After a week at the Lantaka my friends and I flew back to Luzon, where Father Vic's men were waiting for us at the airport.

INDOCHINA REFUGEE CRISIS MOUNTS

BANGKOK (April 30, 1985) — A decade after the end of America's war in Indochina, half a million refugees are still awaiting resettlement, according to a report issued in Bangkok today.

The report, by the New York–based U.S. Committee for Refugees, found that nearly 400,000 refugees remain in camps in Thailand alone. They include 237,000 Cambodians displaced by fighting between Khmer Rouge guerrillas and the Vietnamese-supported government in Phnom Penh and an estimated 150,000 Vietnamese and Laotians.

At least 100,000 more Indochinese are being held in detention centers in Hong Kong, Malaysia and the Philippines.

Since the communist victory over American-backed forces in Indochina in 1975, some 1.7 million Southeast Asians have fled their countries. Roughly 700,000 have been permitted to settle in the United States, with another half million divided primarily between Canada, Australia and Western Europe.

But international aid officials say that the settlement programs have been haphazard at best, and that the refugee crisis shows no sign of abating.

"The past year—as the several that preceded it—has been a time of all too few solutions for the uprooted," said Roger Winter, the committee's director.

THE DRUMS OF BAN VINAI

At first glance, the embroidered scene that hangs on a living room wall in Fresno, California, could be a festival. Across its upper half, two lines of human figures snake toward an abstract river. The needlework of the anonymous Laotian artist is remarkably detailed: men in blousy black silk pajamas and red waist sashes; women in banded multicolored skirts, with children strapped papoose-style to their backs; thickets of foliage broken by a grazing elephant and a leaping stag. It might be a depiction of *boun ok vatsa,* the autumnal celebration of the waters, when great processions wind down from the verdant hills of Laos to greet the end of the rainy season.

But the story the wall hanging tells is of no festival. The year it recalls is 1979. The river is the Mekong. The men at its bank are cutting bamboo, hastily assembling rafts, pushing their women and children into the stream. In the foreground, which represents Thailand, refugee officials in green fatigues stand beside a waiting truck.

The embroidery pictures the end of a world that the artist's tribe, the Hmong, had known since the dawn of time. It also records the first step on an epic journey that forever changed the lives of the people who flee down its needlework paths.

The old haunts of the Hmong lie a long way from the bungalows of Fresno and the pancake-flat San Joaquin Valley, rising more than four thousand feet above the Mekong River in the jungled ridges where Burma, Laos, Thailand, and China's Yunnan Province meet. The western flank of this high frontier is the Golden Triangle, legendary for its opium crop and warlord law. But opium has never been more than a supplementary cash crop for the Hmong, in a mountain fastness more notable for its cashless barter system and preindustrial ways. There was no written Hmong language until the 1930s, when a European anthropologist invented one. There were no tractors or radios in the Hmong highlands until the 1950s.

So isolated were these highlands before the war in Indochina that many Hmong had only the dimmest notion of who the Thais, Vietnamese, and Burmese were, much less the Americans. Their neighbors were other hill tribesmen. They were the Karen, whose men were tattooed from the neck to the knees, and the Lahu, with their beaded vests and bell-clapper earrings. They were the Akha, who wore towering silver-ornamented headdresses, and the Lisu, Lolo, and Khmu, in their elaborate tunics and ritual sashes. They were the Mien, whose blue-turbaned women were swathed in dark robes accented with red wool ruffs. The Hmong themselves favored costumes that were de facto communal treasuries: tribal assets forged into heavy silver rings and chains worn around the necks of married women.

"The Mien people live in B.C. times," an elder in the Thai reaches of the Golden Triangle once told me. "Maybe we Hmong just a little ahead of them. Maybe not."

All the tribes raised their own crops, most of them on ancestral ground. But there was no such thing as ancestral ground for the Hmong; they were nomadic slash-and-burn farmers who torched their fields after each harvest, in a primitive fertilizing technique that rid the soil of nutrients after two or three seasons. Every few years they moved their furrows, until the crops were so far away that they simply packed up and moved the whole village to another mountain slope above the Plain of Jars.

The Hmong were different from their neighbors in one other notable, and in the end catastrophic, trait. They thought of themselves as warriors as much as farmers—a perception that would eventually set them on the long road to California. Although no one then could have foreseen its terrible twists, this destiny began to unfold in the late 1950s, when American missionaries penetrated the hills northeast of the Mekong, and a strange tale appeared in the compendium of local religious beliefs.

The tale had it that a new Christian messiah was about to arrive on the Plain of Jars. He would be driving a U.S. Army jeep, and he would hand out weapons.

It was a bare-bones prophecy, without much more to it than that single image: a holy man in a jeep full of guns. But repeated over and over in tribal councils, it soon took on the power of dogma.

No one is sure who planted the idea of the armed messiah in the Laotian highlands. It may have been overzealous missionaries mixing Cold War politics with Christianity. It may simply have been Hmong converts, who misunderstood or embellished upon a hodgepodge of sermons and rumors that roiled up in the highlands in those years. It may have been American intelligence agents—this is what the Hmong themselves believe—bent on a more devious mission.

Whatever the prophecy's source, there was good reason for the Hmong to reflect on its effects over the next three decades. They are an unusually blunt people, not given to circumlocution, and they make no effort to cloud the basic fact that would eventually land them in the San Joaquin Valley. Moua Dang, a tribal leader who now raises hogs in the valley, put it with typical bluntness: "We worked for your government. We fought what you Americans like to call 'the secret war in Laos.' It was no secret to us."

Washington refused to acknowledge that secret until 1979, although the Laotian war involved thousands of saturation bombing raids, lasted eighteen years, and produced casualties among the Hmong ten times as high as those suffered by American forces in Vietnam. According to testimony before the U.S. Congress delivered almost two decades later, between 1966 and 1975 a load of heavy bombs was dropped from a B-52 on the Hmong districts of Laos an average of every nine minutes, twenty-four hours a day.

The Hmong were a tough, unsophisticated tribal society whose own backyard grievances made them perfect recruits for this brutal clandestine war. Eternal migrants who had only made their way into the Mekong highlands from China in the mid-nineteenth century, they were at constant odds with the lowland ethnic Lao who controlled both the royal government in Vientiane, the Laotian capital, and the communist Pathet Lao insurgency that rose against it in the 1950s. Although Hmong soldiers fought on both sides in the war, the vast majority served against the Pathet Lao in a CIA-funded third force under a Hmong general named Vang Pao.

But their choice of enemy had far less to do with ideology than it did with the fact that the Pathet Lao operated mainly out of the Plain of Jars, where they controlled the market towns and made efforts to rationalize farm production. The plain was Hmong territory in those years, the crossroads of their incessant wandering, and the Hmong don't take lightly to interference with their tribal customs and peregrinations. In all of Asia no culture is more uncompromising in its devotion to pure independence, which has been bred through two thousand years of migration in search of open land. The sedentary Chinese call them *meo*, "barbarians"; *hmong*, their word for themselves, translates simply as "free men."

That ancient, insatiable desire for independence, together with clan loyalties so fierce that they made separation intolerable, were the greatest strengths of their culture, the resources that fueled the Hmong on their journeys and made them Indochina's most tenacious soldiers. For four full years after the fall of Vientiane in May 1975 and the unseemly American scramble to flee Southeast Asia, the Hmong did not even concede that the war was over. On the rugged slopes of Phou Bia Mountain above the Plain of Jars, they kept their pact with the CIA long after the agency itself had cut and run. It wasn't until the end of the decade, when further resistance became impossible, that the decision was reluctantly made to retreat.

According to one of the few recorded accounts of this nearly forgotten battle, sixty thousand Hmong, mostly women and children, were on Phou Bia when the final assaults opened. Defended by three thousand lightly armed soldiers, some as young as fifteen years old, they faced an army of seventy-five thousand Pathet Lao troops, backed up with sustained bombardment from 105-millimeter artillery pieces that had been left behind by the United States and aerial napalm raids supplied from the same abandoned American stockpiles.

Wang Leng Vang was one of those who held out, commanding a resistance unit in the highlands at the age of twenty-two. On a hot summer morning in 1984 he was pointed out to me by a Hmong tribal leader, sitting on a curb in front of the Fresno County unemployment office. I introduced myself and asked him if he would tell me about Phou Bia. After a long pause, he nodded and got up; we walked together, without speaking, to his home six blocks away.

"The Pathet Lao very angry with the Hmong people," he suddenly said as we reached our destination. "But we not leave the mountain."

At thirty-five, Wang was slight of frame, deferential in conversation. His wife, Xia Xiong, who clearly understood more of our exchange than she admitted, stared quietly at the street as we talked; the Hmong consider direct eye contact impolite. Standing before their flat, in a cramped south-side Fresno housing complex where children played tag in a parking lot full of rusty cars with out-of-state plates, they didn't look very militant.

"Until 1978," Wang continued, "we think we can stay. But in the spring Pathet Lao come with many troops, and the fighting is very bad. Pretty soon I see I must find a way out for my family. So with my brother and six other man, we go into the jungle, to make a trail to the Mekong. We are gone almost one year. We return on May 17, 1979, for our people, and we start to Thailand."

He remembered every critical date in the war, and in the exodus that followed it, with this kind of precision. In his generation of Hmong, they all do. But very few will speak of the experience today. It is left mostly to their older children, the ones who can remember, to describe what happened. A number of them did so in essays for a Fresno English language class. Their accounts made chilling reading.

"It was May 10, 1979, and that day was about twelve o'clock midnight," wrote Kha Lee Xiong of his departure from the family village. "All kinds of food were lost. We ate mushroom until we came to the Mekong. When we got in the Mekong, soldiers were walking on the road and they saw us. Then they caught my mother and my younger sister. . . ."

Tua Xiong recalled "walking on a road with no houses. We got bitten by small animals, by snakes. Some people just die, and some lost their child, husband or wife. Some people just die because they got no food or water. Some got killed by gun, mine and bomb. Some of the people get killed and they don't even bury them. They just leave the person laid down in the place that they die."

"I left my girlfriend in Laos," wrote Ai Xiong, nineteen, hardly an adult himself, yet one of the haunted ones. "She is a pretty girl, but I did not know how to kiss her. When we came to Thailand, I never have another girlfriend. I never saw another girl look pretty like my girl in Laos.

"Then we come to the United States of America. In Fresno, they have so many girls, but they do not like me. I want to go back to my country and I go find my girlfriend in Laos and get married to her. But now her kiss me."

The figures measuring the Hmong retreat, the true end of America's war in Indochina, are speculative at best. The most dependable estimates suggest that less than two hundred thousand Hmong remain in Laos today. Perhaps one hundred thousand have been resettled, primarily in the United States and France. That leaves a quarter million of Wang's people, 40 percent of their prewar population in Laos, unaccounted for.

Thousands were lost in the war, thousands more on the trek to the Mekong or in the midnight swim to Thailand. Awaiting them on the other side was the Ban Vinai refugee camp, a place so overcrowded and rife with disease that it left a grisly memory imprinted on all who passed through it in the late 1970s.

When a Hmong dies, his fellow clansmen beat out a dirge on ceremonial drums, announcing his departure for the afterworld. At Ban Vinai they beat ceaselessly, around the clock.

"In the morning, in the night, the drums never stop in the camp," Wang Leng Vang told me during our conversation at the housing project. "Until we leave for America, the drums are in our ears. Even in this country, some Hmong cannot hear anything else."

On a Tuesday morning in April 1976, exactly one year into the siege of Phou Bia, Moua Dang was in a state office building in Richmond, Virginia, picking up his driver's license. That afternoon he bought a 1970 AMC Hornet for $200. The next morning he left for California.

"There were seven of us in the car, my wife and children, and two friends who begged me to take them along. By the time we got to Tennessee, the front end of the Hornet was sticking up so high I couldn't see over the hood. When I pulled into a gas station, the man take one look at it and asks me, 'What in God's name you got in that trunk? Your springs are totally shot.'

"The answer was everything we owned—dishes, pots and pans, TV set, clothes. Not much for seven people, but too much for the Hornet. So I used my last $60 on new springs, borrowed gas money from my friends, and went on. All I knew was to keep following the sun, three days and three nights. I was the only driver."

Moua had been among the first of the Hmong to arrive in the United States, flown directly to Virginia from a Thai camp in the winter of 1975 and plunked into a warehouse job at a Richmond newspaper.

"They told me the job was 'part-time with lots of overtime.' Now that I've been in America awhile, I realize that the 'part-time' bit was to avoid paying any fringe benefits. I worked from noon to six o'clock, and went back from nine at night to four in the morning. It was thirteen hours a day, minimum wage."

Moua was part of the tiny Hmong intelligentsia, an educated son of a clan elder. He had worked in Laos for the U.S. Agency for International Development. His uncle, a prominent politician, was assassinated by the Pathet Lao in Xiengkhouang, the capital of the Plain of Jars region. Moua Dang was born, raised, and schooled to be a leader. And almost alone among the early Hmong arrivals, he could see that storm signals lay ahead.

The federal government was trying to spread Indochinese refugees around, settling the first wave of Hmong, along with thousands of Vietnamese, Cambodians, and lowland Lao, in fifty-three different cities, twenty-five different states.

"They went wherever a church group or local community would agree to sponsor a family," one U.S. official later told me, conceding that the approach had been "a colossal mistake."

Among other things, the federal plan ran up against the Hmong's tribal instincts. It put many of them in northern states, where they found the climate uninhabitable. ("My people never hear of snow before," Na Vang, a Fresno Hmong by way of Minneapolis, remembered. "We arrive at night in some places like Minnesota, wake up in morning and suddenly whole world is white. What is happening?")

The plan landed others in southern states where there was virtually no English language instruction, job training, or public assistance. In Arkansas, where nearly four thousand Southeast Asian refugees were initially settled, welfare regulations required that an applicant have been in the state three of the previous five years to qualify for $40 a month in a maximum of four annual payments. With his thirteen-hour-a-day part-time job in Virginia, Moua was one of Dixie's luckier Hmong.

He was also a very determined man. For it was Moua as much as anybody who set about reinventing the Hmong future when the omens began darkening in the winter of 1976 and word of the siege of Phou Bia reached Virginia. He pored over geography books in the Richmond library, searching for information on climate, soil conditions, and crop yields. He sent his brother, who had been settled in Orange County, on scouting missions to rural California, where the books described exactly the kind of land Moua was seeking.

In March 1976 his brother telephoned: "The San Joaquin Valley is the place."

In April Moua was on the road west in the Hornet with his wife, Palee, their three small children, and two friends.

Red-eyeing it west with his family on Interstate 40 in 1976, Moua Dang was the Hmong Daniel Boone. He was the pathfinder, the first of his tribe to pursue an American dream of his own making. The road carried them to a Del Monte farmworkers' camp in the San

Joaquin Valley, where Moua and Palee found their first California jobs picking figs.

The hill tribesmen were a minor curiosity in America in those years. A scant three thousand of the Hmong, educated leaders like Moua and high-ranking officers of Vang Pao's army, had been airlifted to the United States after the fall of Vientiane. Most people in the valley, where in 1976 the Hmong could be counted on two hands, took Moua and Palee for Mexicans, maybe Indians from Oaxaca, who also worked as pickers and sometimes spoke to each other in a strange language that wasn't Spanish.

They were not long in the fields. Palee, who was the first to master English, took a job as a bilingual interpreter in the county education department in 1978. By 1980 Moua's own language skills had improved to the point that he too was offered a county job as a teacher's aide.

Five years later he was an indispensable man in the valley, the founder of a tribal social agency that handled most Hmong relations with the federal government, an expert on foundations, a master of the grant proposal. It was Moua who organized housing for Hmong newcomers, Moua who beat the bushes for jobs. It was Moua who gave me Wang Leng Vang's name when I asked about the siege of Phou Bia. "Leadership" is an amorphous concept: The capacity behind it resists definition. But its presence in Moua Dang was unmistakable.

Physically, he was small by American standards, no more than five-foot-five. Although he had broad, powerful shoulders and a thick neck, it wasn't the illusion of size that distinguished him from the other Hmong who crowded the county welfare office where we talked. It was that inexplicable capacity. The Hmong themselves couldn't explain it, even though it's what the elders must have aimed at in his education—the highlands tribal blueblood bred to lead. Because even in the Hmong world, such an education doesn't always work, not the way it worked with Moua.

A circle of tribal members almost immediately formed around him when we walked in. They had problems the welfare people would like to solve and seldom could. It wasn't even his office; he had business in Fresno, and it was a convenient place for us to meet. But Moua was a man with answers, a patient man trying to unravel what he—and virtually every Hmong—regarded as a fundamental, devastating betrayal.

"The 'Promise,'" he said to me when we moved to a back room in the office, away from the crowd. "Do you know about the 'Promise'?"

All the Hmong used that precise word to describe the basis of their wartime arrangement with the United States, the covenant that followed the armed messiah into the Plain of Jars. The Promise was the key to every conversation with the Hmong in America, the code that loosened polite discretion. It was also an open sore in the consciences of Americans who knew about it—intelligence officers who had served in Indochina, church workers from the camps, State Department hands on the Asia Desk.

"Countless individuals told of the 'Promise' that the American 'CIA' personnel had given them if they fought with the Americans," note the authors of a secret U.S. government document on the Hmong that one embittered federal official passed on to me. "Former Hmong soldiers can itemize the dates and places that American promises of help were made to them and name the 'CIA' officials who delivered them."

My source had been hearing about the Promise for more than a decade. It haunted him. Long, incriminating passages in the document were highlighted with a yellow marker. He gave me the names of other officials, some of whom were clearly former intelligence agents, who had talked to him about the Hmong.

From time to time after my first articles on the Hmong were syndicated by Pacific News Service, unsolicited packages would arrive in the mail, stuffed with classified reports or the transcripts of interviews that the CIA and other federal departments had conducted in the Thai camps. The packages never carried return addresses or cover letters.

In 1960, "five Americans came from the CIA and had us sign documents," an unnamed clan elder told federal interviewers in one of these transcripts. "We couldn't write, so we put our handprints on it instead."

The terms were quite clearly explained, insisted another. "The Americans in Laos had an agreement, a contract with us: 'You help us fight for your country, and if you can't win, we will take you with us and we will help you live.' "

Although "there are several versions of the 'Promise,' there can be no doubt that assurances were made to support the Hmong during the war, and to provide assistance in the event Laos was lost to the communists," conceded an unpublished U.S. government study.

To the Hmong, the very existence of the Promise meant that the CIA had become part of the tribal family, eligible for a generosity that knew virtually no bounds, and was expected to reciprocate when necessary. In Laos, a Hmong would never consider hiring other Hmong who were down on their luck; they would simply be given whatever was needed, with no questions asked. It had nothing to do with charity, or even with the principle that the rich must help the poor. When one tribesman had problems, it was the duty of another to help. And if the wheel of fortune turned, it was understood that the favor would be returned: that whatever was necessary would be supplied—usually land, an opportunity to farm. An opportunity to remain independent and free.

It was soon evident, even to the earliest Hmong refugees, that it didn't work that way in America, Promise or not.

"The Americans came to my country and built the war there, now I have no country and have nothing," one of them told U.S. government officials in an exchange that was dutifully recorded in the notes of a Refugee Resettlement Office clerk. "When I stayed in Laos I was a farmer. I was stupid, I could do nothing else. I had all the things I wanted. I never begged anyone for food. Only when I came to the country of America I had to beg. . . ."

As the second wave of Hmong refugees broke over the Mekong in the 1980s and was dispersed across the United States, the Hmong tribal chiefs stopped saying that the Promise would solve their problems. They decided to take charge, once again, of their people's future. They listened to the counsel of a few leaders like Moua Dang, who had decided years earlier that the Promise was an illusion: that the tribe would have to look out for itself. That it would have to move on once more.

They looked west, where Moua had looked.

The number of Hmong in the San Joaquin remained stable until 1982. Then, suddenly, to the astonishment and impotent annoyance of Washington, a vast exodus of Hmong tribesmen began streaming into California.

In July 1980 the Hmong in Merced and Fresno counties, the heart of the great agricultural valley, numbered in the low hundreds. By July 1983 there were more than twenty thousand.

Eighteen months later there were fifty thousand.

In an Asian *Grapes of Wrath,* the clans poured west along the route that Moua Dang and Palee had traveled half a decade earlier, west across three thousand miles of mountains and prairies, and more mountains and deserts. Massing fleets of U-hauls and half-junked Fords and Buicks in Rhode Island and New York, Michigan and Indiana, South Carolina and Alabama, the Hmong picked up and moved to the San Joaquin with the same restless determination that propelled them over the mountains of Laos.

But they had known Laos. They knew its ridges and valleys and the trails that pierced its forests. The map of the highlands was second nature. In America the land was unfamiliar and the maps unreadable. The language was foreign, the writing a cloud of indecipherable hieroglyphics.

It was a staggering accomplishment, the American exodus of the Hmong. It was a voyage across time. Simply to imagine it is to defy credibility:

A phone rings in a boarding house in Mobile, Alabama. It is answered by a man who cannot read, who cannot speak English, who doesn't even know what a "state" is. The caller tells the man to bring his family to a place that is known as "California."

The man goes to a used car lot: Already the plot verges on the fantastic. What must the car dealer have made of this client, a man from prehistory come to buy an automobile? And how does the man choose?

The answer is simple, says Wang Leng Vang—for this is his particular tale, the tale of the young commander from Phou Bia, one episode in the fifty thousand—"I had only so much money and I needed a big car."

So the 1975 Oldsmobile it will be, the biggest car, the only big car with a price under $1,000 scrawled on its windshield. But even this simple transaction baffles: How is it done without words? Without language?

Wang: "I pointed at the one I wanted. I knew the American numbers, that's all."

He tells this story three years later, unsmiling. He has the words, but it isn't amusing yet, not for Wang. Maybe that will be for his children and their children—the family comedy that the immigrant saga becomes as the years pass: "Remember Dad buying that enormous, gas-guzzling monster of an Olds? All that crazy sign language and hand-signaling at the car lot?"

Still, the car isn't big enough. So Xia and one daughter have to take the Greyhound, along with twenty-three other Alabama Hmong whom Wang ferries to the Mobile bus station, five at a time. He manages to follow the bus—probably without a license, he politely ignores me when I ask—as far as the Mississippi. Not that he knows its name.

"It is at the very wide river, four or five times wider than the Mekong. I cannot see my wife and daughter anymore."

He loses the Greyhound in a maze of overpasses and freeway exits. Maybe it is Memphis. Maybe St. Louis. Even the road he is on when he loses his family can only be guessed at later—the family he led from Phou Bia to the Mekong and across to Ban Vinai in 1979, after he and his brother spent a year cutting a trail through the Laotian jungle.

He can't ask someone where to look for the bus. There is no way. This is not Moua Dang, who has had an education and held a job in Virginia before his trek west, struggling to hold the Hornet on the road when its shock absorbers fail and pulling into a gas station to find out what's wrong.

This is a man who has lost his family in the heart of an unknown continent, and cannot tell anyone.

He has no choice but to continue. What he remembers of the rest of that journey is the geography of desperation. The large chain of mountains. Then the great desert. Then the second set of mountains. After which he begins to ask, as instructed in the phone call:

"California?" And when the answer is finally yes, the second instructed question: "Fresno?"

All the while he is obsessed with the wife and daughter; with their clothes piled up in the rear seat and the other child whimpering next to him.

When he said "Fresno" to the people at the bus station in Mobile and pointed at his family, did they understand?

On the fourth day out of Alabama, Wang Leng Vang pulls into the Fresno bus station hallucinating from exhaustion, "confused in my head and seeing everything curvy even if it is flat." He is still there on the fifth day as Xia steps off the Greyhound, with their daughter half asleep in her arms, blinking in the noon San Joaquin sun.

City
of the
Main Chance

CITY OF THE MAIN CHANCE

"I'll pick you up in ten minutes," Mr. Chan said over the phone. "Look for silver Mercedes."

When I passed that bit of information on to my companion, she laughed and pointed out our hotel window to Nathan Road. From the tip of the Kowloon Peninsula to the edge of the northern horizon it was a honking river of Mercedes, at least half of them silver. Spotting Chan Fook Cheung's steed in that high-stakes horse race would be about as easy as identifying a single Fiat in Rome.

Fortunately Chan found me, exactly ten minutes later, peering into the traffic from the corner of Nathan and Peking roads; bearded Italian Americans are less common in Hong Kong than the Mercedes Benz. A few minutes more and we were rocketing through the Cross-Harbour Tunnel toward Aberdeen, on the far side of Victoria Peak. It was a white-knuckle flight all the way, with Chan weaving through traffic bottlenecks with the casual finesse of a stock-car driver all alone on the final lap. His left arm rested on the seat behind his younger sister, Mrs. Yung, and his head turned toward me in the rear seat every time he felt the need to emphasize some point in conversation.

As usual in Hong Kong the talk was business and food, and the destination was a restaurant. Not just any restaurant. We were headed for the Jumbo: the largest floating dining room on earth. A culinary palace comparable to virtually nothing else in existence and part-owned, not incidentally, by Mr. Chan Fook Cheung, re-tired chief warden of Hong Kong Traffic Control, chairman of the Royal Hong Kong Police Old Comrades Association, right-hand man to Henry Fok the cement king, manager of the Far East Hy-drofoil Service to Macao, and ex-director of the Hong Kong Soccer Football League.

"Actually, at least thirty different people own a piece of the Jumbo," he noted, screeching to a jaw-wrenching stop in front of the restaurant's parking jockey. "I'm a little guy, but everyone here still calls me Director Chan. It's a big joke with me and the waiters."

From the dock where we waited for a sampan to carry us out to dinner, the Jumbo resembled an Oriental Rose Bowl float built to the dimensions of a convention center. Up and down it rose and fell in Aberdeen Harbour, under a blaze of red-and-gold neon trim.

JUMBO, the skyscraper-sized marquee flashed across the water. JUMBO. JUMBO. JUMBO.

Everything about this restaurant was sui generis Hong Kong: its outsized dimensions, its garish self-congratulation and Byzantine multiple ownership scheme, its odds-be-damned commercial tenacity. The Jumbo had gone up in flames twice in this decade, in kitchen fires that left nothing visible above the waterline except a charred hulk, which was promptly rebuilt and refloated a few months later.

The Jumbo was also quintessential Hong Kong in the staggering cost of a meal—$120 for steamed fish, $100 for a single lobster, $250 for an especially high-quality shark's fin soup; unfathomably, the place still filled up in the afternoons with tables of grannies and their adolescent wards in the modified pajamas that are the everyday garb of the Cantonese working class. None of it added up. It was pure improbability. Pure Hong Kong.

Most of all, what made it Hong Kong was gamblers like Chan, who staked a crazy, improbable bet on some outside prospect, some long shot, and saw their luck come home. I never asked Mr. Chan what his bet was. In Hong Kong, that question is very seldom asked. Whatever it was, it didn't matter. The act itself—the risk—was what counted here. Hong Kong's lights celebrated the dreams of a city of six million gamblers. The city of the main chance.

Even an outsider felt it, the nervous excitement that translated into endless, purposeful motion. The motion of great crowds swarming each morning onto the Star ferries at the foot of Kowloon, disembarking Hong Kong side to mount elevated sidewalks that zigzagged into the office buildings and commercial hubs of Central. At Queen's Road the human flood merged with the stream of 1.5 million people carried daily by the Mass Transit Railway subway and another 4 million aboard buses from instant cities that had sprung up in the New Territories, cheek by jowl with the Chinese border.

Motion. Hong Kong seethed with motion, with raw ambition, with absurd fantasies. Anything could happen here. Anything was possible.

Nighttime Kowloon side, up Nathan Road beyond the tourist traps of Tsim Sha Tsui, the commercial guise of possibility was afire with neon, riotous colors stacked atop each other like some mad work of abstract expressionism, commerce expressed in its own spontaneous art form. Tom Lee's pianos announced themselves in a gargantuan yellow-and-blue blinking Steinway. Panasonic electronics commanded the twenty-five-story face of an entire building in alternating bands of gold and red. Millie's Department Store throbbed with a show-stopping peacock's tail formed of tens of thousands of individual lights.

Under the peacock's tail, at Jordan Road, the human current poured off Nathan Road and into the back alleys of Yaumatei and Mongkok. This was old Kowloon, blocks of ragged concrete tenements where the newcomers and the not-yet-lucky lived, crammed together 543,000 to the square mile, thirty-five times the density of San Francisco. People slept in shifts in the airless rooms above these streets. They worked fourteen-hour days in textile sweatshops. And they gambled—everyone gambled; there were off-track betting shops on nearly every corner. In 1984, Hong Kong bet $2.5 billion a year on the horses, $500 for every man, woman, and child.

Before 6:00 P.M. the streets of Yaumatei and Mongkok served normal retail purposes and flowed with conventional automobile traffic. After six, in fifteen minutes flat, these streets became a bazaar, a thousand *dai pai dong*—market stands—materializing out of thin air, offering every conceivable product. Stir-fried clams and deep-fried pig's intestines were offered alongside Yves St. Laurent three-piece suits, actual and alleged. Souvenir coins from Nixon's visit to Beijing were pyramided next to radios and women's panties, cigarette lighters in pornographic shapes, pirated Rolling Stones cassettes, and hundreds of models of telephones (including one inexplicably equipped with a deodorizer). All of it was sold from commercial operations so compact that they frequently fitted on a two-foot-square folding television table.

But no one could persuade the *dai pai dong* vendors that they were wasting their time. They knew about the Director Chans, whose ships came in on the basis of a stake no bigger than the one they'd earn tonight, a few dollars well placed. And they knew about much bigger people who had started out like this. They knew about Li Kaishing, the land baron of central Hong Kong and quite possibly the richest man on earth, who launched his career peddling plastic flowers in Yaumatei. They knew about Henry Fok, the patron of Director Chan, whose small investment in a lime-rich Pearl Delta sandbar in the 1950s literally became the stuff by which the towers of Hong Kong were built in the 1960s and 1970s. They knew about all the people trading stocks and bonds on the other side of Victoria Harbour who first stepped onto the soil of Hong Kong dripping wet, after an all-night swim from China through the shark-infested waters of Mirs Bay. To a man, and woman, the *dai pai dong* vendors were believers, convinced they would one day be millionaires. They were dizzied by the sheer narcotic rush of Hong Kong. They weren't unlucky. They were the not-yet-lucky: *ting yat dai fook*—"big winner tomorrow."

The vendors remembered Chan Fook Cheung as a Yaumatei beat cop in the days when he too was *ting yat dai fook*. They recognized him when we walked down the street together: "Director Chan, sit down," they yelled from their tables. "*Nei sik joh mei ah?*"—"Have you had dinner yet?" He was a big man now. But jealousy wasn't remotely evident in their greetings. The risks were still available for the taking. The nerve was still there. That's what mattered.

It was all a gamble, Hong Kong reckoned. The ground itself was unstable. Someone else held the deed.

When the British signed the colonial property away to China in the Beijing-London Pact of 1984, giving Hong Kong an ominous thirteen years to put its affairs in order or leave them behind, the bettors should have been scared off. That was the conventional wisdom in conventional Western business circles, in cautious places like New York and Frankfurt. But in Hong Kong the betting went on. They figured, Mr. Chan and everyone like him, that they even had the China angle covered.

They'd buy the place.

More improbable than ever. But that was the plan, if this kind of massive joint gamble could be called a plan. Mr. Chan did his part. He took some of his earnings from the Jumbo and put them into a seafood restaurant up in Shekou, just across Hau Hoi Bay from Hong Kong in China's Guangdong Province. Shekou had been one of the first foreign joint venture sites in the People's Republic, and Chan got in early. Then others followed, thousands of little investors and lots of the biggest: Li Kaishing, Henry Fok, Y. K. Pao the shipping magnate, textile barons, and food-processing magnates by the score.

Soon a critical mass of investment was achieved, a pattern established and, documented. The big hitters had their photographs taken with party chief Hu Yaobang, Prime Minister Zhao Ziyang, and paramount leader Deng Xiaoping, the godfathers of the Special Economic Zones and the open door—the men whose reforms made the investments something more than a fool's bet, if something less than a sure winner.

The nest egg grew and grew; improbably, unbelievably, it grew. By the mid-1980s Hong Kong, with six million people, accounted for three times the combined total of all Japanese and American investments in China. In the Pearl Delta, the most highly developed part of the country, 90 percent of all foreign investment was in the hands of overseas Chinese, some from Taiwan or San Francisco or Singapore, but the vast majority from Hong Kong.

The money piled up and up, until it seemed there was nobody in Hong Kong—which was to be owned by China—who didn't own something in China. And to the astonishment of the cautious money in the West, it was China rather than Hong Kong that was radically transformed, even when the instrument of change was nothing more than a joint venture restaurant like Director Chan's.

I ate lunch at Chan's place across the border in Shekou on a muggy September Tuesday. Shameless, I dropped his name—*Director Chan*—with the hostess. She responded very professionally and discreetly nodded, so I knew there would be either a discount or a special plate delivered. It turned out to be both. Halfway into the meal, a smiling waiter led a parade of three kitchen helpers to the table, along with a cart atop which sat a small burner and a glass bowl of squirming live prawns. Also very professionally, the prawns were anesthetized in the best Shaoxing wine, then quickly poached: the celebrated "drunken shrimp." The discount, marked on the bill but never mentioned aloud, was 25 percent.

My lunch companion was an acquaintance of Chan's named Ho Kimun. He'd invited me to Shekou to see his own piece of the People's Republic, an electronics plant. The gamble here was considerable. Ho was betting he could train Chinese workers to make floppy disk drives that were good enough to be sold as components in IBM clones. If it worked out, the costs of production would be cut to less than a fifth of what he spent manufacturing the same disks in the New Territories, Hong Kong's suburban sprawl south of the Chinese border.

"Otherwise, I'll be marketing a lot of expensive scrap metal," he said.

The performance of the restaurant was a good sign. A few years before, even in Guangdong, mainland restaurants had almost all been in the mode of the Workers', Soldiers', or Peasants' halls favored by Chairman Mao, where clean plates were regarded as a counterrevolutionary frill and diners had to shove piles of discarded bones and scraps off the tables to make room for their meals. Now, in joint venture zones like Shekou, it was getting hard to tell that you were in the workers' paradise. The waiters and hostesses and maîtres d' were sent to Hong Kong for training. Hong Kong architects designed the restaurants. And almost always, the money was from Hong Kong and a Hong Kong cousin sat at the cash register, just to make sure.

By the mid-1980s, the good signs for Hong Kong's China gamblers were piling up as fast as the investments. A brand-new China ferry building was under construction in Kowloon, with computerized schedule boards to handle the mushrooming fleet of hydrofoils loaded with businessmen that already sped back and forth daily and sometimes hourly, from a temporary port terminal to Shekou, Zhongshan, Canton, Jiangmen, Guanghai, Zhuhai—the Pearl Delta funnels into which Hong Kong was pumping its insurance money. Every dollar brought another omen that the plan was solid: smoother handling of materials at the border (the smoothness increased in direct proportion to the customs officers' willingness to be bribed); workers who were better motivated (and better paid, under the table, where the state work unit salary scales were not a problem); and yes, better restaurants.

"You see, it's getting just like Hong Kong," Ho said, manipulating a toothpick into a rear molar as we strolled through downtown Shekou on the way to his plant.

And although Tian Hongqiao wasn't who he was referring to, Tian proved to be the best example I'd seen yet of the effect that Hong Kong's plan was having on its real target, the mentality of China.

Tian was from Beijing, and apart from his Liberation-era given name, which meant "Red Flag," and that unmistakable northern accent with its long drawn-out *r*'s, he was like the new restaurants on the mainland side of the border: You couldn't tell. Could have been Hong Kong. Could have been Taipei.

He was waiting for us in Ho's office, a young man, probably no more than twenty-five, in a nicely cut soft leather jacket and pressed denims. But the clothes weren't the half of it; it was Tian's manner that I really marveled at. There was none of the ramrod straightness, the visible uneasiness this far from the capital, that often made people from Beijing seem like hopeless prigs even when they weren't. Tian put out his hand to shake mine when we were introduced; he didn't wait for a cue. And he shook it seriously, returning the grip rather than doing his best to escape it, as though a foreign palm might carry some disease. He didn't even have the repressed cranelike stride you noticed in Beijing. It was more of a jazzy lope, so replete with bravado that it made me think of John Travolta in *Saturday Night Fever*.

Like everybody with a stake in China, Ho had set his plant up to do import-export as well as manufacturing since he had to pay for an export license anyway. That's what brought Tian down from the north. He had a long, flat box under his arm: the goods. Tian was a sales agent.

"Ho, my friend, this is going to make you rich. And you too, my American friend, rich!"

Ho translated, although in fact Tian spoke an invented-on-the-spot salesman's mélange of Mandarin and Cantonese, aimed at the local market, that was surprisingly close to my own haphazard jumbling of Chinese dialects. My presence didn't bother him at all, especially since Ho had decided to tell him that I was an importer and not a reporter.

Tian yanked a black plastic gizmo out of the box. It was an electronic piano keyboard, a rip-off of the Yamaha instrument that was a big Christmas seller in the States. He set it on Ho's desk and stepped back, looking it up and down the way a Hollywood producer might ogle a starlet on the casting couch, and shook his head admiringly. Then he fumbled with the controls for a moment, and the unit obligingly played a sample piece that had been programmed into its memory. It was Stevie Wonder's "My Cherie Amour."

The device could be adjusted to mimic the sounds of string instruments, the brass section of an orchestra, or a baroque harmonium for those who preferred Bach to Motown. Tian demonstrated them all. It was a pity that the care that went into imitating the Yamaha original had slipped on the choice of a brand name. Someone had convinced the manufacturer up in Beijing to name it the Bony Keyboard, no doubt hoping it would be confused with Sony.

Ho passed on it, and Tian joined the two of us on a tour of the plant. The disk drive-makers were bent to their tasks just like their counterparts across the bay in Hong Kong, where the term "work ethic" was bandied about so often that it had become the most exhausted cliché in the colony. These young women—the workers were mostly women at Ho's plant, in their late teens and early twenties, who had been brought down to Shekou from villages in western Guangdong and neighboring Hunan Province—definitely had the work ethic. It was what happened when young people earned decent wages, and had the means to buy clothes and go to discos. They worked harder.

Ho took us to visit one of the dorms, where two embarrassed girls from the night shift sat on their beds in a room that measured about ten feet by sixteen. They'd decorated it with stuffed animals and frilly bedspreads that might have been found in a California teenager's bedroom.

So much was changing here, thanks to Hong Kong. I remembered the first time I'd visited the Pearl Delta, going into a bank at midday and finding the tellers all sound asleep, their heads resting on the counter. It felt like it must have been decades ago. It was only four years.

Things were moving very quickly indeed now, and the bets seemed safe. Except that there was sometimes the worry—both Ho and Tian expressed it, when we talked over a beer after the tour— the worry that the changes were coming *too* fast. It wasn't a dominant theme in conversation. They were businessmen and found it difficult to restrain their natural impulse to boosterism. The worry lay between the lines, alluded to in scattered observations that measured costs nobody had anticipated.

"We have to have a doctor on call for the girls all the time, you know," Ho said at one juncture.

I wondered if he was gingerly admitting that his plant had a problem with industrial accidents. But that wasn't it at all. The cost that had him worried, the evidence of too much change too fast, wasn't totted up in severed fingers or damaged eyes.

"We need the doctor," Ho said, "because so many girls have gotten pregnant since they came here."

MARCOS FLEES MANILA

MANILA (February 26, 1986) — With his army in revolt and two key advisers calling for his resignation, President Ferdinand Marcos fled the Philippines last night.

While details remain to be worked out, it appears certain that Corazon Aquino will officially assume the duties of the presidency today. Aquino, the widow of assassinated anti-Marcos dissident Benigno "Ninoy" Aquino, ran against Marcos in a disputed February 7 election.

U.S. military helicopters airlifted Marcos and his family from the Malacañang Palace, the presidential residence, as an angry mob surrounded the building.

Manila has been paralyzed by anti-Marcos protesters since Saturday, when Defense Minister Juan Ponce Enrile and the Deputy Armed Forces Chief of Staff, Lieutenant-General Fidel Ramos, seized two military bases in the city and called for the president to step down.

Aquino supporters blocked access to the bases on Epifanio de los Santos Avenue, one of Manila's main thoroughfares, preventing pro-Marcos soldiers from launching an assault on the rebel units.

Marcos has governed under martial law since 1972, asserting that the nation faced a serious uprising by the communist New People's Army. There is speculation that he will be offered asylum in the United States.

ELECTION WEEK

The Philippines was on a wild, uninhibited bender. Along the jammed commercial corridor of Epifanio de los Santos Avenue, Manila newsboys ran down the center lane, holding copies of *Time* aloft like a banner. The photo filled the cover, the photo of Cory Aquino in her yellow dress, Woman of the Year. The newsboys shouted it out in their demi-English street argot: "Cory, wooman of yare!" On the sidewalks of Makati and Quiapo pretty girls hung garlands of fragrant white san pagitas, the national flower, around the necks of perfect strangers. Filipinos were drunk with self-respect.

That was the heart of the matter, self-respect. They had almost given up, and then, behind this unlikely Joan of Arc with her permed hair and her squeaky voice and her matronly yellow dresses, they'd found the energy for one last desperate gesture in the streets. A common gesture, a family gesture. People would show visitors their scrapbooks of the insurrection, with the clippings arranged in chronological order, carefully annotated, like the photographs that recorded their children's baptisms, first communions, confirmations, and marriages.

Father Vic even had a video. He played it over and over in the living room of the house in the cigarette subdivision, where it would sputter and sometimes black out entirely with the shifting fortunes of the Quezon City power supply. There was always a mob in the room, adding spontaneous commentary: nuns, priests, ex-nuns and ex-priests, Doy De Alcuaz and Art Figueroa, Auntie and Father Vic's cousins. And Tony, of course, his brother here, the one who hadn't emigrated. The room dissolved into a pandemonium of quips and shouts as viewers recognized themselves or their friends on the video. But Father Vic and Tony sat quietly, sipping their bottles of San Miguel, eyes glued on the erratic flicker of the screen.

They wanted me there as a kind of professional narrator. My job was to emphasize the importance of the events on the tape, to compare their revolution to the ones I'd seen elsewhere, the ones that had almost always failed. Journalists were the rage now in Manila, especially journalists from San Francisco. Phil Bronstein, from the *Examiner,* had been the first reporter into the Malacañang Palace, just moments after Marcos and Imelda were shoved into the helicopter and whirled off. It was Phil who found the three thousand pairs of women's shoes and the painting that pictured a bare-torsoed Ferdinand Marcos in the guise of Tarzan, and the abandoned plate of caviar on the dining room table.

Epifanio de los Santos Avenue, "Edsa." The images of that dramatic February in the streets still had great power, even after a dozen screenings. The nuns, kneeling on the Edsa pavement before the tanks, saying the rosary. The enormous crowds, two million people swinging back and forth across the avenue between Camp Crame and Camp Aguinaldo, where Juan Ponce Enrile and Fidel Ramos were making their stand. And every now and then a fleeting glimpse of Father Vic, a man possessed, a general charging through the crowd at the head of his own small army of shantytown urchins, the newsboys and cigarette boys and flower girls of Dupax and Santa Cruz. They'd been there for three days without sleep, running lunch bags and smokes past the tanks to the fences, where they pitched them to the rebels holed up in the camps.

The tank crews looked dazed in the video, exhausted, terribly unhappy. I thought about PFC Leo Merced, the gunner's mate I'd shared a cabin with on the rat-infested passage to Zamboanga. Was he was there in the avenue, manning his gun? Or inside the fences with the rebels? He couldn't shoot a nun, I was sure of that.

Tony López had organized the food supply, sending box after box of brown paper bags south from Angeles City. Nobody knew exactly how he came up with the thousands of neatly wrapped sandwiches, each bagged with a Mars bar and a piece of fruit. Nobody asked.

On the evening of the twenty-sixth the helicopter vanished into the eastern horizon, carrying the president and the First Lady to Hawaii, and it was over. The tanks backed away from the fences, the crowds passed from the precipice of death to the summits of elation. It was their moment, their transcendent moment. They believed, fervent Catholics that they were, that it was the moment of resurrection.

The people of Tamarong, a fishing village on the Luzon coast two hundred miles northwest of Manila, hosted three Americans during the week of the constitutional election, two California reporters and a photographer from New York. We drove up with Father Vic and his entourage; Doy, Father's right-hand man, was from Tamarong, and Father Vic had been assigned there by the election commission to monitor the voting. The villagers threw a party for us—or for the election, it wasn't clear—that started the morning of our arrival and continued for a day and a half after the vote.

It was a very poor village, the kind where almost nobody, not even the mayor's wife, had a pair of shoes. Clustered around a small plaza fronting a church and a school, its huts lay at the end of a muddy track that crossed a small stream near its mouth in the South China Sea. The bridge had washed out long ago, and we had to leave the Toyota at the edge of a rice paddy a mile back.

The villagers wouldn't let us buy anything for the party, not even the San Migs that were consumed, warm, in enormous quantities, shouldered in by the case over the river from the truncated road.

"It's the Filipino way," Father Vic said. The phrase was beginning to lose its ironic sting. "Forget it."

But a few hours later, when he thought we were all at the polling site in the school, I saw him trying to press a wad of cash into the salt woman's hand. She wouldn't take it, not even from him. Doy had been born in the village. That was all she said: "Thank you, Father, but Doy was born here."

The salt woman, whose name was Anita, was already working when we arrived, before nine, from the mountains. This was her job: She dug blocks of what looked like yellow mud out of a sun-cracked tidal wash and piled them in a four-foot-high woven basket until, by my reckoning, it weighed around fifty pounds. Then she carried it on her head, a mile or so up the road, to the family compound of three nipa-palm huts. There was a huge black iron cauldron at the center of the compound, balanced on rocks over a fire of dried rice husks. A water pipe jutted from the sandy village main street another half mile to the east. After dumping the contents of the hamper into the cauldron, which was stirred endlessly by a small boy, Anita took an empty ten-gallon food can to the pipe, filled it, and returned to the compound, where another small boy slowly poured the water into the cauldron in a thin stream.

He laughed when I tried to balance the filled water can on my own head and nearly broke my neck under its precarious, shifting weight. Anita missed the comedy. She was on her way to the tidal wash for another load.

It went on like this, all day and most of the night, with a sister spelling Anita after dark and her children gathering the rice husks or whatever else could serve as fuel. The extracted salt was dried on bamboo racks and sifted into a fine mound, where it waited for one of the men to carry it over the river.

I had made a fool of myself at the tidal flat, asking Anita about the salt-panning in carefully phrased pidgin as though I was addressing a Martian.

"Sure, I'll tell you all about it," she answered. "Incidentally, I have a cousin in San Francisco. He lives on McAllister Street. He says he'll sponsor my daughter, pay her way at Berkeley."

The family here in Tamarong lived on the meager earnings from the salt. The money Anita's husband sent from Saudi Arabia (she hadn't seen him in more than three years) went to Manila, where their daughter was studying chemical engineering. Anita knew every-thing about San Francisco—street names, local points of interest, history—and also about Riyadh, where her husband worked on a construction crew, and London, where her brother was a waiter in the fast-food restaurant at Heathrow Airport, and Rome, where her sister was a maid.

"Your name is Italian, isn't it? Have you been to Rome?" she asked me.

I said yes, but wished the answer had been no.

Rome was her dream city, she said. She dreamed of seeing St. Peter's, of standing in the great square when the pope appeared in his little window on Easter Sunday. Staring through the palms at the sea, I tried to picture her in the vast space between Bernini's foun-tains, caressed by the spring breezes from the Tiber, waiting for John Paul II. It was the terrible Filipino curse again: knowing too much.

"Rome," Anita said one more time, whispering the word like a prayer.

The day before the election I borrowed Father Vic's car and drove up the coast, past Vigan into Ilocos Norte. The moment the provin-cial boundary was crossed the washboard highway flattened into smooth, perfectly maintained blacktop.

Along this part of the road people didn't celebrate the toppling of Ferdinand Marcos; they mourned it. He was theirs. They had sent him to Manila, and as he rose he had remembered them with gifts and public works projects and jobs in Manila and the regional capi-tals. The northern Ilocanos had good reason to love Marcos. (They were less enamored of his wife, a Visayan islander from what they regarded as the frivolous south; Ilocanos blamed Imelda for a lot that went wrong, believed that the corruption was her doing, unbe-knownst to her husband.)

Marcos. It was a name to conjure with on this coast, a name that signed the checks for parks, community centers, libraries, and so many salaries that no one could keep count. He was their most famous native son, and he was gone now. Had they been given the opportunity, the people north of Vigan would have willingly risked their skins to return him to the Malacañang Palace. Cory Aquino knew that, and wasn't taking any chances. Massive concrete barriers had been erected across the airport runways at Laoag, Marcos's chief power base. A plane couldn't land there. Ilocos Norte had no air service at all anymore.

That meant no customers for the Fort Ilocandia Hotel, not far from Sarrat, the Marcos vacation home a few miles west of Laoag. The hotel had been built by Marcos too, to provide suitable accommodations for jet-setting guests at his daughter Irene's wedding in 1983. It was Irene and her husband who sang "We Are the World" in the bizarre home video that reporters found in the Malacañang Palace after the family fled Manila.

The hotel was a long, three-storyed affair, built vaguely along pseudo–American colonial lines. The manager trotted out from his office to greet me when I stopped by for a look. He told a bellboy, who was rigged up in a footman's jacket and a pillbox hat, to show me to a room.

"Have a drink. On the house," the manager said.

A band was playing selections from Gershwin in the dining room. There wasn't another guest in sight. No one in the dining room, no one in the lobby, no one in the hall. You could have shot a cannon through the place.

The room turned out to be an immense suite, with a balcony facing the lawn, which swept down past a gazebo to the turquoise South China Sea. In the sitting area, which was outfitted with a wet bar, the bellboy offered me Johnny Walker Black, Sambuca, Martell. The bottles were already open. I asked for Campari, but there was none to be had.

"We've had troubles with deliveries this week," he said, knowing both of us were quite aware that no deliveries had been made since the airport was closed.

There was ice, and the air-conditioning was pleasantly frigid. I asked for a Scotch, neat, with an ice water chaser, and sat down in a wing chair at the window. It was Marcos liquor. But it seemed pointless to let the stuff evaporate.

The manager said I could have the suite for seven hundred pesos a night, about $35, "or $25 if you pay in dollars." But there was an election on, so I drove back to Tamarong.

*   *   *

The fishing hadn't gone well, and José, who was Tamarong's leading fisherman, felt obliged to take special measures or the election week banqueting would suffer. José liked that, because he liked nitroglycerin, liked the idea that everybody else in the village was afraid of the stuff and a bit afraid of him because he enjoyed using it so much. Just for show, he shook the vial around in our faces, laughing with the harsh, slightly maniacal "whoof" of a bully, before he jumped into the dugout and pushed off. He glided about a hundred yards into a lagoon that had been formed by a sandspit at the river mouth, rigged the vial, flipped it into the water, and paddled like hell to the other side, prudently deserting his macho.

Half a minute passed. Then the lagoon rose into the air with a deep, muffled boom.

The explosion netted a mishmash of fingerlings and four or five sizable mackerel, which lay stunned on the lagoon's surface. It was enough for tonight, but just enough. There was little doubt why the village fishermen were having a hard time of it. They'd let José blow things up far too often.

The fish were broiled, over rice husk fires. We also had *lechon,* suckling pig, after which there seemed to be no more pigs in the village. Some may have been in hiding, traumatized by the squealing that had filled the afternoon air and then quite abruptly ceased. In any case, the sound of pigs rooting around under the nipa huts, which was constant before election day, hadn't returned.

People stood in two lines that snaked across the Tamarong plaza. One was for voting; the other was for the buffet table. The buffet had been my introduction to Filipino culture, back in San Francisco. Every week somebody gave one, a potluck, in the back offices of the city's banks and corporations and even at City Hall, where virtually all the clerks and secretaries were from Ilocos or Manila or Cebu. Here in the islands they were arranged on the slightest pretext of celebration.

A week before the election a splinter group of the Moro National Liberation Front had taken several nuns captive. When the church proved unwilling to pay a ransom, the Moros had quickly relented and announced that the sisters would be released the next day. But first they threw a buffet for them. Photos appeared in the Manila papers: the nuns at one end of the table, smiling, the Moro guerrillas lined up behind the buffet table, like contestants in a cooking competition. One of them wore an apron that read CHEFS MAKE BETTER LOVERS.

On Luzon, each of the men in the Lopez circle had a special dish that he'd bring to buffets. It had gotten around that Sharon, the other American journalist, liked crispy *pata,* the deep-fried foreleg of a pig served with vinegar and garlic. At one buffet in the cigarette subdivision, six men showed up with crispy *patas,* each of them presenting one to her the way a beau presents flowers or a box of candy in the States.

"The Filipino way," Father Vic said. He shrugged.

The feasting went on in Tamarong until ten o'clock, when the food was gone and the polling station in the school had been closed for two hours. Most of us were pie-eyed drunk from the boilermakers Doy had been concocting out of palm spirits and San Miguel. It hadn't been established where we'd all sleep; the location seemed to vary from night to night. Basically people curled up wherever they found themselves and drifted off. The informality made it difficult to follow the village's strands of relationship. One night a household had ten or fifteen residents and the next night none.

Somebody grabbed my hand and led me, in a stupor, to the mayor's house, the only building in Tamarong that had two stories. It glowed with the warm, welcoming light of oil lamps. I was led upstairs to the bedroom, which was almost entirely filled by a four-poster that must have been passed down the generations from a Spanish colonist. Sharon, the reporter, and Erica, the American photographer, were sitting on it.

I sat next to them, then looked up at a crowd of two dozen small children who were watching us expectantly, waiting to see what would happen next. Downstairs, I could see the mayor and several other children, staring up through the warped floorboards. They were also waiting to see what would happen.

Except for Erica and Sharon, everybody looked disappointed when I stumbled to my feet and walked down to the beach to sleep in a small hut, where I found Father Vic already stretched out, awake and mulling as usual. He laughed for a good fifteen minutes when I explained why I was joining him, and was still shaking with silent guffaws when I drifted off to sleep. South of Vigan, the voters gave Cory a big majority.

The road into Mountain Province, due east of Tamarong, zigzagged along a sharp ridge high above the rice terraces. At some points it was only wide enough for a single jeepney, one of the reconditioned jeeps that served as buses in the Philippines. But that never troubled the drivers who bounced their way toward Ilocos with Fleetwood Mac or sixties golden oldies blasting from their tape decks, and passengers clinging to the vehicles' flanks and roofs in frantic human pyramids.

Our party—the three American journalists and a Filipino guide—got off at a sharp turn, with the left rear wheel of the jeepney resting a few inches shy of a thousand-foot drop. The driver pointed down into the valley, where smoke curled from cooking fires next to a tight cluster of reddish brown cubes: The hamlet. It lay at the base of an immense green stairway of paddy fields that had been carved centuries ago out of the sheer jungle wall. In the midday sun the flooded paddies formed a mirrored mosaic across which tropical clouds scudded in fragmented disarray.

Word had it that Conrado Balweg, the guerrilla chieftain, was here, trying to figure out what his next move should be. But word also had it that he was up in Abra, seeking sanctuary from the government at a church. Or that he was a Cory supporter now that the election returns were in, and on his way south to Mindanao Island to negotiate an alliance on behalf of the government with the Muslim separatists. There was no telling from the talk in Manila, where reports on the activities of the guerrillas—the Muslim Moros, the communist New People's Army, Balweg and his Cordilleran Liberation Front—invariably blended semi-fact with outright paranoid fantasy. It all sounded as though it had been cooked up on the spot.

So, on Father Vic's advice, we went to Mountain Province. It was more likely than the other possibilities, he said, because it had been Balweg's stronghold, the place he'd wrenched from government control half a dozen years before, when the countless other factions of the Philippine rebellion were hard pressed to claim a few acres of rain forest.

Balweg had been a priest in the beginning, a member of Father Vic's own order: "the Guerrilla Priest of the High Cordillera," a legendary character from the start, perfectly suited to the Latin excesses of the Filipino imagination. He was unmistakably a holdover from the four centuries that Madrid had ruled the Philippines, before Admiral Dewey sank the imperial fleet in Manila Bay in 1898 and ushered in fifty years of American occupation. The Guerrilla Priest of the High Cordillera was the kind of flamboyant popular hero that only the old Spanish empire seems to have produced, with no recognizable counterpart across the Sulu Sea in formerly British Malaysia or just to the north in Chinese Taiwan. It was no less appropriate, from this perspective, that his story eventually carried him out of the priesthood and into a love affair with the daughter of a Tingguan chief that produced both children and wildly romantic revolutionary escapades, embellished over and over again in the retelling by provincial villagers and Manila urbanites alike.

But it was the villagers who claimed him as their own. For Balweg, unlike most of the priests and all of the government administrators sent to these mountains, was himself not an ethnic Filipino but a Tingguan, a member of the indigenous tribe that had lived in these mountains since prehistory and still clung to a form of nature worship that seemed logical in its context—which made his tale even more the stuff of legend. He was a pastiche of Mexico's Emiliano Zapata and Cuba's José Martí, a child of the interior. He was more real—his rebellion was more real—because of that fact.

It took an hour and a half to descend to the hamlet on foot, using the terraces as switchbacks. At five hundred feet or so there was a single nipa hut wedged into the cliff, resting on wooden pilings topped by a circle of spikes meant to keep rats out. Three children sat motionless under the hut, shielded from the sun. The oldest looked to be no more than four years old, the youngest less than a year; there were no adults in sight. The children barely noticed our presence; they didn't make a sound when we arrived or when we left. They had the distended bellies and glazed eyes of famine. Their mouths were encrusted with flies. The place had a horrible stench. We weren't doctors; there was nothing to do but continue the descent.

The cooking fires were smoldering when we reached the valley floor, but the hamlet was empty of people. We made a few half-hearted attempts to find someone, shouting "*Mabuhay*"—"Greetings"—and poking our noses into a few huts. The Tingguans were there, somewhere. They didn't want to be found and wouldn't be.

After an hour we gave up and began the two-hour ascent on the opposite side of the valley, toward another westward bend of the Abra road.

A man was waiting for us at the top, sitting cross-legged inside a one-room shack. He was a Tingguan, about forty-five, I thought, but his lean frame and sun-worn face could have been ten years younger or ten years older. When we introduced ourselves, he smiled and invited us to sit down. He was polite, but didn't offer his name.

"I'm a butterfly man," he said.

The walls of his shack were bamboo mats that had been rolled up to the roof beam. Perched in this eagle's nest, he had a view that extended far beyond the valley and the terraces toward the mountains that formed the great central spine of Luzon.

While we waited for the next jeepney—"It could be an hour or a day," he said—we examined his butterflies. They were carefully preserved in cellophane packets, each affixed with its Latin label, and organized into small, neat piles along the edge of the shack. The largest were the size of nightingales, banded in the same improbable electric colors as the fish that patrolled the Philippines' offshore reefs. He said he sold them to museums, and named a few in the United States, West Germany, Holland.

There was no reason not to believe him, not to believe that he had tired of Manila, where he said he had once studied zoology, and returned to the Mountain Province to make his living as a butterfly man. It was no more implausible than anything else in the Philippines.

A month later, in Manila, Tony showed me a photograph from the 1950s of Father Vic and a group of other seminarians. He said Balweg was the second from the right in the front row: a bit darker than the rest in his long white novitiate's cassock. But the faces were thirty years younger and the picture fuzzy, taken with a Kodak Brownie, and it was impossible to be certain about my crazy notion.

Perched up there in the clouds a thousand feet above the hamlet, watching the Abra road, discreetly polite amidst his butterflies: Was it Balweg?

SINGAPORE SUBWAY OPENS, A FAR CRY FROM NEW YORK

SINGAPORE (January 15, 1987) — An urban rail system that will make its U.S. and European rivals seem hopelessly outdated is nearing completion in this tiny Asian nation.

Yesterday, transportation planners took reporters on a daylong tour of the $3 billion Singapore Mass Rapid Transit (MRT) line's main construction sites. The initial thirteen stations of the system are scheduled to go into service by the end of this year.

The MRT is the first subway system to be built in equatorial Asia. It will also be the first in the world to boast fully air-conditioned underground station platforms along its route, which will eventually stretch for forty-two miles across the bustling city-state of 2.6 million people.

Operation of the entire system, from climate control to speed, will be directed from a computerized control center. Instead of coins, tickets or tokens, riders will use magnetically coded plastic cards to enter the platforms. The cards will be sold from automatic dispensers.

The near absence of personnel in the MRT stations, said a government spokesman, "is possible not just because of technology, but because Singapore has so little crime and vandalism that there is no need for the constant supervision you see in New York or London.

"We don't intend to hire a single transit policeman," he said.

As recently as two years ago, transportation engineers were predicting that the MRT would not carry passengers until 1988. But Singapore has acquired a reputation for completing major transportation projects ahead of schedule.

Construction is also moving toward early completion of a second terminal at Singapore's Changi Airport, already one of the ten busiest on earth despite the nation's small population.

THE SYSTEM

W. K. Kuo had been right. Just a few years after my first visit to Singapore, the hawkers' lot where the two of us had wolfed down mutton *satay* and *Hainan ji fan* with Mr. Goh was gone, replaced by a forty-five-story building. There were no hawkers' stalls left in Temple Street either, the place that had stoked my sentimental memories of old Detroit. "The doomed past," W.K. had called it. Well, it was the literal past now.

The crane forest along the harbor front was gone too. It had moved on to other projects, leaving the world's tallest hotel and several million square feet of climate-controlled commercial space in its wake. Even some of the downtown high rises that had impressed me in 1979 were gone, giving way to the steel skeletons of bigger ones. So, for that matter, was Paya Labar Airport, the modest terminal that had welcomed me with a drenching inundation in the dash to a taxi. It had been succeeded by Changi International.

If there was a single monument that encapsulated what Singapore meant to become, was already becoming, it was Changi. The place was not so much an airport, in the antique sense that the suffix "port" implies, as a machine. A system. The binary-numbered creation of computer design.

Indeed, it was itself a vast computer, hurtling people through its dustless circuits at ever-increasing clock speeds of efficiency. And counting, always counting—calculating the relationship between effort and effect. The arrival bays could handle 8,500 disembarking passengers an hour, 204,000 a day, 75 million a year. No matter that Singapore's population was 2.7 million, or that the annual load was now 10 million. Changi wasn't about today, much less yesterday. It was about tomorrow. It was about speed and numbers. And most of all, it was about control.

"Fascism"—that was what the detractors said. The rap on Singapore was worse now than it had been in the 1970s. It remained the most despised city in Asia. But Lee Kuan Yew's little state still didn't give a damn what outsiders thought; and if fascism was what the ruling party cultivated, it had to be admitted that for most Singaporeans it was fascism of a strangely soothing variety.

At Changi, travelers were spun from the arrival bays onto elevated moving walkways that tripped a light-fantastic voyage through a landscape of manicured indoor gardens, waterfalls, and bubbling fountains. The walkways led to customs checks where there were never any lines and baggage claims where the bags were always waiting. The whole process, from the moment a plane's door opened to the moment a passenger boarded an air-conditioned taxi (or soon, the air-conditioned subway) for the ride to a hotel, took about twenty minutes.

The hawkers had also been systemized. They'd been counted up, all twenty-seven thousand stalls and fifty-six thousand Ma-and-Pa cooks; trained to grill their *satay* and poach their *Hainan ji fan* according to the world's highest sanitation standards; licensed, then moved out of the empty lots and streets and into clinically antiseptic "Food Centres." There was a government Hawkers' Department, part of the Ministry of the Environment, lodged in a new, dazzlingly white marble skyscraper on Scott's Road near the Orchard Road shopping strip. George Yeo, a fatherly bureaucrat in late middle age, had presided over the systemization of the food stalls. It had all gone according to plan, he told me. None of it was happenstance.

"You see, back in the fifties, just after the British left, we had a very big unemployment problem, and hawking was a way for people to make a living without much start-up capital. Besides, it was a cheap source of food and pleasure for the blue-collar workers—a way for us to maintain wage restraints as our economy stabilized and grew. People just wheeled carts into the parking lots and streets at night.

"We let them do it, then. We were liberal with licenses, even though from a health standpoint it was anything but ideal and from a traffic standpoint it was a mess."

Always those twin concerns: cleanliness and efficiency. They were the national obsession.

Yeo continued. "But by the late seventies, we were becoming a middle-class society, so the government took on the task of updating the hawker economy."

Updating. It made sense, the way he described it. Singaporean bureaucrats always made sense. There was no arguing with the basic proposition, with the policy argument for moving the hawkers out of the empty lots and providing them with running water. This was the only place in Asia where you could sit down at a native food stall and eat anything you wanted with no fear of getting the trots.

Singapore had systematized diarrhea into the past.

Systems. Control. Numbers. Conversations with Singaporeans invariably seemed to wend their way into a blizzard of facts and figures.

The bug had even bitten the hawkers. In their spic-and-span new stalls they talked about how many chickens they served a day, how many bowls of Hokkien prawn noodles. Statistics were a kind of liturgy in Singapore, memorized and invoked as though the speakers themselves couldn't quite believe what had happened around them, couldn't believe what they were enumerating, had to take it on pure faith and profess it, the way Catholics used to profess themselves in unintelligible Latin.

One evening I visited Ng Jingloo, an acquaintance who lived up in suburban Hougang New Town, where she shared a flat with her boyfriend, Eddie. I'd met Jing in the autumn of 1986 on a creaky overnight ship from Hong Kong to Shantou, a former European treaty port on the China coast from which her grandfather had taken the coolie passage to Singapore in 1905. She was a classic Teochew beauty, moon-faced and slender-limbed, with the soft ivory complexion that the Chinese regard as ideal.

Jing had been headed for a reunion with family members who had remained in China, and to hear her talk of the experience when I leafed through her snapshots in Hougang, the chief result was six days of acute discomfort. The words "dirty" and "primitive" cropped up in every second sentence.

"I had a much better time last year, when we went to California and Las Vegas," she said, clicking her tongue at a photo of the disorderly Shantou waterfront.

Shantou was classic China coast, full of curving, arcaded shop streets and homey little cafés where the proprietor had worn the same apron since Liberation without bothering to wash it. But Jing wasn't keen on ragged charm—not when it also meant four people to a room in her relatives' Shantou home and reeking public toilets down the street. Her ambivalence was understandable from the perspective of the Hougang flat where we sat, shuffling through a series of photos in which Eddie, a pudgy, prematurely balding Cantonese in his early thirties, tried his luck at twenty-one, poker, baccarat, and the one-armed bandit. It was a breezy floor-through on the eighth story, with five large rooms. The furnishings were pseudo–Danish modern, a reserved choice for East Asia.

"We picked up the idea in L.A.," Eddie said.

Out on the balcony, local taste received its more uninhibited due in the form of a six-foot-high fountain lit in alternating bands of red, blue, and yellow.

It was the kind of flat that would fetch a good $350,000 in Los Angeles, where the Danish modern inspiration struck. Eddie and Jing had bought it for $20,000. Half of that had been covered by a move-in payment drawn from their social security accounts. Incredible though it might seem to anyone familiar with the seamy council estates of Britain or the crack-ridden urban projects of America, this was public housing, subsidized by a government that was landlord to 84 percent of the population. The number came from Jing, who started paging through a glossy government yearbook that sat on her mahogany coffee table when asked about the flat's cost.

"Yes, here it is, 84 percent of all Singaporeans live in public housing estates. In 1986 alone, 63,602 residential units were constructed."

Ten percent of the population had been supplied with new flats in a single year. Jing smiled, contented.

It was pointless to ask her or Eddie about their political views. In the last election a few months earlier, the party of the PM—that's what everyone in Singapore called Prime Minister Lee, "the PM"— had won all but one of the eighty-one parliamentary seats contested.

Unbelievably, the PM had been furious, determined to know why he'd lost that single seat, lost what had been a total electoral monopoly the last six times at the polls. Where had the party failed? Where had *he* failed? How should this challenge be met?

The *Straits Times,* the government-controlled newspaper, reported the loss in dark, ominous headlines, heavy with foreboding. It remained the chief subject of the editorial pages, dissected and analyzed ceaselessly. One seat: Was it the beginning of the end?

The *Times,* which was always peppered with flowcharts and bar graphs, exhorted its readers with even more numbers than usual, desperate to provide unimpeachable statistical proof that the voters who had broken with the People's Action Party were wrong. Mathematically wrong. The quality of average living standards had risen 7.8 percent annually since 1965, 67 percent faster than in Japan, the *Times* pointed out. Two decades ago, the lager turned out by the Tiger Brewery had accounted for three-fourths of all manufacturing output in Singapore. Now the island was the world's number one producer of hard disk drives for computers. It was into bioengineering, lasers, fiber optics. That was why people like Jing, who was a travel agent, and Eddie, who was an ad salesman for the Singapore Yellow Pages, could afford Danish modern and vacations abroad.

The editorials in the *Straits Times* were plaintive: How could the voters be so ungrateful?

It was the question of a parent who felt that nothing had been left to chance—that authority could never be challenged. Singaporeans were raised and instructed, from the cradle to the grave, to appreciate the rewards of efficiency and to honor a powerful, centralized government that protected their every material interest and monitored their every word. (It was amusing, in these years of Washington's Evil Empire rhetoric, to hear Ronald Reagan cite Singapore as a sterling example of the achievements of free enterprise, when it was actually one of the most thoroughly socialistic nations on earth.) There was a variant of fascism at work here, a suspicion of anything that could not be foreseen and programmed. But notwithstanding its distaste for free speech and its paranoid fears of the slightest political challenge, Lee Kuan Yew's Singapore wasn't fascist in the mode of Hitler's Germany or Stalin's Soviet Union or the North Korea of Kim Il Sung. It was something else, and I didn't quite grasp what that something else was until the morning I visited Vincent Yip.

Yip was an articulate pitchman, thirty-eight years old and as smooth-talking as they come. That was the way I had described him in an article for the Sunday magazine section of the *San Francisco Examiner*. A clipping had made its way back to Singapore; in fact, all my articles on Singapore eventually wound up in a file at the Information Ministry there, to be quoted from, accusingly, whenever I sought an official interview. Yip hated that description of himself and sent a letter to Susan Brenneman, the editor, complaining about it and vaguely warning that I might have trouble researching future articles.

But the label fit perfectly, and in fact I had meant Yip no harm. I admired the guy. His job, as director of Singapore's Science Park, a mini–Silicon Valley near the university on the island's west side, was to sell Singapore as a site for top-level technology joint ventures.

He did it very well, with just the right mix of informed boosterism and an understated hipness he'd picked up as a doctoral student at the University of Southern California.

The Silicon Valley parallels at Science Park—the university connection, the union of think tank and industrial lab—were quite deliberate. Most of Yip's targets were deeply rooted in the peculiar culture and life-style of the original Silicon Valley. They were people (and companies) who were almost incapable of justifying the existence of a universe that was markedly different from the one they had designed for themselves in Santa Clara County, California, and then replicated along Route 128 in Massachusetts.

It was an Apple Macintosh universe, aggressively informal, ecologically sound, physically fit.

Yip needed to demonstrate that Singapore was a town where engineers could find jogging trails and Nautilus gyms and aerobic courses. Which they could. And Science Park had to have the same university-campus leafiness, no sign of smokestacks allowed, that you found in Mountain View and Santa Clara. Which it did. Singapore hadn't gone quite as far as Taiwan, where the government had installed an excruciatingly precise imitation of a Santa Clara County condo development in the rolling countryside outside Taipei, right down to the tennis and squash courts and bicycle lanes, to lure engineers back from the real Santa Clara County. But it went far enough to dispel any lingering doubts that equatorial Asia could be user-friendly.

Lure the engineers back: That was the semi-hidden agenda of both Science Park in Singapore and Hsinchu Science-Based Park, its counterpart in Taiwan.

An astonishing percentage of the scientists and engineers who wrought the high-technology revolution in California and Massachusetts were Asia-born overseas Chinese. Taiwan alone had sent more than a hundred thousand of its brightest young people to earn Ph.D.'s in the United States, only to see most of them take up permanent American residence—including a few who eventually became Nobel Prize laureates.

Taiwan wanted them back. Singapore said it could make a

better offer. But neither could rely on simplistic appeals to things like patriotism or ethnic loyalties to Asian roots. For over the years, the electrical engineers and systems designers from Taipei and Penang and Singapore and Hong Kong who had settled in California had become Californian in their tastes. Vincent Yip, USC '74, understood that.

He also understood that these were Californians who were not entirely sure, after many years on the West Coast, just what their prospects were in California. They worried about the "glass ceiling," a tacit assumption in Silicon Valley that a brilliant Asian engineer could rise to vice president, but no higher. They worried that an accent and the leftover cultural differences it implied were terrible handicaps, obstacles blocking the way to the Olympian levels of management. So that was part of the pitch, delivered very deftly.

In his office, which was crowded with photographs of himself with celebrities, Yip gave me a sample reading. It started with the obvious stuff: "You can talk to the people. You can drink the water. You can eat the food and find a luxurious flat."

But there were certain other factors, he added, "subjective" factors.

"We are a young, aggressive country. Here, a bright engineer in his late twenties or early thirties can command a much more important position than someone his age in the United States."

The critique was implicit, it didn't have to be said out loud: America was no longer a young, aggressive country. American business was stuck with rigid policies that worked against a bright fellow under forty. Especially if he happened to be Chinese.

Yip pointed up at the wall, nodding at a photograph of himself shaking hands with Deng Xiaoping.

"That shot was taken when I headed an official scientific exchange mission to Beijing three years ago. It's something that would never have happened to me if I had stayed in a place as big as California."

And then back to the life-style pitch, since it was absolutely essential not to overlook the degree to which these same engineers were also in love with California and all it stood for, despite their career frustrations. That they were creatures of its tastes.

"How often," Yip asked, "does a second-string quarterback over there get a chance to prove how good he really is?"

He grinned at me when I laughed. We both knew that most Chinese engineers in Silicon Valley were devoted followers of the San Francisco Forty-Niners. They were all afraid they'd be lifelong backup pilots to a high-tech Joe Montana.

Yes, Yip understood how to pitch Singapore, and not just to ethnic Chinese engineers who were caught between cultures, but to the companies that employed them and the scouts they were sending all over Asia to pinpoint offshore joint venture sites.

It was in the part of the pitch that involved selling Singapore, pure and simple, that the picture began to come into focus. The hyperefficiency. The order. The mistrust of old-style, combative politics. The impatience with people who didn't understand. The fear that the whole enterprise was at risk from the blunders of someone outside the charmed circle. The wariness of anybody who wasn't part of the team, didn't speak the language, a politician or a journalist who refused to play ball.

I had encountered this package before, recognized it from my days as a feature writer in the Silicon Valley for the *San Jose Mercury News*. It was starting to sound very familiar.

Yip introduced me to a corporate executive, an Irish American about his own age, a pioneer who had brought his company to Science Park from Santa Clara several years earlier. He was still marveling at the way the first day had passed.

"Within an hour of stepping off the plane I was meeting with top people at the Economic Development Board. That afternoon the phone rang in my hotel room. It was a messenger from the board. He had a complete contract for me to examine, spelling out in precise detail the tax breaks and other incentives we would be offered at Science Park.

"Anywhere else the tax terms alone would have taken months, if not years, to work out."

His was a very important company, a high-flyer in the skies where the research minutiae of supercomputing were pondered. A big catch.

"They made us an offer we couldn't refuse. No taxes for ten years. We could import and export anything. The telecommunications are incomparable. We could bring in as many expatriates as we wanted. From the very first we could meet the people we needed right away and get instantaneous decisions."

The executive paused at the end of this list, then threw open his arms and shook his head. "Singapore is an incredibly practical place," he said. "The whole country is run like a company."

A country run like a company: another implicit comparison. This was a man who was tired of the taxes and regulations of California, tired of squabbling with U.S. immigration authorities over green cards for his foreign employees, tired of delaying company decisions while Sacramento or Washington slept at the wheel.

In 1982, Yip informed me as I was getting up to leave, there had been twenty-seven hundred engineers and scientists engaged in research and development in Singapore. It was another dose of statistics, and it was frankly mind-boggling. By 1984, he went on, the count was five thousand and rising.

"In 1986, 1.1 percent of all Singaporean workers were engineers. By the year 2000 the figure will be 2.3 percent. Since 1980 alone, our university enrollments have doubled."

It was just the prescription that Professor M., the academic who sneered at my sentimental attachment to the hawkers, had called for back in 1980. The nation of Singapore was reforging its identity, bound and determined to be the world's first all-professional, all-high-tech society, jogging and bicycling to work in spotless laboratories where no smog was generated and no one ever raised his voice.

Two generations before, Mao Zedong had set out to create a new man. He had failed. Singapore, in its hunger to be the prototype postindustrial state, had embarked on its own quest for that holiest of grails. It did so with an efficiency that knew no limits, with systems that its leaders believed would never fail, with an ideology that was complete down to the smallest detail of everyday life.

No wonder the computer wizards were struck dumb by the place; the narcissistic attraction must have been overwhelming. You could call the inspiration that built Lee Kuan Yew's Singapore—the statistical animus that drove it—fascism if you chose. But in fact it was the politics of neither the right nor the left. It was the absence of them both, the absence of politics. What had replaced them was the mindset of technocracy.

If Silicon Valley could have designed a country and a people to inhabit it, Singapore would have been the result.

OLDEST EUROPEAN COLONY WILL BE
RETURNED TO CHINA

MACAO (April 13, 1987) — China and Portugal today signed an accord that will officially end Lisbon's 430-year-old rule over Macao, the oldest European colony in East Asia.

The step became a foregone conclusion in 1984 when Britain agreed to return nearby Hong Kong to Chinese sovereignty in 1997. Macao, which was established by Portuguese explorers in 1557, will be handed over to China on December 20, 1999.

The Macao accord was signed in Beijing by Chinese Prime Minister Zhao Ziyang and his Portuguese counterpart, Prime Minister Anibal Cavaco Silva.

According to the terms of the agreement, Macao will be governed by China as a "Special Administrative Region," with its own currency, economic regulations and judicial system. Beijing will assume control over defense matters and foreign relations.

Anyone born in Macao before 1981 will be entitled to a Portuguese passport, according to Cavaco Silva. The policy extends residency rights to more than 100,000 Chinese residents of Macao, nearly a quarter of the colony's population.

By contrast, Britain has refused to make more than a few thousand of its 5.8 million colonial subjects in Hong Kong eligible for settlement in the United Kingdom.

THE BONES OF
SAINT FRANCIS

He would never go back to Lisbon. That was the thing Mañuel Teixeira was insistent about, so insistent that his face would flush and redden in anger at the mere thought. In the sixty-four years since he had arrived in the Orient, a teenage novitiate awestruck with wonder, he had made the return trip just once, in time to see his mother again before she died. But no more. They couldn't make him leave Macao, and he would never do it voluntarily.

There was no phone number listed for the old seminary that opened onto a cobbled courtyard above the Praia Grande. The Church didn't provide much of a budget anymore, and a telephone must have seemed an unnecessary expense for a building that had just a single resident left in its labyrinth of peeling rooms. I'd hiked up the hillside stairway to São José half a dozen times before the housekeeper said yes, Father was in now, and he came gliding down the hall in his white cassock.

Teixeira gave me a start, that first time I met him in 1986. He was the very picture of Matteo Ricci, with the same waist-length gray beard and hawkish nose, the piercing eyes that look out from the great Jesuit missionary's sixteenth century portraits. It was hard not to stare. Standing in the hallway of the seminary, with its creaky wooden floors and its shelves of books and letters documenting Rome's five-hundred-year effort to convert China, he was the composite ghost of Ricci and Francis Xavier and the legions of others who had followed them east. To meet Mañuel Teixeira, the last Portuguese priest in the last (and first) European colony in China, was to commune with half a millennium of heroic but futile history on the very eve of its disappearance into dusty archives like the ones that lined his solitary retreat on the hill.

The Chinese, for the most part, had already forgotten that history, excised it from public memory. In Shanghai and Beijing and Hunan and Sichuan, where the missionaries had dug deep roots, the Christian legacy included dozens of institutions—churches and seminaries, colleges and orphanages, gymnasiums and hospitals. Without exception, their names had been changed and their commitments recast after the Communist Revolution. People over sixty-five could still dredge up the details, still tell you that the Number Three Elementary School down the road had been called Sacred Heart before 1949. But they were dying off.

That was Teixeira's vocation now: confronting mortality, battling the feebleness of memory. When I met him, the old priest had written more than a hundred books and pamphlets on that long, failed mission in the East. They were books of minute historical reconstruction, books that captured the China coast of the sixteenth and seventeenth centuries in exacting, detailed brush strokes.

He would die here, writing still. He was sure of that.

"They will never make me leave," he said again, speaking with a peculiar accent that added soft Portuguese vowels to the ends of English nouns and rose and fell in a cadence borrowed from Cantonese.

"The Red Guards could not make me leave when the other priests went back to Europe in 1968 and 1969. They all tried, my son, even my superiors in Rome tried to convince me then that it was for the best . . ."

Thousands of Red Guards had stormed across the border into the colony during the Cultural Revolution, ending any lingering illusion that Lisbon could, or would, defend Macao if China wanted to take it over. The Church had ordered non-Chinese priests to leave afterward. Teixeira regarded the order as a betrayal of his mission and refused point-blank. He still spoke of it as a wound unhealed.

The two great Jesuit predecessors of Teixeira had never gone back to Europe either. Matteo Ricci, for whom Macao was but a preliminary staging ground in a lifelong effort to penetrate the inner sanctum of Chinese civilization, eventually succeeded in his task and became more Chinese than Italian, a valued official in the closed circle around the Ming emperor. There was little recollection of him on the streets off the Praia Grande, save for Teixeira's books and the occasional image of a curiously full-bearded mandarin on some Chinese artifact in a back-alley antique shop.

A more substantial relic remained of Francis Xavier, who died on an island in the South China Sea just a few miles from the colony: a bone of his arm, the humerus to be precise. Ensconced in a chest, it sat in a small pastel church on the Macanese island of Colôane, next to the remains of a group of martyred sixteenth-century Japanese Catholics. The rest of Saint Francis was, in varying amounts, to be found in the Indian state of Goa, in Nagasaki, and in Rome, with alleged bone splinters and locks of hair scattered across the Spice Islands and in an ancient half-abandoned Portuguese village below Malacca where children still greeted visitors with "bom dia" three hundred years after the Portuguese had technically surrendered their outpost on the Malay Peninsula.

Go back? Lost in his reveries on Ricci and Macao and China, sifting through the annals of all the places where Francis Xavier lay scattered, Mañuel Teixeira simply couldn't conceive of a life for himself, after so many years, in contemporary Europe.

"The world I was born to doesn't exist any longer, you see, and I don't know what I would do with myself in the one that replaced it."

Instead, surrounded by the annals of his faith, by its accumulated manuscripts and letters, the last occupant of the Seminary of São José spent his days reconstructing an even earlier world than the Lisbon of his birth.

Teixeira held court on the terrace of the Bela Vista Hotel. The manager, young Pinto-Marques, supplied him with glasses of chilled *vinho verde* and plates of olives or salt cod fritters. There wasn't a *taverna* in the colony that didn't see it as a religious duty to host the last resident of São José. But the old priest's heart was in the Bela Vista, which was the grand hotel of his youth and retained, in its advanced years, a cranky charm much like his own.

He was a boisterous conversationalist, ready to disagree with virtually any proposition, no matter how logical, just for the sake of argument. People who wouldn't argue, who were unduly respectful, plainly disappointed and bored Mañuel Teixeira. He also had a spot in his heart for pretty girls, and a way of putting them at ease with Old World courtesies in Cantonese or Portuguese or English or French, so that they were pleased rather than shocked when he leapt to his feet and embraced them with a warmth that sometimes exceeded decorum.

Down below, the great muddy bay separating the peninsula from Taipa Island was always aswarm with a cloud of dragon-sailed junks and sampans, pierced at fifteen-minute intervals by the sharp white spray of a Hong Kong jet foil cutting through the Pearl Estuary toward the casinos.

The Bela Vista was painted a relatively fresh pastel green, reflecting the Pinto-Marques family's latest—and as it proved, final—attempt at staving off their own departure into the musty oblivion of Macao's history. Three aging Chinese sisters owned the hotel then, and had for as long as anyone but Teixeira could remember. Draped in an intentional obscurity so unremitting that it gave them a certain air of mystery, they never came to the Bela Vista themselves, leaving its management to Pinto-Marques, the Macanese whose family had been its majordomos since the 1920s or maybe before.

"Even I cannot be certain when their tenure began," Teixeira admitted.

For his part, Pinto-Marques turned over the daily operational duties to a sullen elderly Chinese accountant, who invariably miscalculated the room bills and ran a small side business marketing Father Teixeira's more accessible monographs to tourists and reporters.

The best rooms were spread along the southeast side of the hotel and were equipped with small enclosed terraces that produced the sensation of being suspended in space over the weed-choked cliff, where an English sea captain had erected the rambling neoclassical structure as his private mansion in the early nineteenth century. It was the perfect place to write for anyone who preferred idiosyncrasy to strong air-conditioning, and I had developed a habit of taking up residence in the Bela Vista for a week or so whenever I was faced with knocking out a long magazine piece or newspaper series. There are a decade's worth of photos of me on these balconies, snapped roughly every two years, working at an Olivetti portable against a backdrop of the bay and a ridge line of jagged Guangdong hills.

But that's the past now. The Mandarin Group, a corporate hotel giant over in Hong Kong, bought the Bela Vista from the mysterious sisters in 1990 and closed it down, with a view toward reopening it to an international standard. The Macanese, who had seen five hundred years of modernization projects founder in their little backwater, were dubious.

The Macanese: They too didn't want to leave, for many of the same reasons as Father Teixeira, but intensified by their five centuries of generating the very memories he was determined to preserve. In their tiny three-square-mile enclave on the periphery of the immense Middle Kingdom, their ancestors had literally given birth to the European dream of an East Asian empire. The dream was usurped by the Dutch and then the English and the French, who sailed east long after Macao was founded in 1557—usually with Portuguese pilots to guide them and Portuguese interpreters to translate for them—and soon brought to bear an industrial power that Portugal—which with a population of just over one million then ostensibly ruled half the known globe—could never muster.

But the Macanese were still here. The Dutch burghers were gone from their Batavia, now Jakarta; the French *colons* were no longer sipping *pastis* on the Rue Catinat in Saigon, now Dong Khoi, the Street of the People's Revolution in Ho Chi Minh City; and the British *tuans* had been ousted from their verandas in North Borneo, now the Malaysian state of Sabah. But Macao was still Macao.

That was the great difference, or rather, the fruit of a great difference symbolized by the Macanese themselves. They belonged in Asia, in ways that the Dutch, French, and British never did.

The Portuguese had always been too few in number to be rulers in any convincing sense, which left them only one resort, and they abandoned themselves to it. In Macao and Ambon and Flores, in Malacca and Ceylon and Brazil, in Timor and Mozambique and Angola, in the Cape Verdes and Goa, the Portuguese mixed. They married. They spawned. They became history's great enthusiastic miscegenators, going native with such alacrity that surnames like Silva and Nuñes and Perreira are nearly as common today in parts of the Orient as Chang and Lee and far, far more common than Smith or Vandeberg or Martinière.

To a degree that must have shocked the minions of Paris, London, and Amsterdam, their fellow imperialists from Lisbon abandoned their identity as Europeans to immerse themselves in new, synthetic cultures of astonishing richness and fertility. The *colons* and the planters of Malaya were Frenchmen and Britons, transposed through brute force to French imperial Indochina and the rubber plantations on the South China Sea. They were the legates of conquest. The Silvas and the Perreiras of Macao and Malacca, with their almond eyes, sharp Iberian noses, tawny complexions, and curly hair, represented something else—not so much conquest as conjunction. A wild, startling, and often quite beautiful mélange.

The marriage was sculpted into the faces on the Praia Grande. But it was also evident in food and religion, language and art. Indeed, almost everywhere you turned in East Asia, the synthesis spawned by Portugal had become inextricable from the idiom of popular life. The Cantonese called the incense they burned in Buddhist temples *joss,* a word borrowed directly from the Portuguese *dios,* for "gods." The Japanese, who had no indigenous word for "thank you," adopted the Portuguese *obligado,* rendering it as *arigato.* The Javanese and Malays picked up hundreds of Portuguese terms and made them their own: *armada* for "fleet," *roda* for "wheel," *tempo* for "time," *bola* for "ball."

The two-story, balconied shops that lined Asian main streets from the mouth of the Yangtze to the Indonesian Archipelago were of a recognizably Portuguese design. In the Straits Settlements of Penang, Malacca, and Singapore, Chinese merchants covered the facades of their houses with Portuguese flowered tiles and protected their roofs with red terra-cotta in the fashion of the Portuguese Algarve.

The Portuguese carried the chili pepper from Brazil to Thailand and Sichuan. They taught the Tamils to mix the chilies with vinegar and garlic in *vindaloo,* which is based on the Portuguese expression *vinho e alho,* "wine and garlic." They introduced deep-fat frying to Japan, where it took on a Portuguese name, *tempura,* used for a dish that now passes as the most characteristically Japanese item in Japanese cooking.

None of these phenomena, in its Asian setting, was Portuguese alone. They were all part of the conjunction, the marriage, that produced the Macanese and their far-flung cousins. They bespoke a sensibility, and a sensuality, that was a universe apart from what Paris and London and Amsterdam wrought in their empires. A sensibility that could be read in the stubborn will of Mañuel Teixeira, who refused, categorically, to live in Europe.

Mario Lim, a machine parts salesman, had tried. "In 1984 my wife and I put the kids into a Portuguese-language school, and she broke the news to her parents: We were leaving. Then I went on alone, to get things started. But fifteen months later I was in Macao again. My wife still hasn't set foot in Lisbon."

The problem wasn't money. In fact, the little garment factory he set up near the Portuguese capital showed promise very quickly.

"The wages, you know, are actually lower there than they are here. And they work hard, the Portuguese."

We shared a cabin on the overnight ferry from Canton, a flat-bottomed riverboat that floated slowly down the Pearl with the ebb tide and sidled into a wharf at the foot of Avenida Almeida Ribeiro as morning broke over the estuary.

There were four of us in the cabin, scofflaws to a man: I was a journalist traveling on a fraudulent tourist visa; Mario was returning from a trip to Hunan peddling German-made drill bits that were ostensibly banned by Chinese import restrictions. Our bunk mates were a Taiwanese toy manufacturer whose plant in Guangdong was technically prohibited by Taipei, and a cynical ceramics salesman from Shanghai whose night of drinking and unauthorized conversation with a Taiwanese and an American reporter were anathema in the eyes of Beijing.

But official eyes tended to blink in the heyday of China's business frenzy. It was an open secret in Asia that the biggest new factories in the communist People's Republic were financed by the enemy capitalists of Taiwan; that a reporter could get a tourist visa in three hours in Hong Kong or Macao instead of the six months required by the Chinese embassy in Washington for a press pass; that the published Chinese import restrictions were the best possible way of identifying the products that were actually being imported.

The cabin talk was politics. Not long ago the future of Macao had been penned into a contract between Lisbon and Beijing. December 20, 1999, the date when China would reassume control of the colony, loomed—like Karl Marx's proverbial specter—over every conversation. So it soon came out, as we talked, that Mario had once sold everything he owned and gone off to start a new life in Portugal, only to return after fifteen months.

The Shanghainese knew the vagaries of his own country all too well—how the blinking eyes of officialdom could suddenly become fixed, and with what devastating consequences. He scarcely dreamed of such an opportunity for escape, and couldn't imagine why anyone would pass it up.

"And now," he asked, incredulous, "do you feel you've made a mistake?"

It was the wrong question. Posed strictly in political terms, Mario admitted that he couldn't explain his return to Asia. It made no sense.

"I tried to live in Europe. It didn't work out."

He left it at that.

*   *   *

Mario Lim was not a Macanese creole by blood, not in any genetically measurable way, even if there was some long-forgotten sailor from Oporto or the Azores among the ancestral gods whose shrine occupied the entrance hall of the concrete house on Taipa Island where he took me to meet his wife. Mario was Cantonese; at least 90 percent of the people in Macao were.

Statistically, Macao was as Chinese as Hong Kong. That fact and shared circumstantial details like a European colonial past and a Chinese contractual future—1999 here, 1997 there—made it convenient to lump the two places together. Guidebooks and magazine articles often presented Macao as a kind of down-market annex to Hong Kong.

But beyond the confines of its tacky casinos, its dog track, and a few international hotels on the waterfront, Macao wasn't Hong Kong, even writ small. And the Cantonese here were nothing like their cousins across the estuary. As much as the first Portuguese colonizers and their mixed-blood offspring, they had been altered, transformed by the temper of the place.

On Taipa, one of the two tiny offshore islands that made up Macao's rural hinterland (the other was Colôane, the last resting place of Francis Xavier's humerus) the differences were vivid. Along the village main street where the Lims lived, Chinese family life had blended almost imperceptibly into its Mediterranean equivalent. Shop houses and ancestral halls were jumbled side by side with whitewashed cottages and churches. At night everyone was in the street, Chinese and Portuguese and creole, their children's endless game of tag dodging through a tangle of chairs and card tables brought out into the warm evening air, where the sweet smell of Cantonese roast duck was folded into the salty codfish steam rising from pots of poached *bacalao*.

At Pinocchio's, the Macanese *taverna* at the end of the main street, you knew who was from Hong Kong and who was from Macao by the pace of the meal. The visitors gulped down their chili prawns and grilled sardines, called for the bill, and headed back to the casinos in half an hour. The Macao Chinese spent entire languorous afternoons dawdling over one course, then another, slipping into a doze that nobody cared to shake off as the *vinho verde* took hold.

Across the big arched bridge that connected Taipa to the city, urban Macao looked, from a distance, like the spin-off of Hong Kong the travel literature alleged it to be. At night it was a row of high rises flashing the same lurid neon welcome over the estuary that was mirrored in Victoria Harbour. But even in the central city, the differences between Macao and Hong Kong were far more evident than the similarities. The high rises were a thin facade of modern sheen behind which the Macao of Matteo Ricci and Francis Xavier lived on in a tangle of dimly lit alleys and courtyards that snoozed, like the Pinocchio's diners, in a haze of wine and insouciance and the dusty clutter of the past. Hong Kong, by contrast, had no history, no past, only a fealty to the wrecking ball. You could hardly find a twenty-year-old building in Hong Kong, much less a quiet sixteenth-century square or a ramshackle seminary inhabited by a single old eccentric.

Most of Macao's people were of the very same stock as the Cantonese who made Hong Kong one of the world's most electric, most frantic, cities. But they were also of the same, unhurried race that the Portuguese themselves had become as they drifted through their long, sleepy Asian sojourn.

It was doubly ironic. In Hong Kong, where the British made it virtually impossible for all but the wealthiest to acquire British citizenship, there was a nonstop accounting of the merits of emigration and overseas investment. A Hong Kong business executive could reckon, to the dollar, how much profit might be extracted from a base of operations in the borderless Mecca of the European Economic Community. In Macao they understood all that. They understood that a home in Portugal meant the freedom to climb, if one wanted, to the prosperous pinnacles of Germany or France. And the Portuguese, unlike the British, were obliging. Macao-born Chinese were welcome to apply for Portuguese citizenship and were generally granted it.

They had a thousand reasons to pick up stakes and move to Europe. But like the Macanese, like Father Mañuel Teixeira and Matteo Ricci before him, they seldom acted on them. For reasons no anthropologist and certainly no economist had ever calculated, they were different from their cousins across the estuary in Hong Kong and up the Pearl River in China, whatever the blood said.

The Macao Chinese just weren't suited to leaving. Mario Lim had tried. It didn't work out.

TAIWAN'S CHIANG DIES,
ENDING DYNASTY

TAIPEI (January 14, 1988) — President Chiang Ching-kuo, who presided over the emergence of Taiwan as a global industrial power, died of a heart attack in Taipei yesterday.

His vice president, Lee Teng-hui, was immediately sworn in as the new leader of the Nationalist Chinese island republic.

Chiang, 77, had been confined to a wheelchair for the past four months, suffering from acute diabetes. He served as Taiwan's president for 10 years, succeeding his father, the late General Chiang Kai-shek, in 1978.

As a young man, Chiang Ching-kuo rejected his father's conservative views and left China in 1925 to study political theory in the Soviet Union, where he married a Russian and remained a dozen years. But after a period of forced labor in a Siberian gold mine for his public criticism of Soviet leader Josef Stalin, he returned to China in 1937 as a fierce anti-communist.

From the end of the Second World War to the 1970s, Chiang was a top political aide to his father's government and directed military security operations for Taiwan.

The sixty-five-year-old President Lee is the nation's first Taiwan-born leader. An agricultural economist who was educated in the United States, he was hand-picked by Chiang to be vice president in 1984.

SONS

I asked only at the end of the interview if the rumor was true: Was he the president's son? John Chang nodded once without saying anything, the slightest affirmative gesture he could make.

It was enough; there wasn't any point in pursuing the matter beyond simple confirmation. Even the powerful have some right to nurse private pain away from public eyes. In the silence that followed I noticed the photographs that covered the walls of his office. They were all of Chiang Kai-shek, the grandfather. There wasn't a single image of C. K. Chiang, the second president of the Republic of China on Taiwan, the man whom John Chang now acknowledged to be his father.

For more than forty years his existence had been a closely guarded secret. The papers in Taipei were front-paging the story, which had broken a few days earlier. Most pictured it not as John Chang's burden, but as evidence of the late president's virility and superior guile. A deep capacity for guile would certainly have been necessary to hide a compromising mistress and illegitimate son from not only his wife but also his formidable stepmother, whom even he addressed as Madame Chiang Kai-shek.

The big Taiwan publishers had loved the old man, especially at the end, when he began to open things up, so much so that many people began to forget the dark days less than a decade before when Chiang's opponents were still disappearing mysteriously in the middle of the night. Just a few years earlier, in October of 1984, Henry Liu, a Taiwanese journalist in California who made a career of investigating and writing about the Chiang family's foibles, had been gunned down by two assassins in the driveway of his suburban San Francisco home. At the trial the Liu murder had been hung on a Taiwan gang. But there was little doubt that the Chiangs were somewhere in the background.

Already that seemed a distant epoch. In his waning years C. K. Chiang had made one of Asian history's great about-faces, introducing constitutional reforms, dropping the four-decade-old martial law with its restrictions on the press and the political opposition, even permitting his people to vacation on the communist mainland. Roughly half a million made the crossing the first year it was legal. The world was changing, and when Chiang suddenly collapsed from a heart attack and passed away, he went with the reputation of a progressive.

There were those who credited the opening entirely to his personal vision, and those who credited it to a moment in history that C. K. Chiang, whatever he might have preferred, was unable to resist. And there were those like John Chang, his illegitimate son and the vice minister for foreign affairs in the Republic of China, who credited a much more unexpected source.

"China has had three revolutions," he said when we were deep in a conversation about the reformist wave. "The first was the one that my grandfather and Sun Yat-sen made. The second was the one that pushed the Nationalists onto Taiwan. And the third, the one that is breaking all around us today, was made in America."

He meant a very specific America. That was the unexpected part.

The new Taiwan, in John Chang's estimate, was born in Berkeley and Cambridge and Ann Arbor in the sixties.

He himself had seen it, Chang said. He had watched the wave mount on the radical American campuses during the Vietnam War, then crest over places like Georgetown, which he entered the year of the Tet offensive, 1968, and left in 1971, the year after the U.S. invasion of Cambodia. Roughly seventy-five thousand students from Taiwan attended American universities between 1964 and 1975.

"We were bystanders, we had to be under the circumstances. And at first we hardly knew what to make of it. Nothing in our own experience had prepared us for what we saw on those campuses during the war.

"But it's impossible to exaggerate the impact it had, witnessing that kind of freedom. Every Taiwan student who was in America then will tell you the same thing. Because we talked about it all the time. We talked about what it meant to live in a democracy."

Chang stopped for a moment and smiled—at some memory, perhaps, one he didn't want to share. "The life-style, too," he went on. "It had an enormous impact on us."

The college students who had watched the protesters seize the Columbia University president's office in New York and People's Park in Berkeley were the government and business elite of Taiwan now. For two decades their altered worldview had been like the secret of John Chang's birth, a revolution concealed in privacy, nurtured in the hidden corners of Chiang Kai-shek's island fortress. But now it was out in the open, everywhere in sight.

Thousands of them—especially the engineers—had remained in America, to the chagrin of Taiwan's scientific establishment. But thousands of others had come home, with political science and economics degrees, and by the mid-1980s they were claiming power. It was as though the stony gerontocracy of Chiang Kai-shek's Nationalist exiles had been suddenly shoved into the wings and replaced by the Big Ten and the Ivies. The growing fleet of private cars that struggled to work each morning, negotiating seas of honking taxis and buses on Chung Hsiao Road, carried stickers in their rear windows that displayed the Georgia Bulldog and the Florida 'Gator. There were bars that catered to Columbia and Texas A & M grads, and a clinic on Tung Hua Road in flashy new East Taipei that called itself the Michigan Wolverine Dental Hospital; it was plastered with Rose Bowl pennants and bumper stickers reading LET'S GO BLUE.

A third or more of the American-educated elite in Taiwan had attended universities in California, and they had organized themselves into Stanford, Cal, and UCLA clubs that were not simply social groups but powerful forces in Taipei's politics and corporate affairs—old-boy clubs in precisely the sense that their American equivalents were. A Cal rep tie covered with golden bears and tied loosely at the neck marked someone to be reckoned with at high levels of the bureaucracy. Even if you weren't really a Stanford man, it was useful to make passing allusions in conversation to the Big Game—Stanford versus Cal—or to mention some well-known Palo Alto beer joint.

The older old-boy schools had their followings too. The current president of the Republic of China, C. K. Chiang's low-key reformist successor, Lee Teng-hui, was a 1969 graduate of Cornell. Nearly two-thirds of his top-level appointments went to other American university alumni, most of them Ivy League grads from the Vietnam War years. The new premier, Yu Kuo-hwa, was a Harvard man. So was Ma Ying-jeou, the de facto presidential chief of staff. The booming city of Taipei was managed by a former pal of Lee's in Ithaca, Huang Ta-chou (Cornell '71).

The list was nearly endless. The Taiwan economy was being shepherded into the twenty-first century by a think tank, the Development and Investment Center, run by John C. I. Ni (Stanford '69). The chief spokesman for the rapidly growing environmentalist lobby was legislator Jaw Shau-kong (Clemson '75), who self-consciously combed his hair in a bushy Kennedy mop and told me his current political hero was Jesse Jackson. The fastest rising star in the biggest opposition group, the Democratic Progressive Party, was Tsai Shih-yuan (American University '79), who introduced himself as "Jimmy" and described the platform of the ruling Kuomintang Party as "unadulterated bullshit."

They argued incessantly, with each other and with the oldsters who clung to power in the Legislative Yuan, the Taiwan national congress. That was their distinctive touch, the habit they brought back from the tumultuous years in America. They were always ready for an argument, ready to the point of literally picking fistfights and engaging in physical shoving matches on the floor of the assembly.

It was enough to make an American reporter who'd spent six years in Ann Arbor (Michigan '69) downright homesick.

The combativeness, the willingness to drag political controversy out in the open, was very new in Taiwan. It was something new, for that matter, everywhere in the Chinese-speaking world. China wasn't ready for it. You couldn't imagine it, at least not yet, in Singapore or Hong Kong. But it was happening in Taiwan: The students who returned from American campuses in the late 1960s and 1970s were, in John Chang's words, the vanguard of a third revolution. They were genuinely different people.

At the heart of their difference was the refusal to accept a subtle compromise that had governed behavior in East Asia for as long as anyone could remember. The compromise said there could be Chinese business in Hong Kong, but that government should be left to the British. It said that debate and factiousness would be mortally dangerous to Singapore's economic miracle. For four decades it had stifled the political opposition within Taiwan to maintain a solid front against the communist enemy across the strait. At its most fundamental level this compromise was a bargained silence, passive acceptance of the political status quo in the interest of prosperity. It was in force not only in Singapore, Hong Kong, and Taiwan, but in the large Chinese communities that dominated business in Indonesia, the Philippines, Malaysia, and Thailand.

Remain silent, get rich: It worked.

It made the forty-five million ethnic Chinese outside mainland China into a staggering success story. Silent and invisible in politics, bold and omnipresent in business affairs, they emerged as the grand back-room power brokers of the Pacific boom, the indispensable middlemen without whom Japanese manufactured goods and American technology might never have wrought the miracle that made the Pacific the center of global economic gravity in the 1980s.

By the end of that decade, Taiwan, with one-fifth of Japan's population, had larger foreign reserves than Tokyo—indeed, at some $90 billion, the largest in the world. Singapore, a racially tense, deteriorating port in 1958, was now a telecommunications giant with a standard of living that made America's look anemic. Hong Kong, still a colony and roughly the size of metropolitan Philadelphia, ranked among the major trading powers on earth, with annual export figures rivaling those of France, Italy, and its own erstwhile imperial master, Great Britain. Chinese families in Jakarta, Bangkok, and Kuala Lumpur owned American banks, German manufacturing plants, office buildings in Toronto, Los Angeles, Tokyo, and Paris.

Remain silent, get rich: It worked.

But under the wrong circumstances it could also be a misjudgment, which was what the ethnic Chinese were learning from Dr. Mahathir in Malaysia—and what they had learned at much greater cost in Indonesia in 1965 and Vietnam in the late 1970s. The Chinese there had quiety grown so successful in the postwar decades that they controlled entire economies, and when the Javanese and Vietnamese finally took notice the result was violent resentment—the horrifying explosions that took at least half a million Chinese lives in Indonesia in 1965, and prompted more than six hundred thousand Vietnamese Chinese to become refugees.

But even in these places the bargain reasserted itself and prosperity returned, so that by 1987 the Sino-Vietnamese boat people of 1979 were coming back to Saigon and opening successful businesses, in tacit cooperation with the same communist bureaucrats who had pushed them into the sea. A single Chinese Indonesian family, the Liems, seemed to own (in partnership with the children of President Suharto) every major industry in Indonesia, not to mention one of California's oldest banks and an investment house that was a key— though often invisible—player in building, buying, and trading transactions in every Pacific capital.

It had all been built on peculiarities that other nations—conventional nations whose cultural identities were framed by geography, by a specific set of borders, by a *state*—couldn't match. The overseas Chinese were a stateless nation, a singular culture that had no home of its own save for the ancestral Middle Kingdom that had spawned it.

Taiwan, officially, was just one part of one Chinese province, awaiting the day when its ruling party, Chiang's Nationalists, would reassume power in Beijing. No assertion was more fiercely prohibited in the Chiang era than to call Taiwan a country. Singapore was 75 percent overseas Chinese, but its position at the heart of the racial tinderbox that is Southeast Asia made it impolitic, to say the least, to call it Chinese. The state ideology was rigorously multicultural, even if state practice had often given the nod to the interests of a Chinese majority.

There were another twenty-two million overseas Chinese spread around the Pacific—a million in San Francisco and Los Angeles, six million in Indonesia, six million in Malaysia, pockets big and small in every country from the Solomon Islands to Canada and from Peru to Burma, for whom there was not even the official nod to mitigate statelessness. There was only the sense of a nation in diaspora, adapted to local circumstances but almost always and everywhere connected to the rest of that disenfranchised Chinese world outside China.

The great genius of this world was to make an advantage of disadvantage. In much of the Pacific, Chinese could not own land or enter politics; they were virtually banned from the decision-making levels of bureaucracy. So they went into business, running the tiny shops that kept rural Indonesians and Thais supplied with canned mackerel and cigarettes, saving money, following the fluctuation of prices and the movement of commodities with intense care. Because there was no choice.

The tiny shops dug in, held, multiplied. Their owners paid close attention to the market, to what people around them needed and to what was available—not just in the next valley, but across the strait or the sea in the places where products were designed and manufactured.

It was an anomaly, one of the strange paradoxes of European imperialism, that made the Chinese effective traders. The anomaly rested on language.

In the colonial epoch an ambitious young Vietnamese, someone who would one day make the decisions in postcolonial Vietnam, was educated in French. His counterpart in nearby Malaysia learned English. Across the Riau Archipelago in Jakarta it was Dutch. When independence came, when the colonial vacuum left behind by the Second World War was filled with a checkerboard of self-governing states, the ambitious of Vietnam and Malaysia and Indonesia couldn't talk, couldn't bargain, with their neighbors.

Unless, that is, they were ethnic Chinese.

Chinese everywhere read the same written language; even when their dialects are mutually unintelligible, as they often are, the ideograms are the same everywhere. And everywhere in the overseas Chinese world in the 1950s there were Chinese newspapers that reported, in that uniform Chinese written language, minute details on things like commodities prices, local political conditions, stock market performance, industrial developments, growth rates, investment costs. All you needed to know to bargain and trade.

The little family businesses took root because there was no choice. They became chains of businesses. They moved products— Liem Sioe Leong, the founder of that Indonesian business dynasty, traveled the back roads of Java for years as a peanut oil peddler, making his first fortune. They created a business and trade network of their own that was, in many ways, the framework for the global economy that would emerge in the Pacific in the mid-1970s.

They brokered the birth of the Pacific Century, careful, mortally careful, to observe discretion at all times. They kept their silence and they prospered.

"This man and this man, and every man in this picture," Mike Chen said. "And all but two in the next."

We were leafing through a well-worn copy of *Sports Illustrated,* and Mike was identifying his clients. A smile lit up his face when we came to a shot of Terry Steinbach, the Oakland A's catcher, flipping off his mask and somersaulting gymnastically over the plate to tag a sliding Minnesota Twin.

"Steinbach!" he exclaimed in a half-shout, pretending he'd never noticed this page before. "My jock strap and my catcher's mask, too!"

It wasn't difficult to find Mike's customers in the magazine. He'd sold 1.5 million athletic supporters in the United States the year before and manufactured the masks worn by seventy major-league catchers and 90 percent of all major-league umpires. I had a fleeting mental image of them lined up, page after page, in their jocks and masks, seeing them the way Mike obviously did, shorn of the uniforms that obscured his accomplishment.

Ten years ago, before he started calling himself "Mike," Chen Qianfang had been a vegetable farmer, raising *bok choy* on this same plot of land outside Taipei. Today, at fifty-one, he was the globe's leading manufacturer of athletic supporters. The undisputed jock strap king of the world.

He had been plowing, getting ready to sow the next crop, on that day in 1979 when a group of fliers from the nearby American air base drove up across the road and began tossing a ball around in a pickup game. One of them was a brigadier general who could speak a little Mandarin, and he and Mike got to talking about baseball, and about the difficulty his boys were having finding protective equipment in Taiwan that would fit them.

On a sudden impulse, Mike said, "I told him I could solve his problem—that my wife and I had a side business, a small textile factory."

Of course there was no factory then, not yet, just the family house, the same farmer's cottage we were sitting in, although another floor had since been added and there wasn't the big color television set in the living room, much less the black sedan in the driveway.

"I really don't know what made me do it," he added.

But he was a Christian and inclined to credit the inspiration to Divine Providence. "Maybe Jesus whispered it to me," he said of that white lie a decade before that shifted his sights from bok choy to jock straps.

His wife was skeptical at first. But the two of them set to work night after night on a borrowed industrial sewing machine, and a few weeks later Mike presented the general with a full complement of athletic supporters with protective cups, and four hand-stitched chest protectors for the catchers and umpires.

A year later, on a second wave of inspiration, he left his plowing once again and spent every cent of the family savings on a trip to an athletic goods convention in Chicago. He would never forget what he saw on the streets of the Windy City.

"It was wintertime, and all of these American people have the money to eat very nice food, maybe so they will stay warm. They are very fat! And I know what they need: exercise. Sports. And I also know that I have not wasted our money. This is the right business for me. Much easier than farming. Much more money to make."

Mike Chen was a natural. He talked a good game, starting that winter in Chicago, and came home with five thousand orders, which were filled in the living room of his cottage.

In the beginning, all Mike did was copy the models sent to Taiwan by U.S. contractors, but that didn't satisfy him. Never stopping to think that design and materials decisions were made by engineers and chemists nowadays, he began puttering around with his jock strap cups and chest protectors, and later a line of masks, trying to find a combination that would make his goods lighter and stronger than the products he was copying. Instead of cotton fill, Mike began to use molded polyurethane, introducing what became a standard design improvement adopted all over the world. That brought him to the attention of a sharp-eyed Boston manufacturer, the patriarch of one of the oldest and best-established sporting goods companies in America, and a partnership was born.

The chart measuring Mike's expansion in the 1980s was an absurdly vertical line: from bok choy farmer to jock strap king of the world in less than ten years. By mid-decade the Boston partner had retired, and without taking a second breath, Mike acquired enough shares to be a major stockholder in a firm that combined parts of the Boston operation with a manufacturer that had been its biggest supplier. In 1987, the firm's sales of baseball protective equipment passed those of Rawlings and Wilson, the household names of the American National Pastime.

But he was a casual guy still, a farmer in a cardigan sweater and baggy pants who couldn't entirely grasp what stroke of fortune had wrenched him out of his fields at forty and made him a millionaire industrialist before his fiftieth birthday.

We walked over to the plant, where I admired the enormous collection of protective pads, cups, and masks that hung from the display walls; the firm churned out a thousand different products now.

Mike took me up to the apartment he'd installed above the plant. There was a very well-stocked wet bar in one corner, another giant television and video deck in the other. He shut the door of the tape cabinet before I could look at the titles. Porn? He blushed when I asked.

"Just some things the Japanese buyers like . . ."

There was a bedroom off to the side, its door half closed, also for buyers and their guests. Christian or not, business could lead businessmen into gray areas.

Business had led Mike to Indonesia. He wasn't terribly comfortable talking about it, but offshoring—setting up plants overseas—was the next logical step. He wasn't a cottage industrialist with a borrowed machine in his living room anymore, he was the jock strap king. And to remain king, he had to watch labor costs.

The math was simple. In Taiwan a factory worker was paid around $600 a month, as opposed to $25 to $40 in Jakarta, where he was shifting most of his operations. Didn't matter if the Indonesians were only half as productive; the profit margin was still enormous.

He was aware of the risks. Most Taiwan industrialists were going to Fujian Province in China, which was closer and spoke the same dialect as Taiwan. But Mike's style was to do the unorthodox thing, or he would never have lied to the American general in 1979.

"People in business tell me to attack *here,* and I say, 'No, I'll attack *there* instead.' That's my way."

Besides, he knew someone in Jakarta, "a fellow high in the government."

That was the sine qua non of offshoring to Indonesia: a big man, usually a military officer, who smoothed over potential problems in return for a share of the profits. The arrangement was so normal that hardly anyone in Asia thought of it as corrupt. It was Indonesia's brand of corporate culture.

There was also the fact that, as Mike put it, "there are six million Chinese in Indonesia," which was a sort of business insurance until— and he knew this, too—it suddenly became a dangerous liability.

He could very well lose everything as fast, faster, than he had made it.

"If we have the right partner and the politics are stable, we'll produce more and more and more. If something changes, we lose. Yes, I know that."

He tensed, just slightly, at the thought. "But that's what 'venture' means, doesn't it?"

He must have picked up the definition at one of the sporting goods conventions, where he was now a celebrity. But I remembered that he had also told me he kneeled down on the floor and prayed, every morning, before he got dressed.

It was quite a distance for a bok choy farmer to have covered in less than ten years. We drank a toast to that in his apartment. Mike poured me a Johnny Walker Black, then filled his own glass with ginger ale. He was a Christian, he said again, and didn't drink.

CHINA TENSE AS STUDENTS ERECT
DEMOCRACY STATUE

BEIJING (May 31, 1989) — In a dramatic escalation of the protests that began here in mid-April, student activists yesterday erected a twenty-eight-foot-high statue of the "Goddess of Democracy" in Beijing's Tiananmen Square.

The sculpture, a torch-bearing female figure that resembles the Statue of Liberty in New York Harbor, is the work of students from the city's Central Academy of Fine Arts. It marks the most defiant gesture yet against China's communist government in a month of pro-democracy marches and hunger strikes.

In a statement published in the *People's Daily* last night, the government of Prime Minister Li Peng denounced the statue as a foreign-influenced symbol "totally against the law and against the will of the people."

The Tiananmen demonstrations, which opened with the death of liberal politburo member Hu Yaobang on April 15, have taken special aim at Li, the hard-line Marxist who helped engineer Hu's removal from the post of Communist Party General Secretary in 1988.

Although the Li government declared martial law in Beijing two weeks ago in an effort to stem the protests, the students have refused to leave Tiananmen Square.

Rumors of impending military action against the demonstrators have been rife since May 19, when the current party secretary, Zhao Ziyang, paid a tearful visit to the demonstrators and begged them to go home. Zhao, the nation's leading economic reformer, warned that conservatives in the politburo were calling for violent suppression of the pro-democracy movement.

Zhao has not been seen in public in ten days, and is believed to have offered his resignation.

Inspired by the Tiananmen demonstrations, pro-democracy activities have spread around the nation in recent weeks, with large demonstrations reported in Shanghai, Xi'an, Canton and several other major cities.

DEMOCRACY SPRING

Things were not right in Shanghai. There was an unnerving brittleness in the air, a stiffness to the way people walked along the Bund and up the commercial blocks of Nanjing Road, that belied the constant assertions of the *People's Daily* that all was normal. It wasn't the usual brittleness of the early Yangtze spring, when winter still hangs over the city in a pall of coal smoke and pedestrians huddle for warmth against the street front walls. It was something else: the fear that someone would call a halt to China's spin, the fear that no one would. It was fear mixed with inarticulate anger and expressed in strange, unsettling encounters.

Tom Feng approached me in People's Park, the former Shanghai Race Track, and asked where I was from. After an hour of conversation on a footpath that used to be the backstretch, he invited me to his home for dinner and more talk. A seventy-four-year-old retired electrical engineer, he was the most bitterly alienated man I had ever met, in a nation that seemed to be drowning in bitterness and alienation in the spring of 1989.

Tom never used his Chinese name, although he had spent his entire life in Shanghai and never traveled outside China. With numbing deliberation, he had severed himself as completely as possible from the country in which he was born and had passed all of his days. The instrument of this act was his home.

He was very insistent about that: The small two-story house, just off of Huaihai Road on a narrow lane in the old French Concession, was his private property. It was modest, no more than a simple cottage, the sort of dwelling that was occupied before the Communist Revolution by the mid-level employees of foreign corporations. In the late 1920s, when the house was built, its tenants would likely have been expatriate Armenians or Germans.

By the 1930s, upwardly mobile Chinese professionals like Tom were beginning to crack the barriers that kept Shanghainese out of the city's best neighborhoods. In a sense, the house made Tom as good as a European, the term used at the time he bought it in 1937 for anyone who was not Chinese. He never let go of that image of himself—"as good as a European"—even when the Europeans themselves had all left the city and the revolutionary authorities began moving working-class families into the five-room house on the lane, first one family, then a second and a third and a fourth.

"From 1968 on, we were reduced to one room, one room in our own home," Tom said. "My wife and I"—he introduced her as Jane and insisted that she too spoke English, although she remained silent throughout the evening—"My wife and I raised our two children in this single room."

Both sons, who were in their thirties, had emigrated to the United States. One was in Kansas, the other in Missouri. The room in which they grew up was now the centerpiece in the house that the Fengs had recovered in its totality after an eight-year struggle to remove its other occupants. The struggle began when the municipal government announced that expropriated domestic property would be returned to its original owners under certain special circumstances. The circumstances were left deliberately vague; the announcement was meant more as a reassuring gesture to foreign investors than as a sincere invitation to native residents. But Tom took the announcement at face value, refusing to give up until the house was grudgingly returned to him.

He was as good as a European again, and he set out, in this room, to erase the memory of his humiliation.

Letters from his sons, describing their homes in the American Midwest, were treated as blueprints. Letters back to them were de facto mail-order slips. Soon boxes began arriving in Shanghai from St. Louis and Kansas City. With the right palms greased in the port, Tom had little trouble getting them past the customs desk and into this room.

The room was now America, Europe, Japan. It was every place but China.

Against the far wall, bracketed between a cheap reproduction of a Cézanne still life and a poster advertising a Modigliani exhibition in New York, there was a twenty-six-inch Sony color television set, used almost exclusively with the Magnavox videocassette deck that rested atop it.

"We only watch Shanghai television on Thursday evenings, when 'Falcon Crest' is shown," Tom said, adjusting the contrast as Jane Fonda pulled on a pair of nylon panty hose in *Klute*.

Inside a thick notebook he had written down the titles of all his videotapes, along with the year each film was shot and the day it arrived in the mail from America. There were dozens of entries. He seemed especially fond of Robert di Niro, who was represented by *Mean Streets, Godfather II, Raging Bull, The Deer Hunter,* and *New York, New York.*

Tom had three other notebooks. One listed his music cassettes, the second his compact disks. A Technics tape deck rested in a bookcase, alongside a Technics amplifier and a Sony CD player. The third notebook listed records. It was quite impressive: virtually the entire oeuvre of Mozart, all of Beethoven's piano sonatas and symphonies, the major compositions of Schubert, Saint-Saëns, Chopin, and Telemann, Verdi's complete *La Traviata* and *Otello,* Puccini's *Manon Lascaut, Tosca, La Bohème.* But there was no record turntable in the room.

"We don't have one," Tom said. "Those are the records I collected before 1965. They were all taken away by the Red Guards, broken one by one in the street. I have listed them from my memory."

He was silent for a moment, then looked me straight in the eye.

"My son in Kansas City. He was one of the Red Guards."

A check mark appeared next to the title of each record that had been replaced, in the past half decade, by a tape or compact disk shipped to Shanghai by the Kansas City son. There were no Chinese operas or musical compositions among them.

"I hate Chinese music," Tom said. "It is worthless."

By 1989, tens of thousands of Chinese were embarking on the trek that the sons of Tom Feng had completed—and that Liang Baihua had begun three years before, "just as insurance," she insisted in a letter.

She was my oldest friend in China. Since that letter in late 1987, I hadn't heard a word from her.

A decade earlier, when our friendship began, Shanghai had still been in the throes of the Maoist aesthetic, and so was Liang. She had the plain-Jane haircut of a junior cadre then, and wore what Western reporters called the "perpendicular pants suit," putty beige and severe. In appearance she was indistinguishable from the mind-numbing collective mass of Miss Liangs, Wongs, and Chans who sat at ranks of identical desks in the interminable folds of the municipal bureaucracy.

Except that there was a fierce spark of the unpredictable to her, an uncontrollable curiosity that was risky business for someone in her shoes. Liang Baihua had the habit of visiting foreign friends to watch television, knocking on hotel room doors long after dark, her all-too-audible stage whisper—"It's me. Are you there?"—echoing in the corridor. Even worse, from the standpoint of party conventions, she would invite a few of us over to talk in her room, an austere dorm space that she shared with another cadre in a smog-choked industrial suburb above Suzhou Creek. Thirty years old then, pencil thin and intense, she wanted to know everything about us: what our homes looked like. How we felt about love and marriage, books and movies, Richard Nixon and Jimmy Carter, Chairman Mao and Deng Xiaoping.

Our paths first crossed in one of those comic opera episodes that gave the early years of China's opening to the West the quality of a charming, idiosyncratic fairy tale. The only hotels in Shanghai then were the ones that foreign capital had built decades before: tattered Art Deco palaces like the Peace and the Jin Jiang. They were booked months in advance, and anyone who arrived in the city as I did, stepping off the overnight train from Beijing without a room reservation, was guaranteed to spend many hours in a fruitless search for accommodations.

The search often wound up back at a railroad station bench. But this time a deskman at the Peace had taken pity, and begun making telephone calls around the city on my behalf. About 8:00 P.M. he walked outside, signaled for a driver, and said, without elaboration, that he had "found a place to sleep."

The Red Flag taxi lumbered off into the night.

Half an hour passed before we pulled up at a cyclone fence, where a white-uniformed sailor saluted and waved toward a four-story concrete box at the center of a compound of look-alike buildings. It proved to be a Chinese naval base several miles north of the city on the Yangtze. The military, far from resisting party secretary Deng Xiaoping's attempt to marry profit and dialectic, was already embracing capitalism with the same fervor that once sent human-wave assaults scrambling up the Korean hills. The Chinese air force was about to launch its own civilian carrier, East China Airline. The People's Liberation Army was organizing a travel agency chain. And the Yangtze command of the navy had become a hotelier, sheltering

Japanese businessmen and the occasional reporter in a private guest house attached to the officers' mess.

We rose with the sailors to reveille at 6:00 A.M., gathering strength over a breakfast of crullers and hot soybean milk for the daily battle over seats in the three guest-house taxis. Liang, who was assigned to the base as a translator, was my ally in these struggles. The Japanese, armed with fastidiously wrapped gifts of Sony Walkmen and Shiseido perfume, were doing fine without her help.

Liang had a temper that burned as dangerously as her curiosity, and when someone slighted her friends she was sure to respond. It was like her, in these situations, not to care about appearances, or consequences. The principle was what mattered. The slight.

Once, determined to get me to an interview near the Bund, the downtown Shanghai waterfront, after an hour's wait, she jumped into the front seat of a taxi and wouldn't leave until the driver removed three Matsushita salesmen from his vehicle. "This man is next in line," she said, pointing at me. "He is next even if he hasn't bribed you."

She shot a glance at the beribboned box on the dashboard.

I was ushered into the car amidst a flurry of tight-lipped apologies and stiff bows that I knew Liang (and I) would wind up paying for. After that morning it became almost impossible for me to get a cab. So I'd walk, and whenever she could get away with it, Liang would leave her post and join me for the one-hour stretch to Haikou Park, and then try to shove an opening into the North Sichuan Road bus, using her narrow shoulders as a battering ram on the wall of humanity that filled every available inch of floor space.

The three miles between the base and the bus stop took us through a canyon of ten-story apartment buildings that were permanently enveloped in a cloud of industrial exhaust. The sun never quite penetrated these streets; it hung tentatively in the gray air, a barely discernible yellow circle that cast no shadows and supported no life. There were no trees, no shrubs, not even any weeds. The buildings themselves were unpainted cinder-block slabs, featureless except for assorted missing chunks and jagged cracks that climbed disconcertingly through several floors. They were blackened with soot deposited by the interminable smog.

By the time we reached the park I was usually hacking with a dry, painful cough that took weeks to shake after I left Shanghai. Liang didn't notice the cough any more than she noticed the rubble that passed for home to the city's giant proletariat.

"Mr. Frank," she'd say, as we picked our way around a pile of cinder blocks that were still awaiting use or removal ten years after delivery, "tell me again: How do you pronounce Y-o-k-n-a-p-a-t-a-w-p-h-a?"

Years passed before she could bring herself to call me Frank, without the "Mister."

There were always discussions of Mississippi in our dusty walks. Liang was enthralled by William Faulkner and his fictional Yoknapatawpha County—had consumed every word of *Go Down Moses, The Sound and the Fury,* and *As I Lay Dying,* over and over—in paperback editions so worn from being passed from reader to reader that the pages were now as soft as Kleenex. But you couldn't be too choosy about what you read in China; almost everything between covers in a European language was technically impermissible. Liang's tastes reflected the broad range that a literary black market imposed on its readers.

"What is your opinion of Jacqueline Susann?" she'd abruptly ask. Or: "Do think John O'Hara's books are pornographic?"

Hidden under her bed she had stacks of Henry James and Erskine Caldwell novels piled next to Harlequin romances and James Bond thrillers. I'd never met anyone, in America or Britain, who believed so rapturously in the printed English word.

I had sent Liang two books from Hong Kong in the summer of 1985, when things had begun to loosen up and it no longer seemed dangerous for a Chinese citizen to receive such a gift. One was *Gone with the Wind,* which she had asked for during my previous visit to Shanghai. The other was a volume of John Cheever's short stories; I thought of it as a double corrective to the postbellum angst of Faulkner and the plantation reveries of Margaret Mitchell, a taste of a more contemporary America, a subject that endlessly fascinated her. We corresponded often, discussing Cheever's acerbic portraits of suburbia, then a series of other books I mailed to her. Liang's life slowly took fuller shape for me in these letters.

She could read the books only because of her father, a scientist who had been trained in the late 1930s, when Shanghai was still the cosmopolitan Queen City of the East. He held on to the English he had learned from the Jesuits at Fudan University, and when his lab was closed during the Cultural Revolution, along with Liang's school and the entire educational system of Shanghai, he taught it to his children.

The Liang family had passed those years in a strange, unfathomable netherworld. By day Liang and her sister were Red Guards like Tom Feng's sons—it was expected of them—denouncing teachers and scientists, hunting out the vestigial remnants of Western influence in Shanghai. By night they read their father's clandestine volumes of Hemingway and Shakespeare. I learned secondhand that Liang had eventually been shipped off—for "reeducation"—to Manchuria, where she spent eight years working in a steel plant. She was evasive whenever I brought it up.

"What I can tell you? There isn't anything to say," she snapped the last time I tried to pry the memory out of her. "None of it made any sense. Even now, it all seems impossible. A nightmare. Something that could not have happened."

But the Great Proletarian Cultural Revolution did happen, and the Red Guards were among its chief victims, a generation far more lost than the one Hemingway had chronicled. You saw them on the street corners of every large Chinese city by the mid-1980s: men and women in their thirties and forties, few of them educated, hawking cheap clothes or plastic trinkets to eke out a living. In the new, profit-minded China there wasn't much else they could do. Nobody, in the party or out of it, trusted them. Nobody had much use for them.

If you were lucky, you also encountered the Liangs, the few who had survived with spirits intact. Mostly they wanted to get out.

Ever since 1986, slowly, methodically, Liang had been accumulating the necessary papers and, more important, the *guanxi*, "connections," that greased the wheels of the exit permit office. Collecting the countless official stamps and permissions from work units. Acquiring a passport, a three-year task. Applying to American universities—a monumental undertaking, with each application fee representing up to two months' wages in China.

Student visas to the United States were not easy to come by, especially for the children of crowded, ambitious Shanghai. In the first eight years of the 1980s, the People's Republic of China had sent more than seventy thousand students to the United States, including Deng Xiaoping's daughter and the children and grandchildren of hundreds of other high-ranking Communist Party and military officials. This was one reason why the People's Liberation Army, the navy, and the air force went into the hotel and travel business. Foreign currency profits translated into tuition for the progeny of the high command.

Much like their counterparts from Taiwan, few of the students returned after graduation—so few that in 1988 the government felt obliged to announce cutbacks in the number of student passports. The cutbacks were almost immediately rescinded after a public uproar. American education commanded an enormous, powerful constituency in China.

"We know damn well that most of these students will overstay their visas," a consular official in Canton told me over a beer in the cavernous lobby of the Garden Hotel.

But he admitted that he himself granted them by the score. For all of its own bureaucratic strictures, the diplomatic corps had the sympathetic ears that Liang was looking for. She found one, right there in Canton. It might have been the officer I drank a beer with at the Garden.

In 1988, I learned later, Liang's purse had been snatched on a bus; she lost her address book just a week before she left the north Shanghai dorm for a work-unit room in the city center. In the meantime I changed newspapers. Our correspondence suddenly ended. I grew obsessed with her disappearance.

I began seriously hunting for Liang in early 1989, when an assignment brought me to Shanghai periodically over several months. She had always dreamed of a post with a foreign trading company; without much optimism, I presented myself at the receptionist's desk at one of the best-known firms, the one she had been most anxious to cultivate, and asked if a woman named Liang Baihua worked there.

The receptionist looked around to see if anyone was listening, then turned back to me with a curious expression on her face. Very quietly, she asked half a dozen questions. How did I know Miss Liang? When did I meet her? Why was I looking for her in this office?

Finally she asked, "Are you Mister Frank?"

That night she took me to Liang.

She lived now in a sagging nineteenth-century tenement near the waterfront, at the end of a stairwell so dark that I had to feel my way blindly up to the fifth floor. It smelled of damp mold and rat excrement.

We talked for hours that night, as in the old days. But Liang was different. No longer in a perpendicular pants suit—she wore a blue pullover sweater and a cotton skirt—she was no longer satisfied with only reading about another kind of life.

Liang admitted, when I pressed her, that she didn't have much money. What there was of it had been exchanged for dollars at half the official rate on the black market near the Jin Jiang and deposited by a friend in a Hong Kong bank.

She said she understood what it meant to disappear into another country. She believed she could beat the odds. She wouldn't talk any more about it.

"I'll be all right. I'll be all right . . ."

Outside the building vast crowds surged along Nanjing Road, past the neo-Gothic towers where the old Taipans had schemed before 1949, past the new towers where foreign businesses were returning to the Shanghai scene. It was in one of these offices, Liang said, that she had made her decision to leave.

In 1986 she had been reassigned by her work unit to the Shanghai branch of the foreign firm where I went looking for her. It was one of the great *hongs*, trading houses, that had been booted out by Mao after Liberation. There she became close friends with a Hong Kong colleague—far too close, in the party's estimatation. The friendship was a social error so serious, even in the reformed China of Deng Xiaoping, as to be regarded almost as perversion.

Her voice quaked when she spoke of it.

"There were rumors, terrible rumors about us. None of it was true, but that's not the point. The point is that they wouldn't allow it."

In the midst of the scandal over her Hong Kong friend, she had been given a choice: deliver confidential company files to the work unit, or accept another transfer. Instead she had descended into Shanghai's equivalent of the underground, waiting out what she was determined to make her last days in China.

Young people were marching in Shanghai that tense spring week in 1989 when I found her. Chanting "Science and democracy," they poured through the city streets day and night under a bright canopy of university and work-unit banners. Most were too young to remember the Cultural Revolution clearly. Their history, their grappling with the meaning of freedom, was here and now. But Democracy Spring came too late for Liang Baihua. Her mind was in another place, torn away from Shanghai by a scandal in an office tower and a burning desire to see the world John Cheever described.

On an abstract level, the case the Chinese government made was understandable: "A nation as poor and populous as ours cannot afford Western individualism." It was the official mantra, chanted at some point in nearly every interview, by the very people whose sons and daughters were angling for admission to Stanford and Harvard. But the die had been cast, in part through the power of imported ideas, in part through sheer frustration. A generation was lost.

I went once more to Liang's room, the day before she was to leave. When I arrived she was out negotiating the final indignity, a bribe to move her name up on a standby list for the flight to San Francisco. Her father was there, helping arrange her few things in a small suitcase, folding up the bed linens.

The elder Liang was a small, frail man. We'd never met before, but we had heard a great deal about each other. He let me in, and sat on the edge of the bed while I sat in Liang's single chair.

He knew, he told me, that he would never see his daughter again.

The next morning Liang left for America, and I caught a plane to the city of Xi'an in western China.

*   *   *

June 3, 1989, was a scorching day in Xi'an. Bicycling down Lingyuan Road to the film studio on a rented Flying Pigeon, squeezed onto the shoulder by a line of heavy trucks bound for the outlying cities of Shaanxi Province, I had to stop to catch my breath every ten minutes or so for fear of passing out.

Waves of reflected heat shimmered over the souvenir stalls beside the Small Wild Goose Pagoda, but there was hardly anyone to notice. The tourists had disappeared from Xi'an and everywhere else in China, frightened off by the demonstrations and the relentless buildup of tension.

By the time I reached the film lot, about six miles south of the city wall, rivulets of sweat were inscribing long trails down the back of my polo shirt, and my khaki pants were plastered to my bottom and thighs. The scene inside the lobby restaurant of the studio did nothing to make me less self-conscious. It was a perfect cultural turnabout, exactly as if some uproariously unkempt hayseed from Shaanxi had suddenly walked into the executive dining room at Paramount. Seated over cocktails around half a dozen tables in the frigid air-conditioning were, judging from sheer appearances, Xi'an Film Studios' latest crop of ingenues, casting agents, directors, and producers. A couple of the men had shaved heads. Most of the assembled wore sunglasses, even though they were indoors. White, the year's color, screamed from blindingly laundered Lacoste knock-offs, skimpy summer dresses, pumps. The women looked unintentionally hard and studiously bored. Several hadn't bothered with bras. Someone was even smoking a joint—hash was easy to find in Xi'an, sold in the back alleys by the same Uygur Muslims who dominated the black market in foreign currency and endowed the local mosques.

The characters gathered in the hotel lobby seemed quite oblivious to their country's wild dance toward the abyss. A few of them turned to look at me, then turned back to their colleagues in theatrically muffled laughter. One of the women winked.

China in 1989 was like this: twisted, contorted, sometimes in its desperate resistance to change, at other times in its frantic embrace of it.

Xi'an Studios had forty directors on its payroll, most of them churning their way through kung fu thrillers; but it was known in the West primarily for a small but steady output of serious films, the work of a generation of brilliant young filmmakers who were trained in Beijing and had relocated to Shaanxi because it was far enough from the capital to give them creative rope. The reins were held by an older director, Wu Tianming, who genuinely believed in artistic freedom and set about the deliberate task of putting China on the world cinema map. To a large degree he succeeded, and it was the mountains, deserts, and villages of the impoverished west—not the streets of Beijing or Shanghai—that became the visual stamp of a new Chinese cinema that was arguably the most imaginative in Asia. I'd come down to try to arrange interviews with Wu and his protégés.

I hunted around the first-floor offices until a conservatively dressed woman in her mid-thirties, who wore a simple orange frock and introduced herself as Bonnie, asked if she could help me. She was a studio accountant.

I explained my mission, naming the people I'd like to see, but she began shaking her head halfway through.

"They're not here, none of them," she said.

Wu had gone to Hong Kong. One of the directors I named was in Shenzhen, on the Hong Kong border. Another was in California, a third in France.

"They've all left in the past month."

Bonnie offered to take me on a walk through the back lot, where giant effigies of Guangying, the goddess of mercy, flanked a plywood palace, bleaching in the fierce heat, that was to be used in some costume epic. Nearby, trucks painted with the red star of the People's Liberation Army were lined up next to similar trucks emblazoned with the stylized white sunburst of Chiang Kai-shek's Kuomintang.

Bonnie didn't know what either of the films was to be about; only that they'd both, for the moment, been abandoned.

"The government stopped sending us money. I think they were quite unhappy with some of our films."

I thanked her for the tour, and made my way back across the deserted sets to my bicycle.

*   *   *

The imam of Xi'an, the city's leading Muslim prelate, was visibly delighted when I pushed the Flying Pigeon into the courtyard of the Great Mosque, which was crammed into a neighborhood of baked mud single-story houses five miles north of the film studios. He clearly viewed my sharp nose and dark beard in a more favorable light than the starlets had. Taking me for an Iranian or an Arab, he rushed inside to fetch an album that had been filled with neatly mounted photos of a recent protest demonstration in Xi'an.

At midday there weren't many other people on the grounds. A few men entered the courtyard, glanced briefly at me, then smiled a welcome and bowed piously toward the southwest—toward Mecca—before continuing on into a tile-domed bathhouse. Leftover banners from the demonstration leaned against the wall of the bath. They had nothing to do with the sloganeering for "Science and democracy" that peppered the graffiti of Beijing and Shanghai. WE WILL FIGHT TO THE DEATH TO DEFEND THE HONOR OF ISLAM, one read.

In the imam's photo album, bearded men in white skull caps marched with their families down Dong Wu Avenue, past the provincial government headquarters. The imam smiled over his own wispy goatee and said something to me, repeating it several times, until he realized that I couldn't understand his Shaanxi dialect. Then he scratched the number "30,000" in the baked earth of the mosque courtyard, and pointed approvingly at the marchers pictured in the album.

"May second," he said, speaking very slowly in Mandarin. "Many thousands. One month ago."

The chief purpose of the march, proclaimed from another banner leaning against the courtyard wall, was to call for the assassination of Salman Rushdie and the four Chinese writers who had collaborated—with government approval—on a translation of *The Satanic Verses* .

There are eighty-five million people in China who are not Han Chinese, more than the population of Germany, Great Britain, or France. They include Tibetans, Uygurs and Kazaks, the Yi, the Bai and the Dai, the Lisu, the Naxi and Miao—fifty-five separate "national minorities" in all, thirty-eight of them represented in Xi'an. The Muslims are especially worrisome to Beijing because their faith is understood to be permanently directed across the frontiers, toward Mecca and Iran and the larger Islamic world, where the harbingers are anything but soothing. And they know, too, the party officials, that the Muslims remember; they remember that all fourteen of their mosques in Xi'an were closed by Mao, and that their religious leaders were tossed into prison. The imam still bore the mark of that experience in his gaunt frame and sallow, jaundiced complexion.

Barbarians inside the realm: not so much the people themselves but the ideas they represented, the differing vision, the implicit threat to centralized order. The threat of chaos. It was the classic, the age-old Chinese nightmare, the xenophobic neurosis that led Qin Shi Huangdi, the first Han emperor, to impose a single rule over the sprawling Chinese nation twenty-two hundred years ago and begin constructing the Great Wall across Shaanxi.

But the barbarians hadn't been walled out, and foreign ideas, Western and Eastern alike, were proliferating madly in the disintegrating ruins of Mao's old order.

The imam excused himself, leaving me to flip through the pages of the album. Judging from the photographs, his estimate of thirty thousand marchers didn't seem inflated.

By my own estimate there had been considerably more than thirty thousand people in the demonstration that rolled down Dong Wu Avenue the night of my arrival in Xi'an, May 28. It was a young crowd, mostly students from Xibei University, streaming noisily through the city at 10:00 P.M. The marchers this time had carried the familiar banners: SCIENCE AND DEMOCRACY, DOWN WITH LI PENG, STOP THE CORRUPTION.

Corruption was virtually the first thing a Chinese student wanted to talk about with strangers, as soon as the welcoming niceties had been seen to. First corruption, then, inevitably, the possibility of emigrating to America.

In Xi'an the latest tale involved a fully equipped ambulance that was presented to the municipal fathers by a European charity. Officials at the Foreign Affairs Department, which accepted the gift, were said to have sold it for a hundred thousand yuan, then used the money to buy apartments. Everyone was talking about it, exchanging the latest details: who pocketed the money, where they bought the apartments. People laughed sarcastically when I asked if they expected anyone to be prosecuted.

The Xi'an ambulance scam was small potatoes compared to the rumors elsewhere. Deng Xiaoping's oldest son, a paraplegic who had lost the use of his legs when Red Guards threw him from an upper-story window in the 1960s, headed a special fund for the handicapped that had allegedly "misplaced" millions of yuan. He was widely believed to have raked off much of the cash for himself. Party secretary Zhao Ziyang, the white knight of liberal reform, had his own filial problems. If the rumors were to be believed, one Zhao child had set up shop as an importer in Macao, while a second was deeply involved in smuggling activities in Shenzhen.

The conservatives, the party purists who were Zhao's sworn enemies, fared no better. Their most unreconstructed hard-liner, politburo member Chen Yun—in public, a fierce critic of Western bourgeois liberalism—supposedly used his post to get his daughter out of China and into Stanford. His son, meanwhile, was reported to have put "borrowed" state funds into a private joint venture with Japanese investors.

Many people believed that Hu Yaobang, whose death in April ignited the student demonstrations, had been deposed in 1986 as party chairman for speaking out against the tide of corruption. "Party cadres are using their official posts for private gain and string-pulling," he'd said. "They are raising the cultivation of useful connections to the level of an art."

Hu's mistake was to have left himself vulnerable to criticism for another sort of corruption. He favored Western business suits, and even suggested that China trade in its chopsticks for forks and knives because they were more sanitary. In the party's view he had become un-Chinese. He had worshiped too openly before the idols from beyond the wall.

The day after the May 28 march, I talked to a couple in their early thirties who had participated in the demonstration; they ran a small souvenir stall near the drum tower in central Xi'an.

They'd plowed every fen they could borrow from friends and

relatives into this miniature business, which measured no more than seventy-five square feet and was jammed to its tin eaves with plastic representations of Emperor Qin's buried army of terra cotta soldiers, the attraction that drew most tourists to Xi'an, and a sampling of other local memorabilia. However humble, it was an escape route for them from dead-end Shaanxi village life.

The disappearance of tourism because of the protests meant they wouldn't make it, didn't have a breath of a chance. They knew that.

The husband, who brought me up to date on all of the major corruption scandals shortly into our conversation, was a former schoolteacher. Hu Yaobang had been absolutely right, he said. What it all boiled down to was *guanxi*, pull. The principal players in China's soap opera scandals had it. He, the souvenir peddler, didn't.

"I was the number one student in my class at the normal college, but it wasn't me who got the teaching assignments at Xibei or in the city. Those jobs went to the sons of party officials."

He stopped for a moment, picked up an imitation silk scarf with a phalanx of the terra cotta army stamped on it, and handed it to me.

"Maybe you'd be interested in this? Very cheap today."

His wife smiled, and said in English, "It is okay. You are friend, no buy something."

The teacher continued: "They sent us to a village so far away in the countryside that we could only see our families once a year. Very far in the mountains, very poor. After ten years teaching there, I made seventy yuan a month." The amount worked out to about $19.

They'd decided to change their lives two years ago, taking the reform talk at face value, and asked everyone they knew to chip in a few yuan. It would make them all rich—tourists loved Xi'an, loved that buried army; they would wind up like those peasants you read about every day in the *People's Daily,* the ones who had become millionaires on ideas much less certain than theirs.

"I suppose you must think we were very foolish," the teacher said.

But in fact I was thinking about the march. He and his wife had walked down Dong Wu Avenue in support of the students. They'd been part of the very demonstrations that were bankrupting them. I asked why.

"All our people want is to be more free, more free," the husband said.

In the end I bought the scarf.

PART THREE

Dust in the Wind

JUNE 1989

At 5:00 A.M. on Sunday, June 4, loudspeakers mounted on the bell tower where Xi'an's four main avenues intersect suddenly began playing the socialist "Internationale." A small knot of men gathered at the tower base, talking quietly. When I asked one of them what was happening, he said nothing and looked away.

It was my first inkling that something had gone terribly wrong.

I'd been up all night, trying to get out of western China, shuttling back and forth from the airport to a hotel near the tower. Flights kept being canceled; no one knew why. I heard that the trains were held up too; the entire transportation system seemed to be frozen.

Finally, around 9:00 A.M., a man behind the desk in the hotel lobby, his voice quivering as he spoke, said, "It's Beijing. The tanks have come. They've killed everyone in Tiananmen Square . . ."

He turned his head nervously half a dozen times to see if anybody was watching. Then he showed me a fax that had just come through from Hong Kong. It was a portion of the front page of *Ming Pao*, a Chinese-language newspaper, with a four-inch-high headline in dark black: *Xue,* the ideogram for "blood."

"There is blood everywhere in the streets of Beijing," the deskman said.

At 10:00 A.M. I returned to the airport and managed to get a seat on a rescheduled flight to Changsha, the capital of Hunan Province and the original power base of Mao Zedong. There had been rumors of huge demonstrations there all week. God knew what might be happening this morning.

I never found out. About an hour after takeoff we suddenly banked and made for the airstrip at Wuhan, about 950 miles up the Yangtze River from Shanghai and 200 miles north of our scheduled destination. The pilot made only a curt announcement, something to the effect that we'd land in ten minutes in Wuhan rather than Changsha, and our questions would be answered on the ground.

There were no other foreigners on the packed plane, an aging twin-engined rattletrap that had been copied by Chinese engineers from a Soviet design of the early 1960s. The motors sputtered in flatulent bursts as we began our descent, skipping along on updrafts of ferocious summer heat rising off the valley slopes.

From the air, Wuhan's streets were completely awash with people. A column of smoke rose from the center of the Changjiang Bridge linking the north and south banks of the great river, where there seemed to be a traffic pileup.

The airport was a madhouse. We were conducted into a large transit room, cooled a few inconsequential degrees by ceiling fans, where several hundred marooned passengers milled around in bewilderment. They too had been promised further instruction on the ground, but there was no one to provide it. An information desk next to the landing strip entrance was vacant, as was a counter that advertised soft drinks and cookies in cheery posters taped to a glass display case that offered a selection of dead flies.

At the far end of the room a corridor led to the main hall of the building. It was blocked by the sole representatives of authority in sight: an expressionless People's Liberation Army enlisted man cradling an assault rifle and a middle-aged woman in a blue uniform who bounced nervously from one foot to the other and appeared ready to bolt for the exit at the slightest provocation.

There was little point in remaining in the transit room; the onward flight to Changsha was an extremely dubious bet. I walked up to the uniformed woman, adopting the air of a friendly but hopelessly foolish Western tourist, said, "Wuhan!" and started into the corridor until the soldier barred it with his gun.

It didn't take much wrangling to get past the two of them. The woman examined my ticket, pointing to the scribbled ideograms for Changsha, which she read to me in an unconvincingly stern voice. But when I repeated, much more firmly—in fact loudly—"Wuhan!" half a dozen times, she relented and signaled for the soldier to let me leave.

In the outer waiting room there was even greater confusion. The ticket window would open, sporadically and for no more than five minutes at a time, inspiring an instant crush of would-be passengers—mostly Taiwanese tourists and businessmen—who at this point were trying to get to any port on the coast, any city close to any border. It didn't matter where: Shanghai, Canton, Xiamen, Qingdao. Flights to each place were listed on a signboard above the ticket window. But the schedule was pure fiction. No flights at all had left Wuhan in the past twenty-four hours.

I learned this from the only other Europeans in the airport, three Polish hydroelectric engineers who were deep into the task of getting as drunk as they could. They had a single liter of vodka left, a treasured object from the way they fondled it.

One of the men, Wladislaus, had spent several years in Detroit working at the Dodge Main auto plant back in the 1950s before returning to Warsaw to get an engineering degree. The news that I was, in effect, an honorary Pole—like anybody raised on the east side of Detroit—brought the other two men wobbling to their feet. We kissed and embraced.

They were drinking, Wlad told me, because they were scared to death.

"It is a war out there, my friend. They all have guns or sticks. We were certain we would die. It is a miracle that we didn't. Maybe our countryman the pope is taking care of us, I don't know."

He handed the vodka to me.

The three Poles had come down the river from the big Yangtze dam project at Yichang on Friday morning. All work had ceased on the project the previous week, and word reached the small detachment of Eastern European technical experts that it would be best to get out of China as soon as possible. Wuhan was in an uproar when they arrived, its streets nearly impassable because of the mobs. They'd been trapped in the Qingchuan Hotel on the north bank of the Yangtze until nine o'clock that morning, then narrowly made it across the bridge just before something exploded behind them and sent splinters of wood and metal raining down into the river.

I told Wlad that I had to get into the city. He said I was out of my mind.

I was and I wasn't. I was as frightened as they were, maybe more, because I'd seen wars and insurrections up close before and I had no stomach left for what I expected to find at the river. There were stories I still couldn't tell without crumbling, emotionally, a decade after they'd happened, stories from Nicaragua and Honduras in the late 1970s and from the South China Sea in the last desperate moments of the war in Indochina.

It's not easy to explain. I was a journalist; I was there. I was supposed to observe and report. It wasn't a matter of choosing between courage and cowardice, or more accurately, between madness and discretion. I didn't want to go into the city, to the degree that "wants" were even remotely involved; I felt compelled. Later, in the retelling, the act would take on a certain amount of bravado. But there was no bravado in it at the time. I was terrified, so terrified that I was numbed somehow—the vodka must have played its part— numbed both to fear and to the dictates of discretion.

I suppose Wlad was right. I was out of my mind.

That was certainly the opinion of the drivers who sat in their taxis outside in the parking lot and shook their heads when I explained where I needed to go. To a man, they refused. They'd take me to a hotel nearby, here on the south side of the river, but no place else. They shook their heads and wouldn't discuss it. The sole exception was the single driver who wasn't a man, a twenty-one-year-old woman in a rusted-out Toyota who didn't say no immediately, which I correctly took as an invitation to make a proposal.

Neither of us was in a mood to dicker. I offered fifty American dollars, probably what she earned in two normal months, paid in advance. She accepted. The other drivers ridiculed us as we swung out of the lot.

Wuhan is not one city. The name is an umbrella for three separate municipalities, Wuchang, Hankou, and Hanyang, strung along the banks of the Yangtze and Han rivers at their muddy brown confluence in the heart of China. Each of them holds claim to an important place in modern Chinese history.

The mutiny of the Wuchang imperial army garrison on October 10, 1911, signaled the death throes of the Manchu dynasty and the birth of the Chinese Republic of Sun Yat-sen. Sixteen years later Mao Zedong moved to Wuchang, which lies on the right bank of the

Yangtze, to run the National Peasant Movement Institute, a key training unit of the Chinese Communist Party.

Hanyang, on the opposite bank of the Yangtze and separated
from Hankou by the Han River, was one of the primary centers of
the pre-Republican Self-strengthening Movement, led by a group of
intellectuals who made the first serious attempt to overthrow the
Manchus and bring China into the mainstream of the industrial
world. Many of them paid for it with their heads.

For its part, Hankou was declared a foreign treaty port at the
close of the second Opium War in 1860 and retained a large colony
of Europeans until the Communist Revolution. More recently it had
served as the central command headquarters of the People's Liberation Army. It was here that Deng Xiaoping and other party leaders
had met in mid-May to devise a response to the growing clamor of
pro-democracy demonstrators in the nation's streets.

The nature of their decision was now all too clear.

It was also quite clear why the transportation system was paralyzed. Troops had been moved into Beijing and other cities by the
hundreds of thousands in the past week, transported in sealed truck
convoys and commandeered civilian trains and aircraft. Wuhan's importance in this strategy was considerable. The bridge from Hanyang
to Wuchang, where the airport lies, is the only link between China's
north and south for nearly two thousand miles of the Yangtze, from
Chongqing to Nanjing.

To control the Wuhan Changjiang Bridge was to control the
central artery of the Chinese nation.

Careening uncertainly through the outskirts of Wuchang, we headed
north in the Toyota without seeing another vehicle for about twenty
minutes, until we reached the intersection of Zhongshan and Wuluo
roads near the approaches to the bridge.

There was an extraordinary silence in the air at first, an almost
total absence of sound, except for the chirping of insects. Street
noise—the babble of children, the grinding of truck gears, the thump
of pile drivers—is normally so insistent in a Chinese city, even in
the middle of the night, much less at midday, that its disappearance
left a palpable, unnerving void. But about half a mile from the river

the silence began to give way to a distant, continuous gurgling that swelled to a roar as we drew closer to the Yangtze. It was a harrowing din, a cascade of furious voices merged into a single pulsating shout.

At the corner of Wuluo Road and Shouyi Road, under a monument to the martyrs of 1911, a detachment of white-uniformed police standing behind a line of wooden barricades waved us to the shoulder. I got out of the passenger seat and turned to tell the driver she might as well go back to the airport. It was an unnecessary gesture; she was already jamming the transmission into reverse. A minute later the Toyota was out of sight.

The heat and humidity were appalling. The air seemed to hang inertly in the trees in wet, stagnant clouds. There was no breeze at all off the mile-wide Yangtze. People call Wuhan "the furnace of China"; it was easy to see why.

Once the car was gone, the police unaccountably ignored me. I walked past the barricade and into Jiefang Lu, "Liberation Road," where the outer edges of a vast crowd spilled into the grounds of the monument park and climbed the railroad embankment. Photocopies of the same *Ming Pao* fax I'd seen in Xi'an, with its four-inch-high ideogram for "blood," were tacked to trees and plastered on the walls.

There wasn't another foreign face in sight, which had the curious effect of making me feel insulated rather than conspicuous. The delusion was welcome, and I traded on it consciously and preposterously. I imagined myself encased in an invisible shield like the one that was featured in the television toothpaste commercials of my youth, protecting molars and bicuspids. It was a fine example of the anesthetizing power of banality.

The crowd, which looked to be made up of students and workers from the city's big steel plants, was unlike any I'd seen before, in China or anywhere else. Normally a mass demonstration moves like a sluggish river, flowing purposefully forward to a chorus of programmed chants but leaving a thousand mild eddies of individual conversations and pauses in its wake. There was no conversation and no program on Jiefang Lu as far as I could tell, just a surging, shoulder-to-shoulder push to the bridge amidst that ear-shattering tumult. It was singularly intense. Many of the older men, the ones I took to be workers, carried iron staves. A few others, including some students, shouldered rifles. In the distance there were bursts of gunfire.

I got no closer than a block or so away from the bridge itself, a double-decker that rose three hundred feet above the water in a gradual arc. At the center of the top deck the front ranks of the demonstration were stalled to a complete halt at a jumble of vehicles—public buses drawn across the roadway, probably to prevent military convoys from crossing. At least one had been set afire. Beyond them a phalanx of armored personnel carriers was lined up three abreast, their heavy guns pointed toward our bank.

No one seemed to take notice of me until I pulled a notebook out of my back pocket and began writing, an act that in demonstrations in Beijing and Shanghai had invariably, almost magically, produced an English-speaking representative of the student organizations. They were remarkably adroit in their cultivation of the foreign press. I hoped the notebook would have the same effect here, and somewhat to my surprise, it did. A thin young man in his early twenties walked up and tapped me on the shoulder five minutes later.

"You are a journalist," he said.

He wore the familiar Democracy Spring uniform, a dead ringer for the getup my own generation had favored on American college campuses during the demonstrations of the sixties: jeans, blue work shirt, a bandanna across his forehead, a pair of sneakers. Indeed, he'd come from Tiananmen Square the week before, sent down by the strike committee as a liaison to the steelworkers and the Wuhan University and Central China Teachers' College student groups. The committee had picked him because he was a local, raised downriver from Wuhan in a market town near Huangshi, and he could speak the Hubei dialect.

I asked him about the weapons.

"The railroad station," he said. "On Saturday, after the first time the army try to invade Tiananmen Square, many students want to go to Beijing. They must fight with the soldiers there. Some people steal their guns."

Later the Poles told me that there had been a tremendous clash at the Hanyang terminal early Saturday morning when word arrived of the previous night's humiliation by Beijingers of a detachment of unarmed PLA soldiers dispatched to clear Tiananmen Square. Anxious to participate in what they hoped would be the overthrow of the central government, several thousand students had stormed the rail station. They were eventually repulsed by troops, but a military storeroom was emptied of its contents in the melee.

The student liaison man looked down at my notebook. "Please," he said, "you must write that this action of stealing guns is not approved by our group."

Dutifully I added a sentence to that effect. Then we walked together to an office near the Teachers' College, about two miles east on Wuluo Road, that had a fax machine. It spun out clippings on the Tiananmen assault from Hong Kong newspapers as I pieced together an account of the day's events, writing by hand on a pad of graph paper. After half a dozen failed attempts, we managed to fax it to the *Chronicle*.

It took me two hours to walk to the airport. The Poles were curled up in a corner of the main hall, successfully dead drunk, when I finally got back around 10:00 P.M. I stretched out on the floor beside them but couldn't sleep. A few feet away a pudgy man in his sixties finished one pack of Marlboros and started another. He offered me a cigarette and said, "Where you from?"

I answered in Mandarin, "Jiu Jin Shan"—"Old Gold Mountain," the Chinese name for San Francisco.

"Right. San Francisco. I trained at Hamilton Air Base myself, up in Marin County, in the 1950s. I know 'Frisco very well. Golden Gate Bridge. Herb Caen. Golden Gate Park. Tadich Restaurant."

Old home week at Wuhan Airport, I thought. A Pole who's lived in Detroit and a Taiwanese who knows San Francisco.

He was a retired officer of the Nationalist Chinese air force.

"We just arrived from Taipei, via Hong Kong, Thursday, and now all this has to happen. My wife was born here, in a little village in Hubei. She's waited a very long time, forty years, to come home. We left the village as soon as we heard. Her father is a pretty old guy, you know. He really couldn't understand why she had to leave."

His wife sat next to him, sobbing into a scarf. He patted her gently on the shoulder and lit another cigarette.

At 9:00 A.M. on Tuesday, through a stroke of luck, I was at the head of the ticket line just as a party cadre pushed his way to the window, imperiously demanding to exchange a ticket to Canton—my destination—for a ticket to Shanghai. Thirty minutes later I sat down in the last empty seat of a Boeing 707 bound for the Pearl Delta. We glided uneventfully into Baiyun Airport at noon, and I grabbed a taxi to the Dong Fang.

Ponderously squat in a way that bespoke its Stalinist inspiration, the Dong Fang—"East Wind"—wasn't the leading hotel in Canton anymore, not with the arrival of five-star skyscraper palaces like the Garden and the White Swan. But it had been my base in Guangdong for ten years, and I was used to it. The showers were clean, the televisions and international phone lines worked, and there was—or had been—a public fax machine in the ground-floor business center. It was also the home of the American consulate, where I hoped to get a clearer picture of what was going on.

Clarification was exactly what the desk officer, an old acquaintance, was hoping to get from me when I walked in the door.

"I haven't a goddamned idea what's happening in the rest of China," he said. "Can't get much out of our people in Beijing yet, they're just as confused as I am."

I told him what I knew about Xi'an and Wuhan and what I'd heard from other travelers at the airports. He whistled softly to himself when I described the scene at the Changjiang Bridge.

"So the shit really is hitting the fan. That means there's something to this stuff."

He pointed to a sheaf of faxes: more of the clippings I'd seen in Shaanxi and Hubei. They described demonstrations, some of them violent, all over the country—in eighty cities altogether, according to Ming Pao. The desk officer read me an article from a Taiwan daily that covered the events in Wuhan: It was unmistakably my own account, shorn of its byline and translated into Chinese from the Chronicle. He laughed when I told him.

"At the moment, the truth is whatever you can get your hands on," he said.

In Canton on June 6, that wasn't much. The hotels had cut off their transmissions of Hong Kong television and Cable News Network. A state Public Security officer stood guard over the fax machine. The *South China Morning Post* was not for sale.

"All gone," the salesgirl in the Dong Fang bookstore said.

I asked her what time the next batch would arrive. She didn't answer.

Outside the hotel, Canton—normally the most apathetic of Chinese cities—was in an uproar. Two blocks away on Dong Fang Road, several large articulated public buses had been seized by young people and drawn into a circle, halting all traffic directly in front of the Guangdong provincial government headquarters. Wreaths were placed atop the vehicles, along with banners reading DENG XIAOPING, MURDERER.

Tens of thousands of people, young and old alike, were massed around the sixty-foot-high statue of a PLA soldier that stands in Haizhu Square, at the great northern bend of the Pearl River. The podium served as a speaker's stand, where a student who said he was from Beijing told of the assault at Tiananmen. There were no soldiers in sight. About two blocks above the square, several frightened-looking Public Security officers watched but did nothing.

The demonstration was highly organized. Periodically, student monitors in black arm bands led groups of 250 to 500 people into neighboring streets where police had attempted to detour traffic. The effect was to shut off the detours and bring the entire city to a halt.

A man at the edge of the crowd tugged at my arm. "This is sad day for all Chinese," he said in English.

He was weeping. It is very unusual to see people weep openly in China, but many in the crowd did so as the student from Beijing spoke.

"I am crying for my country," he said. "They have the army, but we are millions of people. They cannot kill us all."

I filed my story by telephone at 1:00 A.M. and went to bed, wondering how long this resolve—the willingness to consider dying for democracy—would last.

Eli Rosenblatt had a reservation on Friday's train to Hong Kong and forty-eight hours to decide whether he would use it. He was a twenty-five-year-old teacher from Milwaukee, just finishing up a year as an English instructor at the South China Agricultural University in Tienhou, a Canton suburb. We'd met in the Dong Fang coffee bar.

"I want to stay on, to stick it out. I feel I owe it to my students," Eli said as he showed me around the leafy campus.

He turned a small cardboard rectangle over and over between his fingers: the train ticket.

On a field below a dormitory a desultory soccer game was under way. A Whitney Houston tape echoed off the walls. It could have been a college campus in America—except for the signs and posters, in red and black, full of that inescapable ideogram for "blood."

Tiananmen Square was written all over the students' faces. We sat in a dorm room, nine of us, including six Chinese students, Eli, and Shaun D'arcy Burke, another foreign teacher, from Lincolnshire, England.

"Use our names. You must use our names in your article," one of the students insisted when Eli explained that I was a reporter.

Later, Eli and Shaun took me aside, separately, and asked me not to use the students' names. They needn't have bothered. I was already haunted by the possible fates of dozens of people I'd quoted by name before June 4. As far as I was concerned, there were only pseudonyms in China now.

Our conversation was a blizzard of rumors. The students said the declaration of martial law, the legal pretext for the assault at Tiananmen, would be extended to Canton tomorrow. They said an army from Sichuan Province had been deployed in the suburbs already, that they'd been put on a "grade two war alert" and issued live ammunition. Tanks were said to be moving into position.

"These are country boys who cannot speak Mandarin and hate us, hate the Cantonese people, because they think we are rich and they are poor," one of the students said. "They will be happy to make Canton another Beijing."

I had heard the same stories at the consulate. No one there could confirm them. Everybody in the dorm room said he knew someone who had seen the Sichuan troops, but nobody had seen them personally. Li Peng, the detested prime minister, was said to have been assassinated—or just lightly wounded. Deng Xiaoping was dead of heart failure, prostrate cancer, or pneumonia—or resting at his summer home. President Yang Shangkun, who sent the Twenty-seventh Army into Beijing, had since fled the capital—or was in complete command of it. Other rumors had the Thirty-eighth Army fighting the Twenty-seventh in support of the ousted Zhao Ziyang, and the Canton garrison rushing north to join in.

We agreed, after about half an hour of this talk, that nobody knew what was happening. A young woman who had sat quietly and listened without adding to the exchange of rumors now admitted that she had tried to leave Canton. It turned out that every one of the students in the room had also tried. But the trains were canceled.

The four students who lived in the room had stockpiled rice and dried greens under their bunks. "In case of a siege," one of them explained.

There was no way to leave, except on the Kowloon-Canton express to Hong Kong. And that was a train for foreigners only—most of whom had already left by now. On a four-hour walk to the Pearl River and back that morning, I had seen no other Westerners on the city streets.

One young man spoke for the others: "We feel safer when we see foreign friends still with us. It is more like the normal." He paused. "But we will understand if you leave."

Like Eli, Shaun had a Friday ticket to Hong Kong. He hadn't made up his mind either.

The students, all of whom were around Eli and Shaun's age, said they planned to participate in a general strike called for the next day. Their teachers were divided on the strike. An older man, a chemistry professor, joined us. He said the students were being rash, that the violence in Beijing was "perpetrated by hooligans in stolen army uniforms."

It was the government's own favorite rumor. He badly wanted to believe it. Eli showed him newspaper clippings, photos of bodies that had been ground under tank treads. The professor looked away, shaken.

We all needed a break from the tension. The Garden Hotel had an Italian restaurant. I offered to treat everyone to pizza. We also invited Chang, an English teacher from Canton who worked at another university. It would be his first pizza, he said.

At the restaurant, he ate one piece, then lapsed into a kind of daze. I joked that it was probably the cheese: "Very hard on a Chinese stomach, huh, Chang?"

No, he said. "It's not the cheese. It's my brother. He is a student in Beijing. We have heard nothing from him since last week."

That night, at 2:00 A.M., and again at 4:00 and 5:00 A.M., the phone rang in my room. Each time a woman's voice, unidentified, said: "Your papers are not in order. You would be well advised to be careful."

The phone rang again. It was Joe Belden, a producer for the NBC affiliate in San Francisco. Emerald Yeh, the news anchor, wanted to do a telephone piece. They had a clear line and could tie in live on the air. I packed my bag while Emerald asked her questions, wondering if I sounded frightened on television. It was hard to concentrate on the interview.

At 6:00 A.M. I left the Dong Fang with my bags, walked to the China Hotel next door to buy a ferry ticket to Hong Kong via Macao, then took a taxi to the White Swan to hide out until departure time.

The *Chronicle* wanted me to go back into China. Dan Rosenheim, my editor, and then Jack Breibart, the news editor, and Bill German, the executive editor, were all on the phone to me in Hong Kong at 2:00 A.M. There was an insatiable appetite in America for news from China, they told me. People were staying up all night watching television, transfixed by the scenes in the streets of Beijing.

Dan came back on the line. "Look, it has to be up to you, Frank. No one is going to hold it against you if decide not to."

Dan had reported from Central America.

In the morning I went to the office of Xinhua, the Chinese news service, to apply for a visa. This time I said I was a journalist and that I planned to file reports. It was getting too dangerous to enter China on a fraudulent tourist visa. The local officials were spooked, weren't getting clear instructions from Beijing, didn't know what they needed to do to prove they were loyal. The government tirades out of the capital had become stridently xenophobic, blaming the disaster on a wild array of foreign conspiracies.

There was a cynical waiting game in progress at the Hong Kong Foreign Correspondents' Club: We were waiting for the regime to start shooting the messengers, placing bets on whether they'd go after a big fish, someone from the *New York Times* or *Le Monde,* or make a lesson of a reporter backed by less institutional power. In the chaos to which China had descended, it was easy to imagine a journalist on a tourist visa being taken for a spy if he asked too many questions. It was easy to imagine what might happen if my papers were still not in order: to imagine myself kneeling in the middle of a stadium field, waiting for a bullet in the back of the neck. That's how capital criminals are executed in China.

I told the Xinhua man exactly who I was and asked for a multi-entry visa, half expecting (and half hoping) that he'd laugh in my face.

He said, "Please return this afternoon."

Either someone at Xinhua wanted journalists in China—someone who supported the students and wanted the truth out—or the crisis had rendered the bureaucracy so dysfunctional that no one was even monitoring the visa applications. Whatever the reason, at 4:00 P.M. on June 12 I had the visa.

I called Jack Breibart in San Francisco and told him I had an idea. I wanted to find Zhao Ziyang, the reformist party secretary whom the hard-liners blamed for the rise of the pro-democracy movement. Zhao had disappeared completely since that last visit to Tiananmen Square on May 19, when he'd wept and begged the students to leave. Hong Kong swirled with news of his whereabouts, all of it entirely speculative. To say he'd been good to the colony was a colossal understatement. Zhao's policies—the liberalization of laws on private investment, the creation of Special Economic Zones all over the coastal south, the official blessing bestowed on trade and profit— had showered money on Victoria Harbour, lined the hills of Aberdeen and Repulse Bay with villas, jammed the streets of the central business district with Mercedes.

I chose my tip from one of the biggest traders, a man who had bought and sold in China, legally and otherwise, through the worst years of the Cultural Revolution. He was on familiar terms with them all: Zhao, Deng, and before them Mao and Zhou Enlai.

The trader said Zhao was in Zhuhai, north of Macao. There was absolute certainty in his voice.

On the thirteenth of June I took the hydrofoil to Macao and

walked to the Chinese border. It was the first time I'd ever crossed from there without having to wait in line; nobody else was in the transit area. The immigration officer silently examined my passport for a very long time. I found myself thinking, once again, that I wouldn't be allowed to enter. Then he stamped me in.

Zhuhai is China's Miami Beach, its Vegas and Honolulu and Atlantic City, all rolled into a single ostentatious package. A laboratory where the new Chinese affluent, the *renminbi* millionaires, can sample Western leisure without leaving the People's Republic. It is everything that the party puritans, the men whose political ideas matured on the Long March and in the caves of revolutionary Yan'an, despise, everything they fear from reform.

"When you open a window, some flies will get in," Deng Xiaoping had warned.

Zhuhai is the flies.

Zhao Ziyang loved the place. He'd been coming for more than a decade, making annual visits since the 1970s, when he was governor of the surrounding Guangdong Province, endorsing its transformation with his presence. If there was a Zhao style, a Zhao vision of what a reformed China might become, it was perfectly embraced in the Zhuhai Holiday Resort, where the general secretary had passed most of his summers in recent years. Although it had both an expensive French restaurant, La Verdure, and an Italian coffee bar complete with espresso and slices of *tiramisu,* the resort borrowed its architectural idiom from nearby Macao. In a clutch of pseudo-Portuguese whitewashed cottages, it climbed a hillside above tennis courts, horse stables, a go-cart track, and the South China Sea.

There was a breath of sin for the Chinese in Zhuhai's very proximity to Macao, with its seedy gambling casinos and nightclubs, a taste of Latin insouciance that was worlds apart from the appeal that Hong Kong held for them. The image of Hong Kong was all business, gray suits, glass-walled towers. But Macao was something else, in its imagined form if not the reality. With its Macanese creoles and its lugubrious ways, it conjured up a fantasy of care-free hedonism that had been more deeply suppressed by Mao than the profit motive. Zhuhai acknowledged that fantasy. It even had its own modest casino, where Zhao's aides were known to be big spenders during the boss's vacations.

The aides tended to stay at one of the "honeymoon hotels"—as the local Chinese called them—that rose in high-rise ranks a few blocks inland from the Zhuhai Holiday Resort and the seashore. They were of a piece, each outfitted with saunas, discos, swimming pools, and Western restaurants that were strong on spaghetti Bolognese, overcooked steak, and banana splits. The splashiest of them, the Yindo, also boasted a nightclub, a bowling alley, a miniature golf course, and a marble lobby encircled by statues of nude women in poses that suggested narcolepsy.

The Yindo lobby was the first place Mr. Jin and Mr. Jiang took me on a morning-long tour of Zhuhai's resort facilities. They were, respectively, the assistant manager and the public relations director of my own hotel, a more restrained establishment that catered to Hong Kong families. Despite the subtropical climate, Mr. Jin wore an imitation sharkskin suit and Mr. Jiang a nicely cut brown leather jacket. Both were in their late twenties.

They hadn't known what to do with me when I showed up at the hotel office and said I was a reporter from San Francisco—a city that had invested a lot of money in this part of Guangdong—and that I wanted to write articles on the effects the "problems" were having on their business. (The answer was obvious: A glance at the daybook told me that there were only twelve rooms occupied in the two-hundred-room hotel.) Jin and Jiang were uneasy and confused, like almost everybody who worked in a post that involved contact with foreigners. For ten years these people had been ordered to hone their skills as exponents of "opening." They didn't know how to speak the language of isolation anymore, or were too young to remember it. So in the end, they swallowed their anxieties and agreed to take me on a tour of Zhuhai's investment sites.

"The troubles will not close our doors. The economic policies will not change," Jiang said over and over, in a way that implied he was trying to convince himself as much as me.

Eventually I maneuvered them into a conversation about Zhao Ziyang, who was, after all, Zhuhai's most famous vacationer. It was a lousy thing to do, cornering them. But there wasn't any other way to begin pursuing my lead, and after a few minutes' hesitation, they talked.

"I think your Hong Kong friend is right. Secretary Zhao is here in Zhuhai," Mr. Jin said.

The reasoning was elaborate, the product of nonstop local gossip since a series of strange events on June 5. Around noon, People's Liberation Army units had suddenly roared up the driveway to Shijingshan, a hilltop resort that was owned by the Communist Party, and then erected a roadblock at the entrance. The troop movements came several hours after Hong Kong television reported that a mysterious convoy of limousines was seen leaving Zhongnanhai, the government residential compound in Beijing, giving rise to intense speculation that a high official was fleeing—or being exiled from—the capital. Everybody with a television in Zhuhai saw the report. Hong Kong was just across the Pearl estuary, within clear broadcast range.

Ten days later Shijingshan was still sealed off by soldiers, who were lounging against the wooden roadblock smoking cigarettes when I passed by the resort in a taxi with Mr. Jin and Mr. Jiang.

There was circumstantial evidence aplenty to support the Shijingshan theory. Guangdong had been Zhao's power base; the province's Forty-second Army was said to be loyal to him. Shanzhao Island, just offshore, had a Second World War Japanese airstrip that was still serviceable. The coast was dotted with scores of harbors. The Macao border and the narrow channels separating the Portuguese enclave from the mainland were notoriously porous.

"It is very easy to get out of China from Zhuhai," Mr. Jin remarked.

Mr. Jiang nodded in agreement. By now the two of them were recklessly warming to their task, trying to figure out ways we could confirm the identity of Shijingshan's mystery resident.

"Maybe we just ask the soldiers," Mr. Jiang mused.

I said we'd better think about that.

We drove up to the provincial government building in Xiangzhou, a few miles to the north. The two Mr. J.'s said there was an economic ministry official there who spoke English and had been most helpful to Hong Kong journalists in the past. "He knows about all the joint ventures," Jiang said.

I asked them to wait in the car and went in. The official was sitting at his desk in a room halfway down the second-floor corridor, staring motionlessly at a sheaf of papers. When he looked up and saw me he involuntarily started, then turned positively ashen-faced after I explained the reason for my visit. He said he wouldn't talk to me, not about business or anything else. He asked me to leave, as soon as possible. He didn't mean his office; he meant Zhuhai, his administrative zone.

"You must go instantly," he said.

I asked if he thought I should register with the Public Security office. An order had come from Beijing to that effect: All journalists must now register their movements. Maybe they'd let me visit one of the joint venture plants. There was lots of San Francisco money in these investments, I reminded him. Didn't our readers have a right to know how things were going?

Instead of answering, he got up, took me by the arm, and guided me into the corridor, pointing to the stairway at its end.

The knock on the door came at 12:50 A.M. on June 15, a persistent rapping that stirred me from a fragile dream. The time was registered in digital precision by an alarm clock on the bedstand. Then more knocking, and several men shouting "Gong An!"—"Security Police!"— and suddenly, a crunching sound as the door was forced open.

I had fallen asleep watching Hong Kong television. A CNN report on the Tiananmen debacle droned accusingly—evidence of my complicity—as the Public Security officers rushed in.

"This is it," I thought.

I wasn't scared at the moment. I don't know why.

There were six of them, carrying long flashlights. One began to interrogate me in Mandarin. He had the harsh, guttural accent of Beijing. I told him I couldn't understand.

The others searched my room. They looked under the bed, in the bathroom, on the balcony, behind the drapes. Somebody turned off the television set. They opened the drawers in the dresser, emptied my suitcase, rifled through my underwear.

At 1:06 A.M. the Beijing man curtly thanked me, and they moved down the hall to the next room. A few minutes later they emerged, shoving a young man ahead of them. When he fell in the corridor, one of the officers kicked him in the groin.

It was impossible not to watch. My door swung uselessly on one broken hinge. The young man moaned, but said nothing. They pulled him back to his feet and continued around the corner, out of sight. I went into the bathroom, crouched over the toilet and threw up.

There was no point in trying to sleep. I turned the television set back on to CNN. Mike Chinoy, the Beijing correspondent, was still on camera, reporting a nationwide manhunt for pro-democracy student leaders escaping from the capital. The police were said to be concentrating on the south coast. The strangeness of it all, the way it had become news that was transmitted around the globe just as I was experiencing it, sent a chill down my spine.

The next morning at breakfast, Jin and Jiang avoided my glance in the restaurant. At the front desk, the manager told me that the police "would appreciate it" if I left Zhuhai. I spent the rest of the day fruitlessly trying to develop sources, then checked out at 6:00 P.M. I never learned whether Zhao Ziyang was the mystery man at Shijingshan.

Jiang, still in his leather jacket, was standing near the door as I walked by. Almost inaudibly he said, "I'm sorry."

MONGOLIA HOLDS COMMUNIST
ASIA'S FIRST VOTE

ULAN BATOR, MONGOLIA (July 29, 1990) — Mongolians
went to the polls today for the first time in their history.

Like other East Bloc countries, this remote nation of two million has been swept by growing sentiment for democracy and Western-style free enterprise in the last year. Massive December
demonstrations in Ulan Bator, the capital, pressured the communist
government here to move toward a democratically elected system.

Five parties, including the ruling People's Revolutionary Party,
are competing in today's vote.

Gomboshaviyn Otshirbat, the current leader of the ruling party,
is a liberal reformer who replaced longtime Party Secretary Jambyn
Batmonh in March and pushed for quick elections.

"We're very encouraged by the speed with which they've undertaken this step," said a Western diplomat in Ulan Bator. "The
Mongolians are showing the Chinese and Vietnamese how it ought
to be done."

The elections will be the first in an Asian communist country.

Wedged between northern China and Russia's Pacific Far East,
the Mongolian People's Republic has been a political satellite of its
powerful neighbors since its founding seven decades ago. The southern half of the country remains a Chinese province.

MONGOLIAN LAMBADA

Five days before the election, Jigeehuu and his cousin Gankhuag,
whose paths hadn't crossed in several years of wandering, were
gloriously and affectionately drunk. They'd pitched their camps
the week before in a velvety green meadow that dipped between
the bare hills near Nalakh, a coal town about forty miles west of
Ulan Bator, then immediately started exchanging celebratory
rounds of *koumis*.

When I reached Jigeehuu's tent the two men were a couple of
stumblebums, hardly able to stand up without collapsing into comical
bear hugs with each other, with their wives and children, and now
with their first American guest. The tent, known in Mongolian as a
gur, was simplicity itself, the home reduced to its barest conceptual
essentials. It was round, about twenty feet in diameter and ten feet

high in the center, propped up against the merciless winds of the grasslands by a skeletal wooden frame and covered with hand-carded felt. There were no windows. A single doorway, about four feet high so that everyone but the children had to stoop low to enter, was positioned on the lee side of the *gur;* a yak skin was thrown over it during storms. A coal-burning stove crackled in the center of the floor, below a hole cut through the felt roof to draw out smoke. Next to it sat two low wooden tables, manufactured in Russia and painted in bright orange enamel, and an oversized shortwave radio whose batteries were dead.

But these were the sole concessions to the industrial revolution. In its composition and design the *gur* hasn't changed since Jigeehuu's thirteenth-century ancestors, the cavalrymen of the Golden Horde, charged behind the Great Khan all the way to the gates of Vienna. As then, the structure could be taken down, packed onto horses, and moved in a few hours.

"We'll stay in this meadow twenty days, no more," Jigeehuu said, theatrically suppressing a burp. "After that, we go to a new place about a day's ride from here."

The barrel of *koumis*—fermented mare's milk—held a place of honor several feet away from the stove. Jigeehuu ambled shakily over to it after our first embrace and ladled out half a pint for me in a rice bowl. It tasted yeasty, with a slight hint of effervescence, and began almost instantly to produce a slow easing of inhibitions. The men's wives, whose names were never offered, watched us from outside the *gur,* politely giggling every time a new round of *koumis* was followed by a new round of embraces. After a second ladle, I giggled back.

At thirty-one, Jigeehuu could be reckoned rich (and in the harsh Mongolian actuarial tables, middle-aged). The *koumis* made him expansive, and he wanted me to understand that I'd happened across a man of substance.

"I have thirty cattle and twenty horses," he said. "About fifteen thousand tugrik in beef alone."

A tugrik was worth about thirty cents.

We spoke through an interpreter, a young woman from Ulan Bator named Malongo who had a modicum of English and French, picked up from friends in Sophia when she was a student in Bulgaria.

She helpfully wrote all of the unpronounceable names in my note-book, rendering them in a labored scrawl that mixed Roman and Cyrillic letters.

Outside, as we drank, the animals grazed in the short grass that blanketed the hills. Jigeehuu and Gankhuag, who was thirty and not as successful as his cousin, judging from his silence when I asked about his own livestock, had two children each, an even two sons and two daughters. One of them, a boy who looked to be no more than seven, cantered around the herd on a horse that was a dozen times his size, wheeling and accelerating with mind-boggling command of his mount. He galloped up at a dead run to greet us, stopped on a dime, and leaned over to stare intently into my face without saying a word. It wasn't hard to imagine such horsemen confounding the armies of China, Central Asia, and Europe seven centuries ago.

But this was the 1990s, not the time of the Great Khan, when the Mongols had been the authors of history rather than its picturesque footnotes. Nomads still made up most of the Mongolian population, which was composed of 1.5 million herdsmen and a few hundred thousand city dwellers scattered across the fifteenth largest country on earth—six hundred thousand square miles of desert, steppe, and forested mountains virtually untouched by the twentieth century. Even in Ulan Bator, the capital and only city, 40 percent of the five hundred thousand residents lived in *gurs*.

Their lives were now confronted by earthshaking change, by the arrival of the modern world. More specifically, by the coming elec-tions—the first ever in Mongolian history—that were supposed to put twentieth-century Mongolia into motion. They knew about it out here, had heard that they would soon be given some sort of voice in how the government was run. They knew that they were supposed to ride into Nalakh Sunday and "vote." But the comprehension of what that actually meant was slim. For starters, they had never met a politician or a bureaucrat who wasn't a member of the Mongolian Communist Party, which had recast itself a few months back as the Mongolian People's Revolutionary Party.

"They are close to us, they understand us," Jigeehuu said when I asked about the ruling party.

And the opposition? What about them? The question seemed to wash away his alcoholic haze. He was almost belligerent.

"These other people: Who are they?"

It was the year of communism's fatal crisis, from the shores of the Adriatic to the shores of the Pacific. The year that the Russians would be re-enclosed within the confines of Russia itself. The year that the geopolitical note came due. But that part of the message hadn't reached the *gurs,* where the Russian-Mongolian-communist axis had been the very definition of public affairs for decades, and hung on, tenaciously, against the current of global decline.

"It dishonors us," Jigeehuu said when I brought up the matter of anti-Russian sentiment, which was dangerously, even violently, evident in Ulan Bator. "We died with them, fighting against the Chinese."

In which war? I wondered. The Mongolians had reason to hate Beijing, which had swallowed up half their country, making it a Chinese province and relocating millions of Han emigrants there. Mongolia was the least known of the world's divided nations; unlike Ireland, Korea, and Germany before 1990, its fratricides had been conducted in a complete media vacuum. Had there actually been a secret war here between a Russo-Mongolian army and the Chinese? Was Jigeehuu confusing China with Japan in the 1940s? Was he alluding to the border war between Beijing and Moscow that flared along the Ussuri and Amur rivers in the 1960s? His chance words spoke of history still to be written. Or soon to be forgotten forever.

"And the doctors," he continued. "Russians are the only doctors my children have ever seen, the only doctors I have ever seen."

As far as he knew, the Russians and their Mongolian communist allies had never done anything to earn his dislike, whatever the opposition might be saying in Ulan Bator. He had heard the phrase "the opposition." It didn't impress him. Nothing in the city impressed him. Opinions changed slowly in these wide-open spaces; they were not subject to the shifting whims of urban taste.

The horses neighed as a north wind swept over the hills.

"But it is very good to have new friends," Jigeehuu said, gently moving us onto more comfortable conversational ground.

He ladled out more *koumis.* "Especially Americans. Much better than China."

Gankhuag joined the conversation for the first time, agreeing with his cousin. "You can't trust them over there," he said, nodding toward the Gobi Desert and the Chinese border.

He mused on that awhile, then asked me where the United States was located, exactly. "Is it near China?"

Ulan Bator translates as "Red Hero." Russians, rather than Mongolians, decided that it should be the Mongolian capital. Its name, its appearance, its very creation were owed to three generations passed in the absolute shadow of Mongolia's giant neighbor to the north. Three generations of imitation so doggedly faithful that it defied credibility.

Sukhebator, who led the Communist Revolution to victory in 1921, was remembered in the Soviet bloc as "Mongolia's Lenin." Obligingly, he had died within months of his mentor in 1923, just as the revolution was being consolidated in the Mongolian People's Republic. He was buried in a gigantic Russian-designed mausoleum in Ulan Bator's central square. The marble mausoleum was a startling, near-perfect facsimile of Lenin's. The square was Ulan Bator's version of Red Square, without the onion domes and saving grace of St. Basil's. The city rising around it was a jumble of Soviet-style apartment blocks designed by Soviet architects, built by Soviet engineers, and very often, inhabited by Soviet technical experts.

After Sukhebator came the darker side of parody: Choibalsan, "Mongolia's Stalin." Choibalsan followed Josef Stalin's policy proscriptions to the letter in the 1930s and 1940s. All potential rivals were discreetly exterminated, usually with the help of Russian security agents. Thousands of Buddhist monks were executed and their monasteries closed. The free-ranging nomadic peasants who were the very definition of Mongolian culture were forced into an industrial collectivization scheme that would have been laughable, given the total absence of industry or an urban proletariat, except for the toll it took in shattered lives. Eventually the scheme had to be dropped and the cattle and yaks and horses returned to the care of individual herdsmen.

It was Choibalsan's single policy difference with Stalin, made in the interest of self-preservation; it was also why the nomads bore the party no animosity.

Like Sukhebator, Choibalsan shuffled off this mortal coil within months of his Russian mentor, in what some Mongolians regard as yet another enormous coincidence and others an unexplained assassination. Whatever the truth, Mongolia's Stalin was eventually succeeded as party secretary by Mongolia's Brezhnev, Yumjaagiyn Tsedenbal. And in the Brezhnevian manner, Mongolia entered into a long, murky twilight of stagnation and ham-handed corruption.

In Moscow, the real Brezhnev collected American, British, and West German limousines in the name of the masses, while his children swung deals with the Uzbekistan mafia to siphon off agricultural income. In Ulan Bator, Tsedenbal made do with less—there wasn't much use for a Cadillac Fleetwood on the steppe; a four-wheel-drive Jeep or Rover was more appropriate. But his Russian-born wife wanted action, and found it in the Mongolian Children's Fund, which she evidently appropriated as a personal budget to be used on frequent state visits to resorts on the Black Sea.

Again like Brezhnev, Tsedenbal descended from the summit in the early 1980s. He was eased out not by death but by a semi-reformer, Jambyn Batmonh (Mongolia's Andropov?), who in turn passed the gauntlet in 1990 to a more aggressive reformer, Gombos-haviyn Otshirbat, surely Mongolia's Gorbachev.

The parallilism was finally too much, too embarrassing, even for the Russians who were the models for this unblinking apery. Vladilen Burov, one of the few Soviet historians I could turn up who had bothered to study the phenomenon in detail, put it bluntly: "The history of present-day Mongolia and the Mongolian People's Revolutionary Party is in its main features a bad copy of the history of the Soviet Union and its Communist Party."

The Kremlin, Burov went on, "didn't even bother to train Ulan Bator–bound diplomats in the Mongolian language." There was often no need to: Most signs, were written in Cyrillic script, Mongolia having traded its own traditional alphabet for the Russian system in 1946. "The view in Moscow," Burov noted, "was that Mongolia was not really a foreign country."

It was a view the West tacitly accepted. The United States didn't formally recognize Mongolia as an independent nation until 1987. The first U.S. ambassador to Mongolia, a good-natured Texan named Joe Lake, didn't arrive until I did, in the summer of 1990.

The mimicry, the numbing dependence, left a more quantifiable mark as well. The two million Mongolians were in hock to the Russians to the tune of $15 billion, a foreign debt that worked out to $7,500 per Mongolian. Taking into account the annual $800 million in Russian aid that accounted for roughly half of Mongolia's gross national product, the debt principal alone equaled almost nineteen years of output by every man, woman, and child in the country. Add in the interest payments and the figures became meaningless; no wonder the Russians and the Americans both found it hard to think of Mongolia as an independent nation.

The turnabout engineered by Otshirbat and his reformers was sudden, and utterly unexpected by the few foreigners who knew anything at all about Mongolia. It was as if the sun set one evening on an Ulan Bator that was a pseudo-Moscow and rose the next morning on a city that looked the same—boxy Stalinist-era apartment blocks in the center, encircled by suburbs of felt-covered *gurs*—but was speaking a radically different language.

The idiom of imitation changed virtually overnight, sweeping away the technical experts from Sophia and Minsk and replacing them with salesmen from the four corners of the Pacific Rim.

In June 1990 the sole air link to Mongolia remained the one that had been established half a century before, an erratic flight from Irkutsk to Beijing that stopped over in Ulan Bator. In July a charter service was opened to Japan, DHL courier jets began arriving from California, and negotiations opened for regular air connections to Singapore and Seoul. A week before I arrived in late July, a fleet of trucks had pulled up to the national museum and carted off all the exhibits hailing the triumph of Marxism-Leninism, leaving most of the building's rooms entirely vacant.

Malongo, the Bulgarian-trained interpreter, was my guide to the future unfolding in these events. In a mixture of franglais and anglicized Russian, she escorted me through the new Ulan. We started with the lambada.

You could hardly start with anything else. Its Afro-Brazilian rhythms shouted from the Japanese and Chinese boomboxes that Mongolian hipsters held on their shoulders as they gathered in the mausoleum square. People hummed the lambada as they walked down the streets. They danced to it—most of them gyrating stiffly, not yet sure of the point—in the bleak proletarian banquet room of the Hotel Ulan Bator, before an audience of diners wolfing down *bootz*, softball-sized mutton dumplings that were the national fast food. Even I danced to it, with Malongo. A large-framed woman in her late twenties, she wasn't any looser than the rest of the dancers, but she felt obliged and dragged me out onto the floor, where we hopped around each other, both of us studiously avoiding the erotic hip-thrusting motions that the dance entailed and that a few of the teenagers around us had somehow picked up.

"I am a yuppie, a Mongolian yuppie!" she shouted, affecting a licentious laugh.

It was what modern people here said about themselves, a word that was making the rounds.

We discussed what a yuppie was in more detail. Malongo was charmed by the idea that it suggested crass ambition and mindless spending on consumer trinkets. The existential question I raised, the notion that such a life might be empty, was irrelevant; after all, Mongolians had their fill of the choice of ideas over objects, that baffling sidetrack that carried dialectical materialism into penury. For Malongo, knowing the word "yuppie" was belonging to the confraternity of the future. It was mastery of a concept that conveyed unique power, the power of familiarity with an outside world that loomed seductively beyond the wide Mongolian horizons. She hoarded words that implied such intimacy.

When I told her where my newspaper was published, she laughed again, really laughed, delighted, because she had the words ready for me: "San Francisco! Chinatown! Jefferson Starship!" And a bit more subtly, "Multinationals!"

But music, not words, was the cultural beachhead of the new invasion. Its guitar-twanging shock troops led the charge away from what Ulan Bator had been, and toward what it was becoming. In one of the few back streets of this city of broad vacant avenues, I went to a video club that played MTV tapes of Madonna and Prince over and over, while a full house of young Mongolians stared mesmerized at the Sony monitor, the veterans among them lip-synching the lyrics.

I attended a competition in the square, in which several dozen young men sang Beatles songs. The object, Malongo told me—with no sense of irony whatsoever—was to identify "Mongolia's John Lennon."

Even the new politics was led by a vanguard of musicians. The Mongolian Democratic Party, the chief opposition force, opened every rally with a performance by its own wildly popular rock group, Honk; their biggest hit was a heavily electrified ballad that recounted the life of Genghis Khan, whose legend had been suppressed under the old regime and was now making a sensational comeback. Images of the fabled conqueror appeared on lapel pins and jacket badges that mini-entrepreneurs sold from card tables next to the sole department store in the nation. The memory of Genghis Khan also figured prominently in a wave of urban graffiti, and in the name of a new joint venture hotel rising behind the Ulan Bator.

The éminence grise of the Mongolian Democrats was a twenty-seven-year-old political whiz kid named Zorig Saanjaasrudden. Malongo took me to meet him.

He sat with his aides at a long table in a dusty, undecorated room that must have been the community center of the gray concrete-block apartment tower it occupied just off the mausoleum square. They nodded in unison as we took seats at the opposite end of the table from Zorig.

"Welcome," he said in English. His face was a frozen mask. "Shall we begin?"

Zorig was famous for his deadpan, let's-get-on-with-it demeanor. It was a trademark, the personal style he had chosen to distinguish himself from other Mongolian politicians, whose effusiveness and desire to be gracious were so pronounced that they found it almost impossible to say no to a visitor. Zorig didn't share this habit. He had something bad to say about everybody.

The Russians, who had provided him with an engineering scholarship and a free education in Moscow, were "dishonest," he said, shifting from English to Russian, which he spoke during the remainder of the interview. The Americans weren't providing the opposition with enough financial support. The Japanese were too interested in their own profit margins. The present government—which had opened the door to foreign business and invited Washington to send in the Peace Corps, not to speak of its legalizing his own party and authorizing the coming election—was "only modestly different" from the regimes that had preceded it.

"They haven't made any real reforms," he said.

It was all couched in very discreet language, the words never inflammatory. But the gist of his observations was clear: The Democrats—and Zorig Saanjaasrudden—were Mongolia's best and brightest, and they deserved better than they were getting.

I was fascinated by his appearance, which was so carefully managed that it distracted me from his pronouncements. He wore a pair of khaki pants—I was almost sure they were from Banana Republic—with ramrod-straight creases, a light blue oxford-cloth shirt left open at the collar, a herringbone sport coat, and wire-rimmed glasses. He looked, in short, exactly like the West Coast yuppies who were Malongo's *beaux idéals,* except for that exaggerated incapacity to demonstrate the slightest warmth. It was an unsettling combination. Half yuppie, half puritan, he reminded me of some of the New Left activists I'd known in the States during the sixties who made a convenient shift to the right in the Reagan years.

The problem wasn't his ideas. He was for all the politically correct things, the whole postcommunist package: a free economy; a freely elected, uncorrupted parliament; a genuine multiparty system; an independent judiciary.

"We have to return Mongolia to the community of global civilization," he said.

Everyone mouthed these phrases in Ulan, but I had to admit that he truly understood them, in a way that government spokesmen often didn't seem to. It was consistent with his manner that Zorig had done his homework.

He complained, when I raised the subject of the rural vote, which accounted for two-thirds of the electorate, that the government had made it impossible for the Democrats to open branch offices outside the city. It was probably true. The idea of democracy was very new in Mongolia. Even in developed countries like my own, which had presumably spent two centuries testing formulae for even-handedness, the rules seemed rigged in favor of incumbents.

But fairness wasn't enough, not in the electoral brand of modern politics to which the Mongolian Democratic Party said it aspired.

Although I could visualize Zorig in the Akasaka district of Tokyo or in Boston's Back Bay, it was impossible to visualize him—the way he looked, the way he talked—winning a constituency on the steppe. It was impossible to imagine him sharing ladles of *koumis* with Jigeehuu and Gankhuag. He had made the jump. He was a man of the Pacific Century, from his button-down collar to his topsiders, which I noticed when he rose to see us off.

Out there on the grasslands, the frame of mind was introspective. It wasn't Pacific; it was continental.

The vote was twenty-four hours away now, but the election commission chairman was cool as a cucumber. The government had made a wise choice. Gurragcha, the commissioner, was the most famous celebrity in Mongolia, the most trusted, the most unflappable by sheer dint of training. He was his country's one and only space traveler, the sole Mongolian cosmonaut. In a brighter era of Soviet-Mongolian relations, he had been propelled into orbit and the affections of his countrymen on a Soyuz mission.

Mongolia's only spaceman was also one of Mongolia's only engineers and, in some ways, his nation's most convincing rendition of a technocrat. He certainly talked like one. When I asked for a briefing the day before the polls opened, he gave me enough numbers to fill my notebook.

"There are fifty thousand people engaged in the campaign work, responsible for four hundred thirty constituencies that will consider twenty-four hundred candidates," he said.

"In forty-four constituencies, there is just one candidate. In two hundred seventy, there are three or more."

I found myself slipping into a doze. It was a funny thing about spacemen, even a Mongolian spaceman. They'd personally experienced one of human history's most soaring achievements, but it seemed to have flattened their personalities.

The commission, Gurragcha went on, had endorsed five parties, counting the ruling Mongolian People's Revolutionary Party—the renamed Communist Party—as well as Labor, the Social Democrats, the rightist National Progress Party, and the Democrats.

One set of figures shook me awake: Zorig had been right about the stacked deck. Of the 2,400 candidates, just 350 represented the opposition, and of these only 90 were running in areas outside Ulan Bator. Listening to the only Mongolian spaceman spew out his numbers, I felt a first pang of sympathy for the opposition. Even without the hearts and minds of the nomads, the government party couldn't lose.

It didn't. On voting day, the relabeled Communists won in a landslide.

That night, indeed every night, the mood in the city was threatening. "It isn't Washington, D.C., yet," a desk hand at the new U.S. embassy wisecracked when I asked about urban violence in Ulan Bator. But there were "difficulties," he allowed, putting it diplomatically.

The difficulties largely had to do with being mistaken for one of the Russians, Armenians, or Uzbekhs who made up most of the foreign technician class that had effectively run Mongolia for decades. Old resentments were now being given scope; scores were being settled. Gangs of young toughs hung out on the department store steps after dark, waiting for anyone with blond Russian hair or an aquiline Armenian nose to pass by. A lot of people—no one knew how many, but the number was thought to be substantial—had been beaten up. One Russian, according to rumor, had died. At first it was sufficient to yell "I'm American"—or "Canadian," or "German"— to put off the gangs in mid-chase. But they'd stopped believing it or didn't care anymore, and it was best to avoid the streets when night fell.

"There are jobs for them, but they don't want them," said a junior official in the Interior Ministry, a renamed Mongolian Communist who sounded like an unreconstructed American Republican. "They want money without working, not a post in a factory or in the countryside."

It was part of the disorienting illusion bred by Mongolia's abrupt opening to the Pacific: that an earthly paradise was within reach, a paradise of effortless gain. Some of the gangsters—that's how people in Ulan referred to them—had a more complicated view of things. They cultivated work of sorts, trading in hashish, black market currency, and smuggled radios and other consumer goods.

I knew one of the gangsters slightly. We met on the Trans-

Siberian Express, somewhere in the bleak forest wastes east of Lake Baikal where every conversation, every meeting, is a safeguard against terminal boredom. Although he was thought by his parents to be a piano student in Tashkent, his real reason for traveling back and forth across the Central Asian republics was contraband. He specialized in wristwatches, which filled the athletic bag he always had sitting at his side on the train. I ran into him on the night of the election standing amidst the Russophobe thugs on the department store steps.

"Farg!" he'd yelled out, pleased at the opportunity to be seen hobnobbing with an American, a pleasure I shared because it meant my Sicilian nose wouldn't be mistaken for that of an Armenian. "Farg" was as close as he could get to Frank.

He had done well, and wore an expensive black leather jacket. But the majority of the young men on the steps were neither as enterprising nor as successful as the pseudopianist. They just hung out, waiting.

The flames of their illusions were readily fanned by Mongolia's chief source of foreign earnings, big game hunters from Western Europe and North America, who drove up to the Hotel Ulan Bator in limos provided by a special government department and unloaded their artillery to an admiring audience of the same young men who chased presumed Russians through the Mongolian night. The hunters were for the most part an unsavory bunch, not just wealthy but crassly, contemptuously so. You had to be crass to fill their shoes, since what the Mongolian government offered—at a price—was a chance to kill animals that no other country permitted to be killed, endangered species like the snow leopard and the ibex.

Slick official guides fluent in English and German and French met the hunters at the airport, flew down with them to the Gobi or up into the mountains in small planes, and made certain that the four-wheel-drive vehicles at the other end were properly outfitted with trekking gear, tents, and Johnny Walker Black. Each hunter paid a per diem price for the trip and a supplement for each animal carcass shipped overseas. Depending on how close the species was to extinction, these supplements could be astronomical. In the hunting department office, which was located in the hotel basement, I saw two Germans peel off $90,000 in crisp new hundred-dollar bills to pay for one such excursion into the wilderness.

*   *   *

The wild game business was also the making of politics, intensely romantic, nationalist politics of a variety that Germany itself knew all too well. The organization with the most clout in the countryside wasn't a political party; it was the Mongolian Association for the Conservation of Nature and the Environment. It had a staggering seven hundred thousand members, a figure that counted more than half of the entire adult population. And unlike the Democrats' proposals, its message rang home loud and clear with the likes of Jigeehuu and Gankhuag. The Mongolian Greens were the high priests of the land, preaching a gospel of the sanctified earth that coincided closely with the views of the nomadic majority. They mixed contemporary environmentalism with the mysticism of the steppe, a potent brew that simmered with unsettling notions like racial destiny and the purification of society. The big game hunters represented everything they hated, everything that menaced the ancient symbiotic relationship between the Mongolian nomad and the Mongolian earth: The hunters were the very epitome of the profiteering rape of the motherland.

The Greens could be a perilous trap for a foreigner, a trap that came very close to ensnaring James Baker until he was saved, at the last possible moment, by Saddam Hussein.

Rumors had begun circulating in Ulan late in July that the American secretary of state was headed for Mongolia, scheduled to arrive a few days after the vote. Joe Lake, the new American ambassador, was dutifully circumspect when I showed up at the embassy in search of a confirmation of the story.

"I can't comment on that," he said.

He didn't need to, because my sources in the Mongolian bureaucracy were providing detailed accounts of the arrangements, which mightily impressed them. American freight planes had already landed more than two tons of communications equipment alone to handle the secretary's needs.

But the interesting part, from the standpoint of Mongolian politics, was that the best hunting guides in the country had been lined up for the visit. I had that on the word of the guides themselves, who had been camped out in the Ulan Bator Hotel lobby for days, buzzing about their good fortune. They were professionally precise about the plans: It would be a five-day trip to the south, with ibex as the main target.

If anything was guaranteed to muff the American bid for influence in Mongolia before it ever had a chance, this trip would do it. Joe Lake certainly knew that, although he wouldn't discuss it. The diplomatic cables to Washington must have been nearly hysterical with pleas to drop the hunting trip. Meanwhile the supply planes kept landing, and the guides kept preparing. The Greens announced a demonstration. There would be thousands of them gathered in the mausoleum square the day Baker arrived.

The date was to be August 2. At dawn that morning the Iraqi army invaded Kuwait. At noon, Baker appeared at a news conference in Irkutsk with Soviet foreign minister Eduard Schevardnadze to announce a joint Soviet-American response, and the maneuvering that led up to the Gulf War began. The Mongolian trip would have to wait.

Seven months later, while sitting out a sandstorm at a refugee camp on the Jordanian-Iraqi border, I picked up a shortwave broadcast from the BBC. Baker was again planning an official visit to Mongolia.

The next week, outside a press conference in Cairo, I asked Baker's spokeswoman, Margaret Tutwiler, whether her boss still had his heart set on hunting ibex. Joe Lake had done his job. "The secretary of state's itinerary will include a camera safari to the Gobi Desert," Tutwiler answered.

She put heavy emphasis on the word "camera."

SINGAPORE CHIEF STEPS DOWN
AFTER 31 YEARS

SINGAPORE (November 28, 1990) — Lee Kuan Yew, the only prime minister Singapore has ever known, stepped down from office today and handed over power to his deputy premier.

The sixty-six-year-old Lee has led his nation ever since it left the British Empire in 1959. The new prime minister, Goh Chok Tong, was only seven years old when Lee and his People's Action Party (PAP) launched their campaign for Singaporean self-rule nearly four decades ago.

Lee will remain in government, holding the post of senior minister in the Goh cabinet.

Under Lee's guidance, the PAP has won every election since 1959, and 'now holds all but one seat in the nation's eighty-one-member Parliament. In the meantime, Singapore's economy has become one of the most vibrant in the world.

Many credit that miracle to Lee's 1965 decision to take his small nation out of the Federation of Malaysia, which was struggling with serious economic and racial problems, and make it a fully independent state.

But the Lee years have also been marked by what many critics regard as heavy-handed efforts to quash dissent and enforce stability in his tiny island city-state of 2.6 million people.

THE SPEECH

Jing and Eddie had been on-again, off-again since 1985, the year I met Jing on the ship to Swatow. I never knew, when I flew into Singapore and called their apartment in Hougang to say hello, if Eddie would be living there or not. This time he wasn't.

Jing wouldn't talk about it on the phone, except to say that she "should have looked for an Australian or an Englishman a long time ago. Or maybe an American, like you . . ."

She invited me to dinner.

The northern line of the Mass Rapid Transit had just opened, and I took it up to Hougang for the first time. The MRT was a big change from the hot, klunky buses that used to ply the road a few years back, dawdling for pedestrians at intersections and dodging their way through all the construction.

The suburban housing estates were complete and the lawns were in. This stretch of the island had a finished, lived-in look, and the MRT got you there in less than fifteen minutes, cool and dry. Even the station quays were air-conditioned, closed off from the tunnels by special automatic doors so that no energy was wasted. I hadn't seen that arrangement on a subway before. They were always tinkering in Singapore, trying to perfect things.

Jing was thirty-two now, which was why she was fed up with Eddie and worried about whether she ought to have looked for someone else a long time ago. She wanted babies, and Eddie couldn't make up his mind. The clock was ticking. It ticked especially loudly for her, not just because she was thirty-two and had a large apartment with rooms to fill, but because of her family. We hadn't discussed these things before, and when she told me I had to ask her to repeat herself twice because I couldn't be hearing right.

"My mother had twenty-four children," she said.

One of the two dozen, a large and jolly sister who was introduced to me only as "Fatty," cooked the dinner: chili prawns, crab sautéed with ginger and scallions, grilled pompano, squid, and greens. Cooking wasn't Jing's forte. There was way too much food for the three of us and Fatty's two little boys, who spent most of the dinner chasing each other around Eddie's tricolored fountain, which still splish-splashed and gurgled out on the balcony. He had left it behind, Jing said, but took the photos of Las Vegas with him.

I gathered that Fatty's marital status was up in the air too. She changed the subject when I posed an oblique question about the boys' father. After the meal she sang Teochew opera pieces in a booming falsetto. She had a grand voice.

Sex and children were on everyone's mind in Singapore these days. Plain and simple, the tinkering in this department had gone awry. The urge to perfection had come a cropper with the urge to procreation. It was as though the entire society had forgotten how it was done or abandoned interest, only to regain it when it was nearly too late. The city was rife with forlorn single women, and there was plenty of blame to go around. Jing, for instance, blamed Chinese men. She said they were "only interested in sex the first time, and lost the knack afterward." I didn't ask how she'd concluded that Australians, Englishmen, or Americans were more dependably randy over the long term.

Others blamed education. Or prosperity. Or the heavy demands of professional careers. But mostly—and this was a startling thing to hear people say in Singapore—single Singaporean women blamed the prime minister for their loneliness. They blamed Lee Kuan Yew.

Lee had inherited an exploding Third World city in the 1950s, when Jing was born, the last of those twenty-four babies. I did some research: Twenty-four was up around record levels, but a neat dozen children was remarkably normal for Singapore in 1955. It had been one of those places that draw the prurient interest of demographers, who love to point out that an enormous chunk of a certain population is under fifteen and wave sheets of carefully calculated projections showing that misery and famine are thus inevitable until the Second Coming. Lee, the Cambridge man, took this kind of thing very seriously.

In effect, he set out to make a family like Jing's, the two-dozen-strong one she was born to, legally impossible. Statutes were enacted by the obedient Parliament of Singapore that forbade paid maternity leave and the use of medical insurance for the delivery and care of any more than two children. College preparatory schools were not allowed to admit more than two children from the same family unless one parent agreed to be sterilized. Television, newspapers, and giant billboards proclaimed the policy: TWO ARE ENOUGH! The ads pictured the ideal Singaporean family: small, modern, prosperous.

There are few people in the world more ceaselessly buffeted with behavioral propaganda than Singaporeans, who have at one time or another been admonished by Lee to: SPEAK MANDARIN, OBSERVE RELIGIOUS FAITH, STOP SMOKING, NEVER SPIT IN PUBLIC, AVOID DRIVING IN THE CENTRAL BUSINESS DISTRICT, GET A HAIRCUT REGULARLY, and DON'T CHEW GUM. Almost all of these campaigns were designed by pricey British and American advertising agencies; Singaporeans who ignored their injunctions risked hefty fines, jail, or both.

None of the Lee campaigns worked the way "Two Are Enough," with its draconian sanctions and saturation advertising, worked. Between 1970 and 1980 the birthrate was cut in half, hardly waving goodbye to the population explosion as it plummeted below ZPG and kept dropping. By 1980, Singapore wasn't even reproducing itself. It was shrinking. Nothing remotely like it had ever been seen in equatorial Asia before.

At the same time, women who were now freed from a future of annual visits to the maternity hospital started filling the higher education system—which, to give Lee his due, was rigorously gender-blind—while many men opted for high-paying jobs that required little education in the booming construction and oil industries. By 1985 the graduating classes of the National University of Singapore were seeing women take home twice as many degrees as men. Indeed, female graduates outnumbered men in virtually every field—not just in "feminine" areas like nursing and literature, but in business administration, economics, mathematics, and the theoretical sciences. This went far beyond a first for equatorial Asia. Nothing remotely like it had been seen in Europe or America either. The new man that Lee Kuan Yew had so firmly and confidently set out to create in the 1950s turned out to be a woman.

What nobody seemed to notice, at least until recently, was that these women weren't finding husbands. It was precisely the university grads, the people who were supposed to build Singapore's future, who were behind the catastrophic decline in child-bearing. One government study predicted that 42 percent of female university graduates would remain single the rest of their lives, as opposed to just 5 percent of male graduates.

The arithmetic was basic. An educated Singaporean woman wouldn't consider marrying an uneducated man, but it didn't work the other way around. Educated Singaporean men actually seemed to prefer uneducated women, for the same reasons that Western men enrolled in lonely hearts clubs that offer introductions to Filipina or Korean women: They wanted a "traditional Asian wife," the kind who would never burn her bra or ask her husband to do the dishes. Or to hear Jing tell it, the kind who would never expect a man to reach across the bed in passion on a moonstruck summer's night—not after the first time, anyway.

Many educated women blamed the prime minister when they hit their lonely thirties, either for tampering too much with the system or for not tampering enough with the mentality of Singaporean men.

*   *   *

Lee didn't take it well, not the criticism or the backfired family policies. He prepared, as always, to confront the criticisms pugnaciously.
As for the policies, he simply installed new ones, almost as though
the first batch had never existed. Down came the TWO ARE ENOUGH!
billboards. Up went another set that read, somewhat less smoothly,
AT LEAST TWO. BETTER THREE. FOUR IF YOU CAN AFFORD IT. Women
like Jing, whose mothers had been declared outlaws by reason of their
fecundity, suddenly found themselves declared outlaws by reason of
their childlessness.

The number of national child-care centers was abruptly doubled
by a special vote of the legislature. Paid maternity leave was enacted.
Cash rewards were offered to the outstandingly fertile. Hefty tax de-
ductions went to large families. Social scientists and pediatricians
were enlisted to appear on television programs warning that an only
child was likely to be spoiled and selfish. More quietly, the Ministry
of Education began to deemphasize language skills on college entrance exams, an area in which women had historically scored much
higher than their male rivals.

Still, nobody was prepared for what has since been referred to
simply as "the Speech," delivered by the prime minister on prime-
time television, so that everyone would realize he was serious. It was
to be Lee's personal reflection on the population problem, and on its
solution. The lights went on, the video cameras rolled, the people of
Singapore adjusted the volume on their television sets.

Then Lee dropped his bomb: "The way the old society did it
was polygamy," he said.

Singaporean officials tend to wince when a reporter brings up
the Speech. They point out that Lee modified his own remarks just
four days later, that he wasn't really advising all those lonely educated
women to double up and share the available educated men.

"It's all too late. We can't go back. It's not possible," he told a
newsman.

But the damage had been done. Even the compliant *Straits Times*
had to acknowledge the furor that the Speech had ignited. A bitter
exchange of letters appeared in the newspaper, embroiling angry

women, defensive men, and beleaguered bureaucrats from a dozen ministries.

"The shrinking violet syndrome is not Grandma's but Grandpa's," sneered one female reader, Lim Ming Geok, in a letter to the editor that aimed suggestively below the belt.

The debate had the effect of reminding Singaporeans of earlier national family spats. Just a few years before, when the prime minister had first raised the matter of what he called "Singapore's lopsided pattern of procreation," the concern had been quality more than quantity. His prescription then had been to offer $5,000 bonuses to uneducated women who would agree to be sterilized as well as preferential treatment for children of college graduates.

It was all very scientific, very Singaporean, very Lee in its cold, high-tech, systematically logical reasonableness. Statistically, educated Singaporean parents raised a higher than average proportion of children who excelled in school. Thus, the reasoning went, if a perfect society was to be the goal, the business of government should include stemming the tide of working-class births while cultivating a flood of pregnancies among the degreed.

There were more than a few observers who noted that college graduates tended to be Chinese, like Lee Kuan Yew, while the working class was drawn heavily from the Malay minority. But anyone who made such an observation did so under his breath if he lived in Singapore. Making remarks like that out loud was a crime: "inflaming community tensions." It led directly to jail.

Singapore did have to do something. It was as obvious as the big signs that hung in front of virtually every electronics plant out in the industrial parks of suburban Ang Mo Kio and Jurong by the beginning of the 1990s: HELP WANTED. TRIPLE BONUSES AT YEAR'S END. ONE MONTH'S EXTRA PAID HOLIDAY.

It was yet another first for equatorial Asia—a labor shortage—and it could only get worse. For the immediate future, companies would have to hire foreign guest workers, more Malays and Thais, always on the understanding that the work would be just temporary. Over the long term . . . well, over the long term, Singaporeans concerned about their country would just have to get back down to basics.

That was where Dr. Eileen Aw came in. It was her task to teach the basics to an entire society: courtship, sex, and marriage. She was to be minister of love, chief of the Department of the Birds and the Bees. Or more officially, director of the Social Development Unit, organized under the most powerful arm of the government, the Ministry of Finance, with one of the stranger mandates in the annals of bureaucracy.

"My job," Dr. Aw told me, "is to provoke an epidemic of weddings and an avalanche of infants."

In other words, the Social Development Unit was a government dating service.

Getting a date with Dr. Aw herself had not been easy. The Ministry of Information was on its guard and very edgy about the Social Development Unit. Singapore had never been the most congenial place to do journalistic business, but things had gotten bad indeed in the late 1980s, when Lee quarreled with the Dow Jones Corporation over coverage of Singapore and essentially banned two of its publications, the *Asian Wall Street Journal* and the *Far Eastern Economic Review*.

It was another of the influential signals that Singapore was sending around the South China Sea: If you have problems with press coverage, step on the press or cut it entirely out of the action. Cory Aquino had picked up that signal in Manila, Hong Kong was beginning to echo it in deference to the press-shy Chinese, and Mahathir Mohamed of Malaysia was carrying it even further than Lee Kuan Yew.

Lee's mouthpieces were very much aware that the proposed cash payments for working-class sterilizations were not material for favorable coverage abroad, so the gauntlet foreign journalists had to run was worse than usual. I'd sent a letter ahead from Hong Kong weeks before, carefully requesting a variety of appointments with economic officials, as well as with Eileen Aw. The assistant state information minister wasn't a bit apologetic when I showed up and found that no interviews had been arranged.

"We had to wait for something in the mail," he said.

The something was my file, updated by the Singaporean embassy staff in Washington to include all recent work on Asia, which in my case was a hefty load since I covered roughly a dozen Far Eastern nations for the *Chronicle*. I could see the stack of clippings on the assistant minister's desk, in a bulging manila folder. Perversely, the sight set me to wondering if I had written anything that could be misconstrued. The situation made me feel like an applicant who is absurdly unqualified for a job—or a felon appearing before a parole board.

The information official spent an hour stretching me on the rack over what he deemed "sensationalized adjectives" in one set of articles and "inappropriate subjects" in others. But I passed the test after all. Eventually the call came through to the hotel; I'd be allowed to see Dr. Aw.

She proved to be a soft-spoken, warm, intelligent woman in her late forties, a pediatrician by training, who was so apologetic about her government assignment that I wound up sympathizing with her— in my experience, definitely another first in Singapore.

"Yes," she said, "I do know how peculiar it all sounds."

To launch the nuptial epidemic and natal avalanche that were her management objectives, Dr. Aw had a staff of twenty-six. There was virtually nothing they wouldn't do to turn Singaporeans' fancies to thoughts of love.

The Social Development Unit hosted dinner balls and afternoon teas. It arranged bridge parties and bowling clinics, provided "appearance analysis" for the unsightly and dancing classes for the ungainly. It sent couples on romantic, government-subsidized excursions to islands on the South China Sea. It published *Link,* a magazine for singles, with cover stories like "Dating: Who Makes the First Move?" More advanced clients were referred to a sister publication, *Becoming: The Magazine of Self-Enhancement and Better Marital and Family Living.*

Dr. Aw told me that SDU-inspired marriages were running at about three hundred a year. She knew that figure was a drop in the bucket; by her own office's count, there were more than a hundred thousand female university graduates looking for husbands. Unless the current trends were reversed, it would take the government until the first quarter of the twenty-fourth century to get them all to the altar.

U.S. TO CLOSE DEVASTATED
BASE IN PHILIPPINES

MANILA (July 16, 1991) — The U.S. Embassy here released a statement late yesterday confirming that the American-run Clark Air Base will be permanently closed.

The announcement came after a month of futile efforts to clear millions of tons of volcanic ash that rained down on the base, sixty miles north of Manila, after the June 18 eruption of nearby Mount Pinatubo.

A U.S. military spokesman described the facility, which is just eight miles from the volcano, as "a total loss."

"Washington believes the cost of clearing and rebuilding the base is simply too great, especially given Clark's ambiguous future," the official said, speaking off the record.

His observations alluded to growing opposition among Filipino legislators to a treaty authorizing the continued presence of U.S. military facilities in the nation.

In addition, analysts point out that Clark has lost much of its strategic value with the end of the Cold War.

The air base was responsible for an estimated 42,000 jobs in the Philippines and $186 million in annual income.

At least two hundred people are known to have died in the catastrophe. Philippine and Red Cross authorities warn that the death toll is likely to climb much higher as search teams scour the devastated region around Mount Pinatubo.

THE GOVERNOR

The mountain blew on a terrifying Monday morning, raining cinder and ash on half of Luzon Island, blackening the skies of the cigarette subdivision, burying Tony López's house in San Fernando. When the Americans announced that Clark Air Base would be closed forever— its runways, six feet deep in volcanic mud, were useless—the word came like one of the eruption's aftershocks. Tony's business was buried now too. There would be no more GIs, no more warehouses to build, no more of the PX radios and Levi's and television sets that had flowed, like manna from consumer heaven, into the shops of San Fernando and Angeles City.

Tony would have to leave. There was no other choice in the

Filipino scheme of things. Disasters were a message from heaven: "Emigrate." He was the last member of Father Victor López's family still living in the Philippines.

It was hard not to see the great spiraling cloud that rose from Mount Pinatubo as a message, a sign, a gargantuan punctuation mark. "But in fact," as Father Vic would say, the process it punctuated in the López family's life had been under way for years. That moment of political euphoria on Epifanio de los Santos Avenue when Marcos fell in February 1986 was the high-water mark of many currents. Not least of them was Father Vic's power, the nervous energy that had driven him and the charisma that had drawn people to him at the gates of Camp Aguinaldo: the flower girls and newsboys from the shantytown of Dupax, the priests who called their parishioners into the streets, and the nuns who knelt before the tanks.

He wasn't even in Manila now. His order had sent him north, to a rural backwater in Cagayan Province on the far tip of Luzon Island just across the channel from Taiwan. Nobody in the church publicly explained it this way, but it was understood that Cardinal Sin, the island's chief prelate, was uncomfortable with his opinionated padres—that he wanted them at arm's length, far enough from the capital to be harmless. In a letter that arrived just before the eruption, Father Vic himself tried to put a good face on things.

"In fact, I'm back doing what I became a priest for. I have a parish of my own. I'm teaching children. I perform the baptisms and the marriages, I go to people's homes to do the last rites. It is good for me to be a parish priest again."

But he wasn't in Manila, and without him Manila wasn't the same for his entourage of church workers, shantytown urchins, and journalists. Father Vic was the organizer. The rest were followers— even I had relied on his contacts for interviews, for meetings with activists, for getting in and out of Manila.

When the mountain blew, with its awful announcement of natural limits, something ended.

There wasn't time for a trip up to Cagayan; the region had no airport, and by bus or car it was a three-day round trip. I called Tony in San Fernando, where he was trying to salvage anything he could from the smoldering ruins of his house. He drove down to Manila and we met at a restaurant that Father Vic liked in the Malate district, facing Manila Bay. About an hour after we arrived, Father's old chums Doy De Alcuaz and Art Figueroa showed up. The two of them stood us to rounds of San Mig, as they had in the old days, and Doy got Art to sing "Jalisco." But neither of them had his heart in it. There was no way to overcome the feeling that we were all at a kind of funeral.

Father Vic's transfer made my work in Manila impossible. I could still function out in the provinces, where local political barons had their own media agendas. But the capital was shut tight, tighter than I had ever known it. Even more than in the Marcos years, you had to have connections to accomplish anything there, and connections were a very scarce commodity.

In the past there had been two sets of options. The connections could be inside insiders, with links of some sort (family, business, school) to the president or a key adviser. Or they could be outside insiders who were plugged into the shadow structures of dissidence. No one had realized it at the time, but Cory Aquino's coming to power made the ground untenable for an effective dissident opposition. Dissidents were now either in the government themselves, building walls of influence that were not terribly different from those that surrounded Marcos's henchmen, or they were stuck in the limbo of discredited movements: rightist anachronisms rallying around the questionable banner of Imelda Marcos, who had returned to the Philippines after her husband died in Hawaii, or leftist anachronisms who had never recovered from the New People's Army's descent into factional bloodletting after the Marcos collapse (not to mention the global demise of Marxism).

So there was only one insider's circuit you could try to tap in Manila these days: that of the inside insiders. But the central government wasn't having anything to do with the press. Cory had never liked the limelight; when reporters started picking on her and the sheer idolization she had received during the election evolved into more objective coverage—when the Saint Corazon period ended— she simply shut the door.

Without the access that Father Vic had arranged for me, I was a fish out of water in Cory Aquino's Manila. That's not an easy thing to admit, because reporters love to be taken for hard-nosed independents who make their own breaks and knock down doors when they don't open. In a town like Manila, nobody reaches first base without connections. Every story, you might say, is a plant. The trick lies in recognizing what's being planted and doing your damnedest to remold the planted material into something that resembles an accurate picture. But nothing is possible without the initial plant, without the people who—to suit their own interests, obviously—are willing to play ball.

It would be great if the truth was merely something to be found rather than bargained over and shaped. That's just not the way it works in Manila. Or, for that matter, in Washington, D.C.

To the disappointment of Auntie and Tony, I decided to forgo the comforts of the cigarette subdivision this trip; the situation was too tenuous to accommodate the lack of a telephone and the ninety-minute slog to official Manila through the endless highway traffic jam. Instead I checked into a midtown Manila hotel within easy walking distance of the ministries and began calling the half-dozen offices I had written, wired, and phoned from abroad over a period of two months in an attempt to arrange interviews.

My efforts had all been inconclusive, and I was ready for problems; the Philippine consul general in San Francisco had been charming and his cook had produced a wonderful dinner in my honor, but I noticed the way he skirted my questions about an interview schedule in Manila. There was no surprise when the phone number he'd given me—"to confirm your appointments when you arrive"—turned out to be a dead line. That's why I'd sent all my own wires and made my own requests for interviews. It hadn't seemed to do any good, though, any more than my reminders, couched discreetly in each letter, that the Filipinos of San Francisco had helped bankroll the election campaign that put the ministers in their chairs. Two weeks of phone calls to half a dozen ministries passed. Every day it was the same: "Please call tomorrow." No one had any record of the wires. No one had any record of a request from the consul general for interviews.

In the cleaned-up government of President Aquino there was no Information Ministry to plead my case to; Cory had called it a propaganda tool and eliminated it. The score was a perfect shutout: Philippine Bureaucracy 6, *San Francisco Chronicle* 0.

I left town for Cebu Island, four hundred miles south of Manila, where I had much better luck on the inside track. On the plane I thought about Father Vic and the old days, and how his face would be twitching through its entire vocabulary of nervous tics when he heard about my useless two weeks in Manila.

Governor Lito Osmena of Cebu Province was not simply an insider. He also had the pedigree of inherited power. That was important, because so much of the new Philippines after Marcos was turning out to be the old Philippines reasserting itself: the Philippines of the *illustrados,* the Spanish and Chinese families who had run and owned just about everything in the islands before 1964, when the upstart lawyer from Ilocos Norte with the showboat beauty-queen wife bullied his way into the Malacañang Palace.

Most foreigners didn't grasp that part of the story. Ferdinand Marcos had imprisoned or exiled nearly an entire generation of the rich and powerful, seized whatever of their assets he could get his hands on, and created his own, much smaller, privileged class of unabashed parasites. In America, at least until the final days of the Marcos regime, the thinking had been that it was the poor and their advocates, the political left and the religious activists—the people who filled Father Vic's circle—who were the anti-Marcos set. Americans were confused when the stockbrokers and bankers of Makati backed the protests. It had been easier to picture the struggle in terms of a conservative tyrant beset by communist guerrillas and leftist padres and nuns.

The New People's Army and the activist priests were there, to be sure, but they weren't alone. Waiting behind the scenes, in their own plush underground of Makati offices and second homes in the States, were the *illustrados:* the Aquinos and the Mitras and the Cojuancos (or at least Cory's half of the Cojuanco family; the other half, the side led by her cousin Eduardo "Danding" Cojuanco, were among the most powerful of the Marcos parasites).

None of them outranked the Osmenas: the princes of Cebu,

the Kennedys of the Philippines. Emilio Mario "Lito" Osmena had achieved virtually everything a politician could aspire to by his fiftieth year, and loved to talk about it, loved especially the Kennedy comparisons, although his own pedigree was arguably more solid than the one that was forged in Boston by the senior Joe Kennedy, a questionable character with questionable friends.

"I suppose you're right about that," he said when I pointed out the contrast. The thought brought a smile to his face.

But it was true. The Osmena saga had a two-generation jump on that of the Kennedys. John Kennedy's grandfather was a rough-and-tumble Irish politician from the immigrant streets, and Joe Kennedy, the president's dad, had reportedly salted away a fortune as a rumrunner during Prohibition. Lito Osmena's grandfather, by contrast, was Sergio Osmena, the second president of the Philippine Republic, and his father was a celebrated surgeon and war hero who had been beheaded by the Japanese. As for the current generation, Lito's brother was Senator John "Sonny" Osmena, one of the most influential politicians in the national legislature. Lito's cousin Tommy Osmena was mayor of Cebu City. Lito himself was the governor of "booming Cebu Province," as the Manila dailies always put it—the crossroads and geographical center of the Philippine Archipelago. The only place in the nation where the fiscal bottom line didn't make economists shrink in horror.

We sat in his office, a second-floor suite in the engagingly grandiose little Cebu capitol building, which had been built during the early years of the U.S. occupation and called to mind the Greek revival courthouses that adorn so many county seats in the American Midwest. The governor said he could do with something to eat. He picked up the telephone and ordered a pizza with mushrooms and pepperoni, and had his aide open a couple of beers.

First we discussed the boom in Cebu. The series of attempted military coups d'état against Cory Aquino, which stopped Manila's economy cold, had barely touched the province. Colon Street, downtown in Cebu City, was jammed with recently smuggled Hondas and Nissans. The governor was an ideal interview subject; he understood the value of being quoted and inserted catchy observations into his comments, speaking slowly to make sure I got it all down in my notes. When I asked about the infrastructure, about the miserable condition of the roads and the communications system, he said, "A boom reaches only as far as the telephone rings." It was a great line, and he knew it.

In his own outer office there were twelve desks but just two telephones. He said he'd take care of all that. He would put in telephones—"fiber optics, none of the old stuff"—pave the roads, wire Cebu with geothermal power generated by the hot springs on neighboring Negros Island. His vision was hard to reconcile with the appalling wreckage of Cebu City; boom or not, many office buildings in the business district were literally crumbling. The electricity failed every night, without exception, plunging the city into darkness until shopkeepers and homeowners could light the candles that every Cebuano purchased by the gross.

Still, the U.S. consulate reckoned that exports from Cebu were running at $500 million a year, a pretty penny for a city of seven hundred thousand people. Timex had set up a plant, along with National Semiconductor. There were jobs here; that in itself was something. Migrants from the neighboring islands were pouring in, camping out on the sidewalks and adding their bedding and baggage to the general disarray. The mess in Cebu City wasn't the desperate negligence you found in Manila. It was the price of sudden prosperity, the unsightly by-product of roaring commerce.

Trade had been mostly underground just a few years ago, when merchants didn't dare export too much—at least not openly—because Marcos's cut would leave them in the poorhouse. A diplomat who knew the place well said the Cebuanos were "magicians when it comes to accounting."

"Absolutely," Lito agreed, then he told me how it worked. The merchants would under-invoice what was shipped and over-invoice expenses. It was all done so adroitly, funneling the money through hundreds of small firms, that even Marcos couldn't follow it, couldn't get his hands on the loot.

They were almost all Chinese Filipinos, the Cebuano merchants. That gave them the right connections in Taipei and Hong Kong and Singapore, with partners who tended not to ask questions. Even Lito's family had its Chinese uncles. He was proud of them, proud of the fact that they had been so much wilier than the Spanish who accounted for the rest of the *illustrado* class.

"Smart people, very smart," he said.

Then he talked about the other part of the pedigree that counted, the years in prison and exile. Even there the details were perfect. "Right next to Ninoy," he said. "My cell was right next to Ninoy Aquino's."

It was a major credential. Like the martyr, he had been imprisoned without charge, tortured, jailed, then released and sent off with his family to exile in America in 1979.

"Nobody expected the troubles in our country to end, not anytime soon. No one expected us to come back."

They had bought land outside Dixon, a small farming town in Solano County northeast of San Francisco, where Lito Osmena and his wife, Annette, set out to start a new life. It was modeled very consciously on the stories he'd heard from his maternal grandfather, a California businessman, who married his daughter into the Cebuano aristocracy. The governor looked dreamy when he described it.

"There was a four-bedroom ranch house and a big pond, almost a lake. I designed both of them myself. We put all these birds in, birds that you don't see in the Philippines. Swans and Muscovy ducks and so forth."

The pizza had arrived. Lito didn't seem to be interested in it.

Life in Solano County had been good for him and Annette, he said. It was the only peaceful life they'd ever really known. He spoke of it the way Cory Aquino sometimes spoke of the years she and Ninoy had spent in Cambridge, Massachusetts, far from the responsibilities and dangers, in a place where their pedigree was nothing more than a curiosity. In Cambridge only the handful of Harvard professors and students who specialized in Southeast Asia knew what an *illustrado* was. In Dixon, aside from Filipino farmworkers, nobody did. The governor said his three children were still there, in the San Francisco suburbs. That clearly pleased him. The link with his California grandfather wasn't broken.

Yes, he remembered Dixon very fondly. They'd had relatives in every weekend for noisy family gatherings. Annette had dozens of cousins, aunts, and uncles in the Bay Area. They were never alone.

He nudged a piece of dry pizza off his desk and back onto its cardboard circle.

"I want you to meet her," he said abruptly. "We'll have dinner at my place."

The governor jumped to his feet. His aide signaled to me to move quickly and followed us out the door.

Four heavyset men stood in the gubernatorial anteroom. They looked as though they had all been stamped from the same corpulent mold and sent to the same workshop for finishing. Each wore a loose, wildly florid tropical shirt over light gray pants. There were ominous bulges under the breast pockets: shoulder holsters.

Lito bounded down the ornate staircase of the Capitol, with the six of us—me, the aide, and the four bodyguards—jockeying for space as we tried to keep up. He threw open a side door off the first-floor hall, and we were bathed in light. It was the Osmena limo and two other cars, all with their head lamps trained on the door. I wondered about the security reasoning behind that; it made us perfect targets.

Then the headlights dimmed and the cars screamed through Cebu City, up and down the washboard side streets, in what was obviously an effort to confuse any potential assassin—so obvious that it was an unmistakable announcement of the passenger's identity. Cringing at the likelihood that this tactic was grounded in unmentioned past events, I asked the governor who might be gunning for him.

He answered honestly: "It could be the left. It could be the right."

The governor handled the violent uncertainties of his country, the incessant bloodletting, a lot better than I did. A few days before, I'd gone to a beach resort on the nearby island of Bohol to unwind. The grounds were guarded around the clock by Philippine infantrymen; the place must have been owned by an *illustrado,* and that should have been reassurance enough. It wasn't. One morning after a swim I came back to my room and walked in on a young man with a bandanna across his face; he swiveled at the sound of the door and waved what looked like a flame thrower in my direction. It's hard to say which of us was more terrified by the ear-shattering "Yoik!" that welled out of me, bringing half a dozen soldiers and the resort manager running. The flame thrower turned out to be bug-spray gear; the masked guerrilla was there to exterminate roaches, not Yankees. The manager insisted that there was no reason to be embarrassed.

At the moment, Lito continued, he was less worried about the left than about the right. He'd worked out some sort of "understand-ing" with the communist guerrillas.

But the right-wingers . . . "Well, I fired quite a few fifteen-thirties, about eight hundred altogether, and they weren't very happy about it."

"Fifteen-thirties" referred to beneficiaries of Marcos's patronage, primarily Ilocanos from Marcos's home province, who had been put on the inflated payroll when a Marcos crony ran Cebu. Most of them had shown up for work only on the fifteenth and thirtieth of each month, when salary checks were distributed.

As we careened out of the city and onto the northbound high-way (pavement for about two miles, then packed earth), the governor returned to the subject of Dixon, and the pond and the house he'd built there. The experience had whetted his taste for self-expression. He fancied himself an architect now, read everything he could on the subject.

"There, look," he ordered, aiming his index finger at a point of light that hung above us in the inky night, adjacent to the slender crescent of the moon. "You'll see. You'll see."

The light grew larger and larger as we climbed the flank of a mountain, winding around narrow curves in fishtail turns that sent showers of gravel into the valley below. I was privately grateful that it was too dark to make out the edge of the precipice. After about forty-five minutes of this, the convoy hurtled down a lane that had been cut between rows of trees and crunched to a gravelly halt at a sixteen-foot cyclone fence. A small army of men toting machine guns stood at the gate, which slowly swung open in front of us.

*   *   *

The house was lit like a Christmas tree and shaped like a gigantic igloo. Improbably, Governor Emilio Mario Osmena had fallen under the spell of Buckminster Fuller and built himself what must have been the biggest residential geodesic dome in the Orient. It was easily sixty feet high, and painted a flat silver from its top to its base.

Annette Osmena waited in the doorway, before a gallery of arches that ringed the entire circumference of the ferro-cement dome at the ground level. We were a good four thousand feet above the tropical floor of Cebu. A frigid wind surged through the arches, producing a ghoulish whine. The First Lady was bundled in a heavy fisherman's sweater, but it wasn't enough; her hand trembled as I shook it. Or maybe it was my hand that was trembling. As soon as we were inside, she sent a servant off to get me a fisherman's sweater of my own.

We sat at the bar, drinking California Chablis and discussing modern architecture. "Fuller," Lito said, "holds all the answers for the developing countries. Simple design, lightweight materials, efficient use of space."

But he conceded that there were some kinks to iron out. One of the most irritating of these was acoustic. The inside of the dome was a colossal echo chamber, capable of transporting the faintest sound on a high-fidelity journey that made privacy impossible. The Osmenas had hung lengths of cloth from the ceiling in overlapping rows as sound baffles. But still, I could hear the cook stirring her pots in the kitchen, each little clink and scape reaching my ears as though she was a yard away instead of seventy-five feet. The puttering echoed around us, mixing its hard metallic ringing with the howl of the wind.

The main course was quail, cooked Filipino style in vinegar, soy, and garlic, and washed down with more Chablis. Annette Osmena looked miserably cold throughout the meal. It was obvious that the dome on the mountain was Lito's fantasy, not hers. She said that she didn't get down into the city very often, and that she often missed the house in Dixon.

The First Lady tried to keep up a proud front, shivering in her sweater in that immense howling egg. But I felt sorry for her. She had been happier—maybe they had both been happier—in exile.

GORBACHEV SAYS COUP WAS
SOVIET LAST GASP

MOSCOW (August 26, 1991) — A somber President Mikhail Gorbachev conceded today that last week's failed coup d'état effectively marked the end of the Soviet Union.

In his lengthiest comment so far on the August 18 attempt by Communist Party conservatives to overthrow him, Gorbachev told members of the national legislature that the central government in Moscow "no longer has the power to control the republics."

The authority of the central government has deteriorated rapidly since the failed coup, which was broken when key military units rallied to the support of democratically elected reformers under Russian Federation President Boris Yeltsin.

Two of the republics, Azerbaijan and Armenia, are already at war with each other. Violence has also raged in Georgia and Moldavia, and across large parts of Soviet Central Asia.

On Saturday, Gorbachev resigned as Communist Party General Secretary and disbanded the party's politburo, terminating its seven-decade monopoly on power.

Yesterday, the actual dismantling of the Soviet Union moved closer to fact with the diplomatic recognition of Latvia, Estonia and Lithuania as independent nations by several Western European governments.

FEVER IN SIBERIA

In the summer the Soviet Union came apart, Irkutsk burned with a dizzying case of Pacific fever. It was measured in kilometers: more than five thousand on the Trans-Siberian Express to Moscow, less than fifteen hundred to the Chinese border.

The city seemed the epitome of nowhere, a sudden clearing in the vast pine forest that springs from the banks of the Amur River and marches north across a wilderness the size of Western Europe before it finally subsides into tundra near the Arctic Circle. But the relative proximity to prosperous East Asia carried enormous emotional weight for Siberians.

Tunneling through the forest depths at the lower end of Lake Baikal and over the frontier to Harbin, the rail line put Irkutsk within a day and a half of the Pacific, within two days of Tokyo and Seoul. The trains focused people's expectations. They pulled into the station on the westbound run mesmerizingly rich (from the Siberian point of view) with Japanese compact disk players, Korean sweatshirts inscribed with nonsensical English phrases, and Chinese imitations of the Sony Walkman and the IBM PC. Packed in the bags of freelance black marketeers—Mongolian students en route from Ulan Bator to Novosibirsk, European punkers on a lark, Chinese scientists and junior diplomats heading for Moscow—the contraband made Irkutsk an entrepôt. A little Hong Kong. A warehouse for the furnishings of consumer delirium.

The contrast with the eastbound run told you all you needed to know about the Soviet collapse. The trains from Moscow brought nothing to Irkutsk except tourists and Muscovites, the latter almost universally intent on tossing their own hoards of sinking rubles into the fire. The going rate then was twenty thousand rubles for a videotape deck—the equivalent of seven years' salary—and eight hundred for a pair of Reebok sneakers, $1,280 at the official exchange rate.

Since a century and a half ago, when its pine houses sheltered the exiled aristocrats of the failed Decembrist rebellion, Irkutsk's gaze had been riveted in bathetic longing toward the West, toward European Russia. But the fever twisted it around 180°. With a very different kind of longing, the city had begun looking to the Orient, and across the great ocean to America. And it was returned, this new longing, because Irkutsk had something to barter. The sole Russian city of any size in the empty reaches of eastern Siberia, it was the gateway to a treasure trove: lumber and coal, gold and iron, diamonds and furs, in such fabulous abundance that it virtually defied measurement. Moscow had barely scratched the surface of this wealth, yet Siberia accounted for more than half of the Soviet Union's $40 billion in annual foreign currency earnings in 1989.

It boggled the Siberian imagination to think what modern business and technology might accomplish. It stoked the Pacific fever.

Alexei Volkov had the unkempt beard, florid complexion, and wild eyes of a survivalist. That was what he instantly reminded me of: the post-hippie mountain men of California's Trinity Alps and Sierra Nevada, the sixties dopers who had decamped from the Haight in the seventies and gone into the high country to wait out the end of the world. He had spent too many of his thirty-eight years in the forest, and it showed, not only in the ravaging of his face and the leanness of his frame, but in a kind of inarticulate fury that overcame him in the presence of company.

There was plenty of company to be had in the dining room of the Irkutsk Intourist Hotel. The place was jammed with traders and prospectors from around the Pacific Rim, the gamblers from Los Angeles and Calgary and Osaka who had returned the eastward gaze of Siberia and followed it back to this clearing in Alexei's forest. Not just rough-and-ready types: If there were wildcatters around, they were seated at the same tables where oil executives in company wind-breakers and neatly pressed khakis chatted with their counterparts from the local bureaucracy. I sat in on a few of the conversations, not by invitation but simply because every table was a negotiating table, and no matter where you ate lunch you were privy to details. The talk was direct: options, leases, extraction rights, the repatriation of profit.

The Siberians were willing to promise anything. "All can be done" was a stock phrase, muttered with fiercely affirmative nodding by men who understood no other words in English: It was the fever.

The Siberians needed Alexei because he had picked up a more complete, if decidedly raw, brand of English from Canadian contract workers who had been wafted by the first winds of *perestroika* into a joint venture in Siberia's Kuzbas coalfields. Alexei was a mining engineer in the Kuzbas, but he had more or less refashioned himself into a translator.

It was an education, listening to him. "Deeze vucking guys, dey have deir heads up deir asses," I heard him tell a group of West Coast suits.

He was speaking of his own erstwhile employers, four Economic Ministry officials who grinned in amiable ignorance while he slandered them a hundred different ways, punctuating every assertion with "vucking" this and "vucking" that. It was remarkable that they didn't grasp the contempt in which he held them. Eventually some vucking guy would acquire enough English to grasp the essentials of these diatribes.

The source of Alexei's scorn was simple. It was a practical man's, a frontiersman's, contempt. The Canadians and Americans and Japanese he'd met got things done, which was in itself such a vast departure from Soviet practice that the sheer observance of the phenomenon had permanently ruined Alexei for everything Russian. He'd say so, flat out, because nobody cared anymore what you said. That was also the fever at work.

Once, in the midst of a long night's argument about what had gone wrong, why everything had been such a miserable failure, Alexei climbed onto the table top and started shouting "shit on you, shit on you vucking KGB" at several startled men at the dining room entrance. He was an embarrassment, even to the foreigners of whom he was enamored. But he knew everything about Siberia that one man could know, and they needed him.

Alexei made Joe Blake laugh like hell. Joe was one of the most outrageous of the gamblers, not least of all in his choice of conveyance. He was exploring Siberian investment possibilities on a Harley-Davidson, which he'd shipped to Rotterdam from New York, throttled across the Urals and the steppes, and planned to unload at Vladivostok on the Pacific. Joe was an investor and a writer; he made money on everything from junk bonds to sow belly futures and then told people about it in a South Carolina drawl, mapping the path to success in videos that were aired on cable television.

His confidence was the objective correlative of Alexei's fury, so blatant and uncontained that it made you nervous. The two of them, Alexei and Joe, fed on each other in an idiosyncratic dialogue between the self-appointed saved and the self-pitying damned. The self-pity only brought paralysis for Alexei. But the brashness, the confidence, had brought Joe Blake a big house, celebrity, and a desire to spread the gospel of risk to the four corners of the fading Socialist bloc from the seat of his motorcycle. Given the times, given the fever, it was almost reasonable.

I was stuck between stories in Siberia, marooned by some snafu in rail arrangements that made Joe impossibly smug about his Harley hog, and wound up spending a fair amount of time with the two of them. We went together to the new Irkutsk supermarket shortly after it opened. In one respect it was a showcase: There was a checkout stand. That was a lot more radical than it might seem because the drill in Russian cities was lines, lines, lines, so many of them that they engendered the most familiar cliché in the entire vocabulary of foreign journalism during the Gorbachev-Yeltsin revolution—Russians waiting in line. Usually the lines pictured on the evening news were just the ones that snaked outside store entrances. Inside it was infinitely worse because it was incomprehensible. For reasons no one could explain, shoppers waited in one line to ask what was available, joined another to pay for it, then beat their way through a gauntlet of sharp-elbowed *babushkas* in a third to pick up their packages. The internal lines were gone in the new Irkutsk supermarket. Clients circulated freely, grabbed what they wanted from the shelves, then passed through the checkout, just like in Frankfurt or Santa Monica.

Visiting the supermarket might have been a transforming moment for Alexei, a way of easing his contempt and shattering his paralysis. A renewal of faith. There were no lines, not even at the checkout. But there was also no food, or close to none, despite the fact that the shelves were groaning. They looked to be an absolute cornucopia by Russian standards—until we got closer. It was all mackerel, every single can on every single shelf, labeled in a rainbow of different colors that from a distance had produced the semblance of variety. There was nothing else, not a vegetable or a sausage to be had.

"Vucking canned fish," Alexei said. "Shit, Joe."

Joe laughed like hell.

The Irkutsk hotel, eastern Siberia's finest, was a creation of the early 1960s, caught somewhere in the void between pure function and a clumsy stab at higher aesthetic purpose. It loomed over the Angara River like a great rectangular tombstone, moldering toward oblivion in stunning disrepair.

The door handles fell out of their doors when guests turned them to enter their rooms. The faucets were often permanently stuck open, so that the sound of the river outside, coursing by in its futile effort to drain the oceanic depths of Lake Baikal, was echoed by the sloosh of water pouring into the sink of an empty bathroom. Closet doors were missing altogether. The bedding was shredded by field mice. The windows would neither entirely open nor entirely closed.

There were four elevators, but there was never more than one in operation; it was invariably loaded with suitcases that traveled up and down between the upper floors and the lobby until a bellhop could be coaxed away from the samovar to clear the deck. The stairways reeked with the stale tobacco smoke and perspiration of overweight Central European tourists huffing their way up to their accommodations.

At the official exchange rate, the only transaction that could reserve a room for a Western traveler, it cost $220 a night. But the view of the Angara, a classic frontier river if there ever was one, made it worthwhile. The river cut through Irkutsk in a great slash under the enormous, luminous Siberian skies, rushing past a sawtoothed crest of pine ridges that filled the eastern horizon.

To the hotel's immediate left, just visible from the guestroom windows, the western bank was crowded with the elegant mansions and public buildings that the Decembrists had erected to recall St. Petersburg.

They had tried to overthrow the czar in the last month of 1825—hence the name of their failed coup d'état—and were deported to Irkutsk for their pains. Those who were still alive were allowed to return to European Russia three decades later.

There were sadder mementos in the city's streets. A nineteenth-century Polish Catholic church rose above the rooftops a few blocks from the river. It was red brick and twin-steepled, in faithful homage to the churches of Cracow and Warsaw, and dozens just like them that more fortunate Polish émigrés built in Chicago and Detroit. Stalin had turned the building into a concert hall, and it was still described as such—with no mention made of its ecclesiastical origins—in the sole guidebook to Irkutsk, a 1976 volume that perfectly captured the obscurantism of the Brezhnev epoch.

The church had been built by intellectuals from Warsaw. Caught up in yet another of the seductive gales of liberal optimism that blew through the czarist empire—and then abruptly stopped dead, leaving nothing but Cossack atrocities in their wake—they were sent here after their own failed uprising against the regime in St. Petersburg five years after the Decembrists. Unlike the Decembrists, they never went back.

Standing in the chill morning air outside the church, I felt I could sense their presence. Their isolation. Their wavering between unnerving despair and a resigned determination—there was no other choice—to build a new life. Today, little tangible remained of the Polish exiles except this church and a clutch of displaced family names that had been scattered across Siberia after a century of frontier marriages. The church wasn't even a concert hall now. Abandoned, boarded up, the bricks beginning to merge with the soil, it was an unintended symbol of the Pacific fever's effect on Irkutsk, a visible erosion of the heart-wrenching links that had once tied this forest clearing to distant Europe.

The vanished Poles at least had their monument, that tangible brick icon of exile and pain, and an honored place in Polish, if not Russian, history books. The Yakuts had nothing.

A Yakut tribesman was out of place in Irkutsk. The local indigenous tribe, the aboriginal people of the Baikal shores, were the Buryats, cousins of the Mongols. So Sergei Muravyov was a surprise. We fell into conversation in a small public square on the left bank of the Angara early in my second anxious day in the city, before I had tapped into the dining room negotiations and gotten to know Alexei.

There's a chronic nightmare that many journalists have, even after years on the road. In my version I arrive in a new town, an utter stranger—"unsourced," in the jargon—and nothing happens. I meet no one; I talk to no one; no one will agree to an interview. There is no story. The longer the journey, the darker the nightmare. It's one thing to be sent from San Francisco to Los Angeles by an editor and return empty-handed; it's quite another to be sent to eastern Siberia and wire your regrets.

For me the panic sets in immediately, rolls up on the baggage belt with my suitcase nearly every time an assignment is to begin. And then something happens, something unexpected. Something that gives shape and meaning to the amorphous experience of waking up in a strange hotel room in a strange city. It can't be depended on; to take it for granted would mean the end of a career. But my fortune had held for a long time, and on the morning of my second day in Irkutsk, my wholly unexpected stroke of luck was Sergei Muravyov.

He was short and stocky, a man in his mid-forties who closely resembled an Aleut (a native of coastal Alaska) in his tawny complexion, slightly almond-shaped eyes, and jet-black hair. He was wearing a thick wool sport coat with a few medals pinned to the right breast, a detail that, even more than his Asiatic features, made it surprising when he walked up and asked if I was an American. Normally English speakers in Siberia were European Russians like Alexei; very seldom, in these cynical times, were they Russians who still wore party medals on their chests. But that was in Moscow. In Siberia the signs couldn't be read the same way. Like everything else, they had their own meaning on the frontier.

Also frontierlike, Sergei got right to the point. "Do you have an Apple computer with you?"

Then he apologized, understanding from my confused reaction that I wasn't one of the freelance traders after all, and that the rumors he'd heard about how easy it was to find things in Irkutsk might be exaggerated. For he too had just arrived here, from Yakutsk, a thousand miles to the north and four hundred miles below the Arctic Circle, where he was the only English teacher and had been for fifteen years.

I had seen the booty on the Trans-Siberian and told him that the Apple was doubtful. But he had a backup plan; you had to if you came this far. If there were no Apples in Irkutsk, he would go on to the Chinese border.

I'd also heard about this: that there was a roaring electronic supply line between Blagoveshchensk in the Russian Far East and the Manchurian city of Aihu, just across the Amur River. You could get a one-day visa by paying a bribe to the Chinese border guards. It was an abysmally expensive proposition because the Chinese black marketeers would reckon a ruble at four or five American cents, while the official rate then was $1.60.

"But they say you can buy the right things there," Sergei mused.

That, above all, was the point: finding the Apple. He was on a mission, sent by the Yakuts of the Lena Valley to buy a machine that, according to all they had heard, required no special training to use and could put them at one leap into the Pacific mainstream. Sergei explained this in careful sentences, strung along a conversation on the riverbank that lasted three hours—the two of us standing there, not even bothering to look for a park bench, in mutual fascination. He had never spoken to a native speaker of English before. I had never spoken to someone who expressed so unabashedly the hopes that the computer age was arousing everywhere I traveled in the late 1980s and early 1990s. It wasn't until after we parted, after it was too late, that I thought to ask how he had learned about Apples, about the possibilities of the new technology. The computer gospel was everywhere, but nobody really understood how it made its way to places like the Lena Valley.

I did ask about the medals. The answer was complicated and poetic. He sucked in a breath, and began.

"I wear them," he said, "because I knew who I was a few years ago, and right now I only know who I am not."

Sergei Muravyov was the third and last son of a Yakut tribal elder, born to parents who had lost their first two children to an exile that virtually no one outside the tribe remembered, no one mourned, even while the Decembrists and the Poles of a century earlier were being elevated to post-*glasnost* sainthood by revisionist historians.

"The troops came to the Lena in the winter of 1942," Sergei said. "They rounded everyone up, put them in trucks, and drove north for several days. Then they stopped, above the tundra line, and built a camp. Tents and latrines. Not much else."

Scholars have yet to fathom the full depths of Josef Stalin's paranoia, the waking nightmares that led him into the labyrinth of the Doctors' Trials and the army purges—the madness that was observed. The Yakut deportation was an unobserved madness, ordered for reasons that were never given. Was it their Asian faces, the genetic evidence of some fantasized allegiance to the Japanese? Was it a plan to build a last secure bunker in the Lena Valley if Leningrad and Moscow fell to the blitzkrieg? Was it anything that could be rendered in words? If the words existed, no one, least of all the Yakuts, ever heard them.

"My father was not the same man after those four years in the camp. He almost never talked again, about anything. I know from my mother that my two brothers, both small children, are buried where the camps were. One of them froze to death in 1943. The other died a year later from a flu.

"Then, in 1946, our people were allowed to return to the Lena Valley. And it was as if nothing had happened: The government officials were absolutely silent about it. The teachers in our schools did not teach it. I did not teach it.

"After Khrushchev, much was written about what Stalin did, about how many of his own friends he had killed, about the people who died at his hands in European Russia. But nobody wrote about the Yakuts."

The northern evening began to fall as he spoke. The Angara rushed by, its torrents spinning wheels of flotsam from the immense lake to the north as the hills beyond the river took on the somber twilight glow that would last here through much of the summer night.

Amidst the great silence, the Yakuts had drifted into a loyal coma over the years, uncomplaining, mute, as the madness of Stalin faded into the restless meanderings of Khrushchev and then the long gray numbness of Brezhnev.

Sergei: "We were perfectly orthodox, good communists. I'm still in the party, you see. I know that is very hard to understand, but it was what we were, what had been made of us. To be cooperative."

He waved a hand over the medals on his right breast. It wasn't a dismissive gesture.

"And then the changes started—the news of Gorbachev and *perestroika* started to come from Moscow. How can I explain? It made everything a lie, very quickly. It made all that I had been teaching a lie. So we had to look at the ground we were standing on more carefully."

His father was gone, but his mother talked of the camps, slowly at first, and then in more detail until, Sergei said, "for the first time in my life I saw her weep."

I thought about China, just to the south, where also for the first time I had seen people weep openly the year before. It was something I knew I would always remember of this moment at the decade's turn, so heavy with promise and regret: the weeping of the stoic.

"After that there was no turning back. We talked to Yakut boys who had been in Afghanistan about what they had seen. We talked about the corruption in Moscow, about how poor we were in Yakutsk. We talked about the world. It was not easy for us, you see, because everything we had always known was at stake, and very soon there was nothing left of it."

The Yakuts, who number 250,000 in a riverine basin six times the size of France, with winter temperatures dropping to as much as 60° below zero, were throwing words like "independence" around now, telling the few foreigners who passed through the Lena Valley that it would one day be a sovereign kingdom, "Yakutia."

It was too much, too soon, in Sergei's estimate.

"We know what we once were, but not what we are becoming. There was only the lie then, and the uncertainty now."

He carried the contradiction with him, wore it as a badge: the medals, with their ambiguous announcement of his years of orthodoxy and service, hanging from his breast pocket on the trip south to Manchuria, where he hoped to find an Apple Macintosh. He was in a hurry, he told me as we shook hands and parted. He would take the next train toward Blagoveshchensk, toward the border.

CHINESE HARD-LINERS
EMBRACE FREE MARKET

BEIJING (June 4, 1992) — Three years after China shocked the world with its bloody crackdown on the pro-democracy movement, top Chinese officials are pushing the very reforms they once blamed for the Tiananmen protests.

At the National People's Congress in late March, according to documents now circulating here, General Yang Baibing announced that the People's Liberation Army would "serve as a protector and escort" for expanded economic reforms.

Yang directed a hard-line Marxist re-indoctrination program for military officers after the Tiananmen incident. His half-brother, President and Central Military Commission chief Yang Shangkun, is believed to have supervised the army assault on the demonstrators.

After the military crackdown, which resulted in hundreds of deaths, the Yangs were among many Chinese officials who condemned the economic reforms of the 1980s for introducing "bourgeois liberalism," and called for a return to Marxist orthodoxy.

But behind the scenes, say analysts, the army itself increased its investments in joint ventures with foreign partners, and turned a blind eye on the nation's growing ranks of private entrepreneurs.

"If anything," said a Western diplomat here, "doing business in China has gotten easier, rather than harder, since Tiananmen."

Recent economic figures indicate that the Chinese economy is growing at a double-digit pace, fueled by a rush of foreign capital into the country's rapidly growing private sector. A new issue of shares by Shanghai's government-approved stock market this week led to a near riot of would-be investors competing to make bids.

AFTER THE REVOLUTION

A year passed after the killings. Then a second and a third. Few people had believed, in the bloody summer of 1989, that the party would ever put Tiananmen Square behind it. But it did. It dulled the memory of the demonstrations and the shootings with money. With hardly a backward glance at the ghost of Mao Zedong, it abandoned the last shreds of economic principle that could rightly be called communist.

The Communist Party of China—which had dismantled the communes, opened stock markets, and formed partnerships with legions of Western plutocrats even before the tanks of June blew away the Goddess of Liberty—was now running a national fire sale. Everything in the country was up for grabs, being put on the block at markdown prices.

Nowhere was the grabbing cruder, more obvious, than in the city of Xiamen, on the southeastern coast of Fujian Province directly across the Formosa Strait from Taiwan.

Like everyone else in the bar of the Lujiang Hotel, Tan Xihu was a businessman of sorts—an "import-export consultant," as his card read—and not what his visa said he was: a tourist, come to visit the old port town that the taipans had called Amoy, the Hokkien dialect name for Xiamen. Tourist visas, as always, were easy to come by in China. They were stamped into the passports of every guest in the Lujiang, although the hotel had canceled its bus tours because no one seemed interested.

The men in the bar were nominally residents of Taipei and Kaohsiung, Bangkok, Hong Kong, Jakarta, Manila. But they were the kind of people who lived out of suitcases for months, sometimes years, at a time. Home was wherever their suitcases took them, usually to second-rank waterfront hotels like the Lujiang and bars like this one, where good Scotch was served neat from 10:00 A.M. on and the cigarette smoke was so thick that the bartenders' eyes were permanently bloodshot. Many of the bar's clients were regulars. They knew each other, and they had similar interests and wore similar clothes that more or less announced their business approach. It was the uniform of Southeast Asian wheeling and dealing: tropical silk shirts open to the chest, tapered linen trousers, a gold chain around the neck, a big gold Rolex on the wrist, dark glasses indoors and out. The Lujiang was B movie all the way, right down to the Chinese hookers being treated by their johns to dishes of spaghetti or Australian T-bone steak, and a comically obvious pair of undercover police in sappy Hawaiian shirts who were ignored by everyone they were there to watch.

Tan, who was himself Taiwanese but spent more time in Los Angeles than Taipei, was a versatile guy. He dabbled in everything from bicycle exports to large-scale commodities purchases. On this particular junket to Xiamen he was shopping for real estate. The whole bar clientele was; the Chinese yuan had halved in value since the troubles at Tiananmen Square, while the Taiwan dollar had risen astronomically. By Taipei or L.A. standards, land was ridiculously cheap in Xiamen—"a steal," Tan said.

He pointed the cops out to me and laughed.

"Poor bastards," he said in perfect Angelino. "They don't even know what they're supposed to be watching out for."

It was true. Nobody could tell what might be illegal in Xiamen because everything was out in the open, and even the strictly above-board stuff was tantamount to highway robbery—"a steal." After Tiananmen, the government had allowed the city fathers to institute a flat 15 percent corporate tax rate to attract foreign capital. When that didn't work, they suspended the tax entirely for the first two years of a venture and held it to 7.5 percent for the following three—by which time most foreigners would have shoveled out their profits and sold the enterprise to the next wheeler-dealer in line. The buyer, in turn, would rename the business and enjoy another five-year tax break.

Sweetheart deals like the tax breaks were now drawing clouds of investors. Money was pouring into Xiamen at the rate of more than $4 billion a year. Some of it was respectable investment: a Coca-Cola plant, a San Francisco bank, a Camel cigarette factory, a Filipino brewery. More of it was wheeler-dealer.

Mabel introduced me to Tan. I'd met her on a Xiamen city bus. She sat down next to me on the rear seat, shoving her narrow hips into a tiny space beside the window, and opened an English grammar book with a busy flourish that was intended to catch my attention. The gesture was superfluous; she was packed into a denim miniskirt so tight that she could only walk in a shuffle. We were soon deep in conversation.

Contrary to appearances, Mabel was a business student pursuing an advanced degree in international trade at Xiamen University. She and her classmates were among the most avid devotees of Western style I'd encountered in China. Maybe it was the proximity of the Coca-Cola and Camel plants; maybe it was the sense that their chosen careers could be defined only in borrowed symbols. But it was also typical of them to miss the mark slightly—to acquire names like

Mabel and Percy that were hopelessly archaic and clothes more appropriate for gigolos or streetwalkers than young executives. (Mabel's male friends at the university business school went to class in tee shirts, with cigarette packs tucked into their turned-up sleeves à la James Dean.)

Curiously, the real tarts over in the Lujiang bar and the Mandarin Hotel Disco tended to wear fussy lace dresses that would have appealed to prim young New England maidens on an outing from boarding school.

If there was a logic to any of it, it was that everyone in Xiamen seemed to be in some sort of disguise. The men who resembled racetrack touts and whose papers read "tourist" were actually investors. The whores looked like ladies and the ladies looked like whores. The cops in the bar were trying desperately to pass as barflies. Before I left town I also met a French Catholic priest who had assumed the identity of an engineering consultant, and a couple of Mormon missionaries from Utah who had passed themselves off as yacht manufacturers in search of a joint venture site. As for me, I had resurrected a brief career I'd deserted almost two decades earlier and told the Chinese visa authorities I was a hospital administrator, a subterfuge that obliged me to pay occasional fact-finding visits to medical clinics just in case someone was keeping track of my activities.

Xiamen, during the Chinese fire sale, was a big, slightly mad costume party.

Mabel had an uncle in Los Angeles who worked for a company that did business with Tan. The uncle thought it a good idea for the two of them to get together when Tan passed through Xiamen. In theory, Mabel was supposed to help him find the right contacts in the municipal government, although in practice it was Tan who knew instinctively which doors had to be knocked on, which bureaucrats taken to dinner.

With me Mabel talked college more than business. She was determined, for reasons I never understood, to continue her studies in the accounting department at the University of Texas at El Paso after she finished at Xiamen U. She was precise about that: It had to be the El Paso campus. The main branch of the University of Texas

in Austin—not to mention some university other than Texas—just
wouldn't do. I advised her to consider broadening the range of possibilities. She was dubious.

"El Paso," she'd say once in a while, out of the blue, when the
conversation flagged. "El Paso."

Whatever its source, the desire to go there had become an obsession with her. Every other Chinese student I'd met was hell-bent on
Berkeley or Stanford, with Harvard or Princeton a distant third
choice. Not Mabel. She lived for the day when she could crunch
numbers in the dry air of West Texas.

I ate dinner most nights with her and Tan. They were an enter-
taining pair in their respective oversupplies of flighty naïveté and
hard-bitten worldliness, and Tan had a real knack for spotting the
best restaurants. He either bought my line about hospital administration or didn't give a damn what I was. Probably the latter. Still, I
didn't have the guts to admit I was a journalist. Appearances were
so uniformly deceiving in Xiamen that I wondered from time to time
if Mabel was a Public Security gumshoe, or Tan a Taiwan spook. Or
vice versa.

One night, halfway into a bottle of Grant's bourbon at a cocktail
lounge in Huli, a new subdivision for overseas Chinese that was
materializing helter-skelter on a hill east of the port, Tan looked
down at his Rolex, smiled across the table at Mabel and me, and
said, "I've got some shopping to do. Like to come?"

A few minutes later we were speeding north along Zhongshan
Lu, Xiamen's main drag, dodging pedestrians and smuggled Taiwanese motorcycles in the air-conditioned comfort of a Toyota taxi. It
was a right-hand drive model, bought at a used car lot in Tokyo by
a Thai-Chinese investor and shipped to his cousin, a Singaporean
who was backing a private taxi venture here in Fujian Province.
China, unlike Japan, drives American style, on the right side of the
road, not the left, which meant that our driver was on the wrong
side of the car and had to guess at the exact location of the center
dividing line. He kept fading into the oncoming traffic or blindly
passing slower vehicles at the most inopportune moments. The ride
was an exercise in terror.

Taxi rides could be dangerous for other reasons in the super-
charged, money-maddened atmosphere of Xiamen. Gangs were known

to block roads in the dark countryside beyond the new subdivisions, then surround halted vehicles and rob their occupants. People who resisted were sometimes stabbed. A few taxi drivers and their passengers had been killed in recent months.

Eventually we pulled up at a six-story hotel in another new part of town, a scattering of mid-rise apartment buildings and office towers that backed up against a joint venture plant. The hotel was the chunk of Xiamen that Tan was thinking of buying. "It's for sale, cheap. Maybe too cheap. But let's take a look."

We went inside and walked up to the desk. Tan didn't say why we were there. Instead, in the Hokkien dialect that Taiwan shares with Xiamen, he began to negotiate for a room.

"I told him it has to be large enough for the three of us," he said to me.

The deskman didn't skip a beat at the notion of our ménage à trois. He showed us up to a corner suite, a two-room executive pad equipped with a marble bath, wet bar, four easy chairs, two studio couches, and a king-size bed.

In the suite, the bargaining went on. When the price descended to two hundred Hong Kong dollars or twenty-five U.S. dollars a night—nobody wanted to deal in Chinese money in Xiamen—Tan abruptly called a halt to the negotiations and we left.

"Just what I was afraid of," he said, back in the street. "No matter how cheap I buy it, I can't make a profit here. There's no margin in a hotel so desperate for customers that it can be talked into renting a suite for twenty-five bucks."

Tan wasn't worried about the collapse of the hotel balloon. His backup was cement, and he knew exactly what profit margin to expect on it. He had explained the angle to me over an earlier dinner. There was a contract with an agency in Keelung, the main harbor of northern Taiwan, to ship cement produced in Fujian to the booming building sites of Taipei. The transaction was part of the most elaborate Xiamen masquerade of all, the disguised commerce that was making the city into an industrial and raw materials subsidiary of Taiwan, to the tune of several billion dollars' worth of imports and exports every year. Since Tiananmen Square and the start of the fire sale, this trade had grown at a breakneck pace, even though it remained technically as illegal as it had been in the 1950s, when

Chiang Kai-shek and Mao Zedong were pitching artillery shells at each other over the Formosa Strait, at Xiamen's very front door.

"No problem," Tan said. "No problem at all."

The cement would be loaded onto a ship in Xiamen, he said, then unloaded and reloaded at some small port elsewhere in Southeast Asia. For security's sake, Tan himself didn't know which port would handle the transaction. It was better for him not to know.

"What happens next," he continued, "is that new papers will be drawn up. Officially the cement won't be coming from China anymore. It will come from the other port."

That is, if the loading and unloading actually occurred. My own hunch was that Tan was telling more than there was to the story—that the middle port didn't exist. That it was as fictional as the paper identities of the men in the Lujiang Bar, and the priest and the Mormons, and myself. The cement—like the hundreds of Chinese construction workers who crossed the strait in the holds of Taiwanese fishing boats to work in Taipei—almost certainly made a beeline for Keelung.

The fire sale appeared to serve everyone's interests, Taiwan's as much as China's. Why bother with technicalities? Why share the loot with another port?

The fire sale was cynical stuff, all right. That wasn't lost on the Chinese who had been true believers. Especially the ones who had stopped believing and were drowning in their own reservoirs of cynicism.

Wei Dongli lived in an airy apartment in west Beijing, just off Fuxingmenwai Dajie, the broad central avenue of the capital that led straight to Tiananmen Square. She'd seen the May demonstrations in 1989 and heard the tanks rumble down Fuxingmenwai in the early morning hours of June 4, their treads crushing the street barricades the students had erected a few days earlier.

Two decades ago she had been a Red Guard, like my friend Liang Baihua, like all the big-city kids of her generation. Now she was an investment banker and an American citizen, a friend of a friend who'd given me her phone number in Beijing.

It would be an understatement to say that Dongli lacked sympathy for the students who seized Tiananmen Square and died in it. She hated them, she told me. "I wish more of them had been killed. I wish they'd really gotten the lesson they need."

But Dongli also hated, with passionate contempt, the government that sent the tanks into the square. She had equal measures of scorn for Li Peng, the hard-line premier, and Zhao Ziyang, the deposed reformer. She had learned to swear in New York, where she lived for six years with her now-divorced American husband, and she did it even better than Tan, especially when she got going on the subject of Tiananmen Square.

"The little fucks. They deserve each other."

That was Dongli's assessment of the confrontation between the pro-democracy movement and the government, and also of the whole cast of characters who attended the tragedy: the foreign diplomats, the nervous Hong Kong investors, and most assuredly, the Western press. We were all little fucks. She was a coldly unsentimental woman, except on a single unlikely topic. She missed the Cultural Revolution.

Wei Dongli had been fourteen, a Beijing middle school student, when she was recruited by the Red Guards in 1966 after Mao's famous swim in the Yangtze—that metaphorical dog paddle against the current that had been the signal for the youth of China to follow the party's radical line, to tear down the imprisoning structures of tradition and reason. A year later she was sent to a village in the province of Heilongjiang, "Black Dragon River," in the Chinese far north. She and her fellow students were told that their mission was to free the peasants from feudalism.

Then they were forgotten.

For six years Dongli and the other middle school children who'd been sent to the village lived in a vacuum. The peasants ignored them. The local party leaders, anxious to rock no ideological boats in the unstable times, left them alone.

These were teenagers, fourteen- and fifteen-year-old kids at the outset, imbued with a grossly exaggerated sense of their historical importance, dispatched beyond the reach of their parents and saddled with no teachers or any other adults to tell them what to do. And left to their own devices, they constructed what might have been the only truly communist society China ever knew.

It didn't work that way everywhere. Dongli's memory certainly wasn't Liang Baihua's—Dongli had been lucky enough to be sent to the countryside before the spasm of violence that was 1967 and 1968. But there's no doubt that what happened to her also happened to some of the others who wound up, ignored and forgotten, in rural outposts where there was nothing to do but make fantasy real.

"I was fifteen, remember. Very young. And I was totally on my own. I was happy."

We sat in a Korean restaurant, a joint venture backed by a Seoul investor, talking over a plate of grilled beef ribs. Dongli's office was in the same building, a block above the grim black tower on Jianguo-menwai Avenue that housed the China Investment and Trust Corporation.

It was a dream, when you thought about it: to be that age, in an autonomous world populated almost entirely by other teenagers. They made the best of it.

"We discovered, on our own terms, all the things that you are usually taught. Nobody explained to us how to act, what to think. Nobody preached. It was the most complete experience of freedom I will ever have, I know that."

Being fourteen and fifteen, they discovered sex very quickly. As much as Haight Ashbury in those same years, the China that Dongli and millions of others knew in their rural exile was a group grope, a wildly experimental introduction to carnal knowledge.

"Everybody slept with everybody else. All the girls with all the boys, some of the girls with other girls, some of the boys with other boys."

Who would have believed it, beyond the wall that then sepa-rated China from the rest of the world? Who would have imagined that those marching hordes in their baggy Mao suits, waving their little red books in the air, were consumed with good old-fashioned lust? But it wasn't just sex. There was that sense of mission, the mandate to construct a new society.

"Whatever we had, the few possessions that we carried north and the little food that was available, especially in the winter—it all had to be shared. Nothing was private, nothing was personal. People lived in one hut, in a group. We cooked together, worked out in the fields together. There wasn't room for jealousy or greed. There wasn't much to be greedy about. Cabbage and tofu and wheat noodles were what we ate, with maybe an egg once a month. Everyone had the same clothes."

Perfect communism. The withering away of the state. The final stage of the dialectic that Marx had envisioned, after the long painful struggle to eliminate exactly the things that Dongli and her friends had no room for in Heilongjiang. Society without jealousy, greed, or possessions.

Then one day in her twenty-first year, a party official came to the village. The antifeudalism campaign was over, he said. They could go back home now, to Beijing and Shanghai and wherever else they had come from.

Mao was in his dotage. Henry Kissinger and Richard Nixon were being feted in the Great Hall of the People. The line had changed. And before too long, even at party headquarters, they were saying that the old line, the one that sent them north, hadn't been just a mistake. It had been a catastrophe.

After the line changed, Dongli began to grow hard, to nourish the seeds of hatred for anyone who failed to comprehend that what had been taken away from her was freedom. Perfection. A life without conventional restraints.

Her parents in Beijing were strangers, and more than a little afraid of her. She tried living with the family of one of her lovers from Heilongjiang, the son of a high party official in Tianjin. The official wasn't crazy about the idea, but he couldn't control his son. He pulled strings to get the two of them into a university. It was a way of getting rid of them.

At the university, Dongli met Glen, one of the first U.S. students allowed to enter a formal course of studies at a Chinese institution. This was around 1978. They were married in 1980. I wanted to know more about the marriage, about the six years in New York. It made for such neat symmetry: six years on the Black Dragon River reinventing communism, then six years of reforging in the crucible of capitalism. But she brushed the questions aside.

"He said he loved me. I wanted to get out of China. We got married. We separated. I came back."

She came back on an American passport with an American economics degree, very useful instruments when the reforms of the 1980s took hold. She started using her given name in the Western manner rather than her family name, Wei.

Dongli acquired the reputation of a steely, dependable broker between the state bureaucracies that authorized joint ventures and the foreign investors who were once again knocking at China's door. She invested money of her own, and bought the apartment off Fuxingmenwai Dajie, in a complex built for the foreign residents of a reinternationalized Beijing.

But inside, she hated it all. Inside, she was in a village in Heilongjiang, free from all constraints, constructing the perfect communist society. Inside, she was living without jealousy, greed, and possessions, or the rage that consumed her when a new generation of the Chinese young shouted slogans about "democracy" and blindly aped the clothing and thinking of the West. They were everything she had been, turned inside out. "The little fucks," she called them. She was openly pleased when they were shot in the streets.

Wei Dongli made a great deal of money in the pump-primed economy that the party engineered after June 4, 1989. She knew she was a hypocrite. But the perfect communist state had been destroyed, and for her there was no longer any difference between hypocrisy and survival.

One week before the assault on Tiananmen Square—on the morning after I last saw her in Shanghai—Liang Baihua had flown nonstop into San Francisco Airport. She asked for and got a window seat, forgetting that it would be worthless on the eighteen-hour marathon over the empty North Pacific. Still, she couldn't sleep, and despite her anxieties—the possibility that there would be a final unexpected hitch in her escape from China—she shuffled through U.S. Immigration in a daze.

Maybe it was better that way. Maybe she seemed relaxed, less suspicious, less certain to be among the tens of thousands of Chinese whose student visas provided the thinnest of pretexts for disappearing into America's vast netherworld of the undocumented. An hour after she cleared customs she was on a Northwest flight to Detroit, the city I was raised in.

That wasn't my doing. If anything, I would have tried my best to discourage her, on the assumption that she would be more comfortable in California or New York, where there were plenty of other Chinese around. But the destination was already a fait accompli when I found her in that grim Shanghai walk-up at the end of May in 1989; it had been arranged by another of her American friends, a businessman who agreed to sponsor her university application and offered her a room in his suburban Detroit house.

She had been in America a year and a half when she told me about the arrival: The long sleepless flight. Her groggy answers to the U.S. Immigration officer's questions. The first glimpse of Michigan from the air, a patchwork quilt of small farms that stretched from the big lake to the sudden wall of factories and single-story suburbs that surrounded Metropolitan Airport.

We sat in a café in Greektown, a two-block island of ouzo bars, restaurants, and belly dance nightclubs near downtown Detroit. Liang sipped gingerly on the Turkish coffee I suggested. Some things were glossed over in the telling. Unspecified problems, for instance, had prompted her to move out of her sponsor's home within weeks of settling in.

"He was married when I met him in Shanghai. But now he is a bachelor again."

I told her I got the idea.

She was renting a two-room apartment on Cass Avenue, halfway between downtown, where she had found a job as a shipping clerk, and the campus of Wayne State University. It was convenient, within walking distance of the job and her business administration classes at Wayne, and it was much bigger and better furnished than the place in Shanghai. But standards are nothing if not relative, and in the American context there was no mistaking the symbolism of the boarded-up grocery store on the apartment building's street level and the dirt-streaked, peeling walls in her rooms. Liang had left a slum in Shanghai for one in Detroit.

The classes had at least brought Andrew into her life. Not that Andrew was an unmixed blessing. He was a professor at another university in southeast Michigan who did a guest spot in one of Liang's courses; she had stayed on, when the lecture was over, to ask him some questions, and wound up being invited to lunch. Things moved on apace after that.

From the first, whatever comforts Andrew offered were offset by the endless supply of confusions that he strewed in Liang's path. He was in fact confused himself, not entirely sure how his career had carried him here. The America he had aimed at back in Edinburgh was New York or Boston—Columbia or Harvard—and decidedly not a commuter university in the heart of the Rust Belt.

Andrew and Liang were actually rather alike in this matter. They had both been determined to escape something—in Andrew's case, it was the stagnant air of British politics in the 1970s and British scholarship in general. And they both landed by happenstance rather than design in the Motor City. A Detroiter happened to sponsor Liang's visa application; Detroit happened to be where Andrew was offered a job in 1977, when U.S. universities were not hiring as they had been.

It had backfired, of course. He was stuck in an irresolvable paradox now: a Marxist economist teaching marketing—marketing!—in the United States because that was what his department needed to have taught. For a Marxist there was no question, not after Gorbachev, of being able to move on to a different university. Andrew had begun his career believing he was in the vanguard of the future, and two decades later he was dead in his ideological tracks, a passenger on a parked caboose.

"I love the way he teaches his marketing classes," Liang told me in the café. "I ask him all the time, 'Why are you so unhappy?' He is a very good professor. He really understands how to sell things. His ideas about advertising are . . ."

She paused, searching for the word.

"His advertising ideas are dynamite!"

Liang beamed. It was exactly the word she wanted. I didn't know Andrew—their relationship was on a back burner the week I visited Detroit—but I could imagine how he'd feel about being described as a dynamite ad man.

The Marxism espoused by Andrew was among the more disconcerting of Liang Baihua's confusions in America. It had so many crevices, so many nooks and crannies that hadn't been part of the Marxism she knew in China. The ethnic and racial issues especially threw her. She was never quite clear on when you were supposed to bring ethnicity and race up and when you weren't.

"One night at a party I said I had been to a big Jewish department store in New York when I went to visit a cousin who lives there. The Jewish people at the party got very angry with me. They said it was anti-Semitic to call the department store Jewish. But the owners *are* Jewish, aren't they? Why are Jewish people ashamed of the store? It's so luxurious."

In an effort to make amends, she had only made matters worse: "I thought to myself, 'Liang, now you must show them you aren't against the Jewish people at all.' So I said how ashamed I was that my country had supported the PLO against Israel. But they were against Israel too!"

She had learned, on another uncomfortable evening, not to voice her fears of the young black men who hung out on her street corner late at night selling crack to the neighbors. Or at least, not to mention that they were black.

This America, with its (to her) unpredictable political sensitivities, hadn't figured in her plans any more than Detroit had in Andrew's. It was a mine field, but as long as she was seeing Andrew there was no avoiding it. All of his friends—in fact, it sometimes seemed to her, all of the professors she met at Wayne State and at Andrew's university—said they were Marxists, socialists, or sometimes even communists.

They bewildered her, and Liang in turn bewildered them. She was the first former Red Guard to enter their circle, to wile away the weekend evenings arguing politics over cheap red wine and overcooked spaghetti at Andrew's apartment. Liang was a woman who had been part of a moment that was engraved in their youths, a sister who had waved the little red book and trashed the establishment and combed her hair like Jiang Qing. She was one of the characters who appeared in the posters they'd hung on their dormitory walls in the sixties.

What an opportunity she was. What a disappointment.

I have this not from Liang, but from a mutual friend at Wayne, who observed her erratic passage through Andrew's tight little universe with a mixture of bemusement and embarrassment—for everyone.

"They'd try to trap her, you know. To get her to admit that Mao was on to something crucial, the genuine remaking of society. That maybe it all went awry because of CIA meddling or—just as Jiang Qing said—because of a rightist counterrevolution. But she never rose to the bait. And she'd say the damnedest things, almost as though *she* was trying to bait *them*. But she wasn't. She was just trying to be straight with them."

The most stubborn of Liang's persecutors, he said, was a fortyish woman named Lucy.

" 'But Liang,' Lucy would say, 'surely it wasn't all a mistake. Surely the idea of communal enterprise, communal action in the interest of society, is more just than the dog-eat-dog individualism we have in this country.'

"And then from Liang: 'What does that mean—"dog eat dog"?'

"Lucy was always throwing idioms at her that required explanation, and there would be a big detour in the conversation, with Liang asking about things like attitudes toward dogs and laughing in pleasure when she finally mastered the idiom and could use it herself in a future conversation. But finally she'd get back to the point, because Lucy wouldn't let go. And she'd say something like: 'Nobody was allowed to own their own house,' or 'The prices were set by the state and no matter how hard you worked or how smart you were, you couldn't get richer than anybody else.' "

The conversations always wound up at such dead ends, he said, with an uncomfortable silence broken only by Lucy's sotto voce whispers.

"She'd turn to Andrew or one of the other Saturday night regulars and say, just loud enough so that everyone could hear it, 'My God, she's a total reactionary.' "

Liang heard too. She was nobody's fool.

"Some of them don't care for me," she told me when I mentioned hearing from our mutual friend and alluded obliquely to some of the difficulties he had described.

"Some of the people I've met here have been nice for a while, but then it goes bad. We can't talk to each other frankly."

But how could she explain it to them? They lived in their words—they were the creatures of ideological abstraction. How could she explain what had happened with such words and abstractions in China, the violence they had wrought in her own life? The one time my friend was able to bring her out of the shell of silence she'd constructed around her past, Liang talked briefly about her years in the Manchurian steel plant.

"Eight years without hope," she told him. "It was eight years without any hope."

How could she explain it? Liang was no innocent. She knew that these people had their own struggles, that they were right to be concerned about justice. They were good people. Lucy was a good woman. But the issues had been simpler, much simpler, in China during the Cultural Revolution, when justice was meted out with a bullet in the back of the neck after trials that weren't trials, for crimes that had to do with words and phrases. In the China of the 1960s and 1970s there was only the broad concept of social justice, the "people's interest"—the very thing that seemed to be missing in America, as Lucy constantly said. But there was no justice for someone who began, for whatever reason, to feel separate from the mass. There was no justice for someone who longed for freedom.

How could she explain that?

The longing had brought her to America, which wasn't what she had expected. She hadn't expected the baffling arguments. She hadn't expected the blasted landscape of central Detroit, where the decline of the auto industry had driven out half the population and left hundreds of blocks of abandoned buildings in its wake. There were large parts of the city that were in far worse shape than Shanghai.

"It makes me ill to see it, Frank."

Finally, after all these years, she had stopped calling me "Mister."

"Many of these houses are larger than the largest flats in Shanghai, places that twenty Chinese would live in. And they are empty. The children set fire to them for play."

I felt ashamed, listening to her. The sheer waste of it was horrifying when you viewed it from her perspective. When you looked at it frontally, with the immediacy of a newcomer. When, as Lucy put it in an uncharacteristically charitable moment, you saw America with the eyes of someone "who doesn't know the history."

Liang hadn't reckoned on an America in decline. She hadn't anticipated the way her own ambitions, which were so fierce in China, could be suffocated by a lame employment market. She hated her job at the shipping firm, which exploited her intelligence with long hours and her fuzzy immigration status with low pay. She couldn't find anything else; she was stuck there, much as Andrew was stuck teaching marketing.

None of it was what Liang expected. But she would continue forward. She had come too far to turn back.

ASIAN NEWCOMERS
TOPS IN MONEY AND NUMBERS

WASHINGTON, D.C. (July 25, 1992) — For the first time in history, the number of Asian immigrants to the United States in the past decade exceeded those of all other groups, according to a new report on the 1990 census.

The report, issued by demographers Jeffrey Passel and Barry Edmonston of the Washington-based Urban Institute, noted that 37.3 percent of the nation's 7.3 million immigrants in the 1980s were born in Asia. Latin Americans were second with 35.3 percent of the total.

Well into the 1950s, the vast majority of America's immigrants came from Europe and Canada, the report's authors noted. "That ceased being true in the 1960s and it's not even close now," said Passel.

The Asian population in the United States doubled in the last ten years, to 7.3 million. An estimated 66 percent of Asian Americans are foreign-born.

In a related census study, the University of Louisville's Urban Research Institute reported that the median income of Asian American households soared to a level 18 percent above that of non-Hispanic white Americans during the 1980s. The finding reinforces a widely held view that Asians comprise the most outstanding economic success story in the long annals of U.S. immigration.

But researchers caution that the success has not been uniform. Census figures also show that the Asian poverty rate of 12.2 percent is almost 50 percent higher than that of whites.

DUST IN THE WIND

Floating. Always floating. It was the image that invariably came to mind when you read court transcripts on kids like Nam Tran. Up and down the West Coast they floated, stopping to knock off a gas station or a Seven-Eleven, then floating on, never lingering in any one place longer than it took to catch a few nights' sleep and find another car to hot-wire onto Route 5.

The cops in Orange County and San Jose and all the way up to British Columbia put the incident reports in the gang files, wedging them into the juvenile subset of organized crime that accommodated the Bloods and the East Side Locos and the Joe Boys. But the label didn't really fit. The term the Vietnamese used—the term that was tattooed on Tran's arm—was a lot closer to the truth: *bui doi*, "dust in the wind."

"Gang," after all, is a pretty specific concept. What's a gang without turf? What's a gang without a membership? That was the strangest thing about the *bui doi*, the thing that made it impossible for the police and everyone else to get a handle on the problem. They had no territory and no loyalties, not even to each other.

Tran had been implicated in an impressive string of crimes when the police caught up with him—extortion, burglaries, weapons violations, armed robberies. They were all in different cities, all with different partners, and under four different names: Nam Tran, Nam Sang, Nam Van, Xuan Huynh. His mug shot framed a painfully bony nineteen-year-old, with a perm combed back into gelled waves from a forehead rooster tail. When he was booked, the assistant D.A. told me, Tran answered questions in a sullen monotone, looking no one in the eye. I had been given the go-ahead to ask him a few questions of my own in the visitors' room at the Santa Clara County Jail, but Tran declined my invitation to tell his side of the story. He knew I wasn't a cop, that he didn't have to talk to me. All I could learn of him was what appeared in the D.A.'s computer printout and in a thick stack of faxed file pages from other police departments.

They drew a dot-matrix portrait of a life without connections. A life whose only structure seemed to be an archipelago of cheap motels that stretched from the Mexican border to Vancouver, the same motels that turned up again and again in the files on other Southeast Asian juveniles. Yet even this bare-bones framework bespoke the random.

As far as the cops could tell, a Vietnamese or Cambodian teenager would just check into one of the motels and wait. And when a couple more Asian kids checked in, kids who affected a certain recognizable style and manner, an understanding of sorts might ensue. An arrangement. A division of labor. A car would be acquired for the job, a target selected, plans laid.

You couldn't call it a bond. It was an understanding, that's all, valid no longer than it took to complete the job. It ended as soon as the money was on the motel room table. Some of the *bui doi* were girls who turned tricks at the motels to stay alive between robberies, and usually they took the boys as lovers. But that always ended too. After the job it was back on the float, alone. The car was left somewhere on a dark street in the next city up the freeway. It was the last thing they had in common.

Tran wouldn't name names for the cops when they grabbed him in San Jose and a computer check sketched his trail up and down the motel archipelago. He never identified his partners, not a single one. He couldn't. He didn't know any of their names. They were all dust in the wind.

The wind had begun blowing a decade before Tran was born, in fierce draughts of chemical fire that carried away families, villages, whole towns, leaving the occasional infant alive by sheer chance under a toppled piece of furniture or out in a paddy field, alone among the corpses. A few of them would be found by a mop-up squad and sent to a hospital in Saigon or Da Nang. Later some would ride a second gust of the wind, blown in a fleet of ramshackle refugee boats over the South China Sea.

That was one starting point, the randomness of airborne death, the randomness of survival. But it was not the only one.

For others in the archipelago the floating began in a night of momentary passion, riven of all attachment, in a Saigon bordello—a foreshadowing, in its way, of those nameless motel room couplings in America a generation later. These lovers were also teenagers: a Vietnamese girl lost to the wartime streets, a boy of eighteen or nineteen from a midwestern suburb or a Bronx housing project. Their children were the first to be called *bui doi,* in Vietnam itself, where they were despised, abandoned by both of the worlds that had spawned them, caught between irreconcilable opposites. They lived in the streets, on handouts, until a guilt-stricken American government packed them onto chartered planes in the late 1980s and ferried them to the United States. The flights came too late; in the heart, where it mattered, a lot of Amerasian kids still couldn't reconcile their Asian eyes with fawn-blond hair or a head of tight African curls. Halfway around the world from Vietnam, they went back to the streets.

Finally there was the line that led to Tran, the Chinese line.

Tran's grandparents were Cantonese who'd probably come to French Indochina in the 1930s, fleeing from the chaos of civil war. They settled in Cholon, the Chinatown of a million people across the river from Saigon. There was never any love lost between the Chinese of Cholon and their reluctant Vietnamese hosts; after the French left, the distaste grew as Chinese merchants acquired enormous real estate holdings and supplanted Europeans in Saigon's trading firms and rice brokerages. It was the old story in Southeast Asia: To the Vietnamese way of thinking, the Chinese were and always would be different.

But by the late 1970s, when Tran was born, it was hard to pinpoint what these differences were, beyond money, because most second-generation Chinese in Saigon could neither speak Chinese nor read it. Almost as much as the Amerasians, they struggled in the currents between two cultures, too Vietnamese for their own families and too Chinese for Vietnam. Saigon provided their primary education in floating, an education they brought to the boats and the camps and on to America—often with no more than one parent left alive, or an uncle, loosely defined.

The wind of chance carried them to the West Coast, the same random wind that deposited the half-breed GI babies and the orphans of chemical war. Then it picked them up again and sent them spinning into the inconceivable void of the motel archipelago.

When the wind first began pushing fleets of refugees over the South China Sea at the end of the 1970s, there were no Southeast Asians in San Jose and only 135,000 in the entire United States.

Ten years later there were nearly a million Southeast Asians in America, and in some city neighborhoods, especially in California, Vietnamese was now the most common language spoken at home. Across the greater San Francisco Bay Area, with San Jose at its southern flank, one hundred thousand Vietnamese had settled in by 1990—more than in any other two U.S. states combined. Of twenty-two Vietnamese daily newspapers, magazines, and regularly scheduled television programs in the United States, fifteen were based in the Bay Area. Their pages and broadcasts carried advertisements for Vietnamese lawyers, car dealers, insurance agents, and financial consultants; they ran reviews of Vietnamese country and western, blues, and rap concerts; their classified sections were crammed with ads, in both English and Vietnamese, for homes and businesses.

It was a whole society layered over the existing social landscape of northern California and adopting wholesale its characteristic features—so much so that it seemed that most Vietnamese had Americanized effortlessly, that they had moved, without a backward glance, from refugee despair to solid middle-class respectability. These were the images that charmed the media: Immigrant Vietnamese businessmen who founded computer firms in the Silicon Valley half a dozen years after they landed in the United States. Immigrant students who had arrived in America at thirteen speaking no English at all and graduated at the top of their high school classes, National Merit finalists with Harvard and Stanford scholarships waiting for them.

There was nothing false about these images or the phenomenal resolve that made them possible. But they were incomplete, and not only because the "model minority" (the favored media term) they summed up ignored the existence of the motel archipelago. Whatever the appearances, Vietnamese America was in fact a society of its own, a model of nothing. It had to be, because the inner life of a people, its sense of distinctiveness, is too tenacious to disappear in ten years. Vietnamese America was a separate society, with profound internal complexities that outsiders seldom recognized. And more: It was an emblem of a separate universe, transported over the Pacific in what sometimes seemed a single enormous wave, but weighted down with the nuances of three thousand years of history. Put simply, the wave made the San Francisco Bay Area the most Asian city in the world outside Asia, a city with close to 1.5 million residents of Chinese, Filipino, Korean, Japanese, Indian, or Indochinese ancestry, six times the number in 1970.

But it couldn't be put simply, not when the immigrants pouring into California included people like the fifty thousand Laotian Hmong who had time-traveled from prehistory to the San Joaquin Valley, and the ten thousand engineers from Taiwan and Hong Kong who made up the backbone of the advanced research work force in the Silicon Valley.

Nothing about this patchwork quilt of new immigrantion was simple. What did it mean, for instance, to say that the Chinese were now the largest single ethnic group in the Bay Area? The Chinese of the new California were Cantonese and Hokkien and Hakka and Teochew from the south, twice-immigrant Chinese sojourners, like Tran, from all over Southeast Asia, northern Manchurians and Shandongese from Korea, Shanghainese and Beijingers from both China and Taiwan. They spoke languages most Californians had never heard of: Putonghua Mandarin, Shanghaihua, Fukienhua, Teochew, Kechia, and at least four separate dialects of Cantonese, in variations so infinite that a Cantonese from Thailand often couldn't understand a Cantonese from Canton, and a Cantonese from Hong Kong or San Francisco's Chinatown couldn't understand either one.

All of these newcomers were governed by their own traditional behavioral codes, their own webs of rules. None was more Byzantine than the one that ensnared the Vietnamese; it was a web laden not only with the weight of an ancient culture, but also with a terrible recent history.

They even had a term for it: *nho nha,* which translates literally as "remembering home."

Although the term conveys something of the universal exile's longing for the lost past, *nho nha* differed from its analogues among other exile groups in its rigid refusal to surrender to fatalism. It implied that the past wasn't, would never be allowed to be, lost. To respect *nho nha* was to support a parallel—but to the outsider invisible—Vietnamese society that was imported intact from Vietnam and was as complete as the hyphenated American society of Vietnamese law firms, Vietnamese car dealerships, and Vietnamese beauty queens and high school valedictorians. It was complete down to an imported political order that ruled an imported world.

In the 1970s, Do Khien Nhieu had been the mayor of Saigon, running a city of two million that was then the hub of Southeast Asia. In 1990, a tip led me to him in the mail room of San Francisco's City Hall, where he sorted letters to the mayor of a city of 735,000. He wasn't happy about being found, proving only marginally more talkative than Nam Tran. "Ever since I come to America," he said, "I follow a policy of keeping a low profile."

That was it, period. He told me he had nothing more to say, and was true to his succinct word.

Mayor Do was the embodiment of the parallel society of *nho nha.* By day, he was a mail room clerk. By night, according to my sources, he was a member of a group of former South Vietnamese army officers making plans for retaking the homeland from the communists. People called them "the old comrades."

They were one of several—nobody knew exactly how many—Vietnamese paramilitary organizations that operated out of the San Francisco Bay Area. Most were headed by high officials like Do who had been the warlords of the toppled regime. One answered to former vice air marshal Nguyen Cao Ky, who lived in Westminster, an Orange County suburb of Los Angeles. A second was loyal to former president Nguyen Van Thieu, who ostensibly resided in a Florida retirement community but was said to spend most of his time in San Jose, which was so rife with ex–South Vietnamese military that Vietnamese referred to it as "the city of the colonels."

That San Jose was invisible to non-Vietnamese. It was *nho nha,* and so were its rules. The most important of these were uncompromising hostility to the communists and unblinking insistence that there be no relations, diplomatic or otherwise, between Washington and Hanoi. In the late 1980s, a few Vietnamese newspaper editors and journalists who tested that rule, suggesting that it was time to build bridges to the homeland, were maimed or killed by car bombs or shot down by masked assassins in front of their families.

There was also money to be made on *nho nha,* a fact that bothered the believers because it sapped their cause. The grapevine hummed with suspicion that the cash collected by some of the colonels went to real estate brokers in Orange County and Miami Beach instead of to the purchase of weapons and ammunition. There was a Vietnamese restaurant chain that had grown into an empire in a few short years, with outlets in six American cities, on capital that had no apparent explanation or source. There were plenty of small merchants who made regular "contributions" to "cultural funds" that built no monuments—or funded no successful sabotage operations in Vietnam, which was understood to be their hidden purpose—a decade after young toughs had begun showing up each month on collection rounds.

Indictments were seldom, if ever, issued in these cases. Nobody, even in the families that had lost husbands and fathers, seemed to know anything about the killings. None of the merchants lodged complaints against the collection racketeers. From the Vietnamese point of view it was all an internal matter, part of that separate world just below the surface where the immigrant striving, the hard work, took on a separate meaning. To respect *nho nha* was to build in America, but only for the day of return to Vietnam. It was to acknowledge the power of a bitter, unforgiving violence.

That was the meeting point between the paramilitary groups and the *bui doi,* who sometimes served as collection agents for the rackets and always limited their own crimes to the refugee community; even the Seven-Elevens they robbed were franchises held by Cambodians or Vietnamese. It was an internal matter, not part of the visible world, and in its own way an expression of *nho nha.* A refusal to forget.

The simple facts, the population figures and rising incomes, were just numbers. They didn't explain anything as relatively straightforward as the languages the new California spoke, much less something as murky as *nho nha* or the motel archipelago. It was all a puzzle, and most other Californians were willing to shrug their shoulders at it, to write it off as inscrutable or to ignore it altogether. Very few made any effort to pick up the puzzle's pieces, turn them in the light, edge them into a decipherable pattern.

Officer Richard Calderon of the San Jose Police Department, the man who arrested Nam Tran, was not most Californians. He stuck out like a sore thumb at the Thanh Hung Sports Club, and he knew it. A six-foot-two-inch, two-hundred-pound Chicano cop fills a lot of space in a Vietnamese pool hall. Across the cavernous room, men glanced up discreetly from eleven billiard tables, then bent back over the games. The proprietor self-consciously arranged and rearranged a cluster of pencils on his counter. Shots collided and caromed, echoing off the walls. Seated under a portrait of Pope John Paul II and a clock made of billiard balls, a wispy boy tried to look older than his twelve years.

The kid could be a runaway, and on a later pass through the room, Rich planned to talk with him. But that wasn't why he was showing the flag, walking ostentatiously back and forth through a warrenlike commercial mall off First Street with a reporter in tow. Between stops at the Thanh Hung, a couple of Vietnamese-Chinese video shops, a shoe stall, an aquarium, and a noodle joint, the cop was watching a young man we'll call Sonny Minh, who may or may not have been the cocaine dealer that the Street Crimes Detail had been hearing about.

"I've seen him hanging out in too many places downtown," Rich said. "Something about him doesn't add up, and I want him to know that I'm interested."

An hour passed, then a second hour. Sonny wandered into the pool hall. A short distance behind, we followed. Sonny stopped to shoot the breeze with the noodle man. Rich joined them. On the surface everything was cool. Sonny told Rich that he was in the clothing business, apropos of nothing. Rich asked if he could order a suit.

"Sure, anytime."

Sonny shrugged and walked slowly away.

"I'd like this guy to get a little nervous and head for his car," Rich told me. "A license plate number can be a handy thing."

But the cat-and-mouse game was wearing thin, reaching the point of diminishing returns. We exited into the blazing noonday sun. A few blocks down First, we entered a small restaurant.

"Nong lam," Rich said, wiping his brow.

"Nong lam," the fry chef answered. "Yes, yes, Richard, very hot today."

This was a different Rich, all smiles through a lengthy conversation in Vietnamese that, he later explained, touched variously on the price of pork, wedding customs, children, and rice noodles, as well as the torrid temperature. It was only at the very end of the discussion, seemingly as an inconsequential afterthought, that the chef gently nudged him into the men's room for a look at some fresh graffiti. But the message Rich was looking for—the signature of one of the collection rackets—wasn't there.

"It's just kids, harmless stuff. No one's after you."

The cook was visibly relieved. "I've got to move on now, Chef," Rich said, "but I'll check back with you again in a couple of days."

The shift was just beginning for Officer Richard Calderon, the man that San Jose's Little Saigon calls Cao Van Duc: "Mister Virtue."

*   *   *

Mister Virtue's story began on a rainy winter night in 1970, when Richard Calderon was handcuffed in the back seat of a police squad car and a cop named Bob Grant caught something, some nuance, in the way this tough Chicano kid moved and talked. A reason to throw away the department book. Grant took it on himself to accept responsibility for Rich Calderon. The two officers who'd picked him up, after a bloody altercation at a party, knew enough of Grant's successes with such oddball impulses to go along with the idea, and released their prisoner to his custody.

He was taking a big chance. The San Jose police records identified Rich Calderon with the gang scene, and on this particular night he had nearly brained somebody in a fight. Rich was a hard case. He understood what it was like to find yourself on the wrong street and have a knife stuck into you. Like Nam Tran, he knew how it felt when assault charges were read to you by an assistant D.A. anxious to reserve a bunk in your name at Folsom State Prison. But that's where the similarity ended. In most ways, Richard Calderon in 1970 was the mirror image of Nam Tran: alike only in a broad reflection whose pertinent details were reversed.

On the East Side of San Jose where Rich grew up, "gang" wasn't a grab-bag label; it meant something solid, permanent, fixed. There were Chicano gangs in the flatlands south of San Francisco Bay that dated back three generations, with sons succeeding fathers in the ranks and grandfathers waxing nostalgic over memories of the same battle nicknames that their grandsons now carried into street fights. These were real gangs, classics in the genre; they were about turf and tradition and belonging to something bigger than yourself and being willing to do anything, absolutely anything, to maintain connection.

For Rich Calderon, who was already a muscular 190 pounds at seventeen and as quick on his feet as a sprinter, "anything" could be plenty, certainly enough to crack a skull and earn that bunk at Folsom. And as it happened, to catch Bob Grant's eye. Grant was a wrestling buff. Not the kind who sits in front of a television set watching overmuscled costume actors dance around a circus ring. He was the kind who can spot genuine athletes and light the fire of serious ambition under them. It wasn't just the size of this kid that he noticed, although that was the first thing. It was that and the way he answered questions, with a sharpness that said his mind was as quick as his feet.

Bob Grant talked to Rich. And in the beginning, like Nam Tran, Rich answered because he figured he didn't have any choice. But Grant wasn't about to be satisfied with that. He pushed for more. He pushed for real conversation. And he didn't just talk. He listened. He was determined to get to this kid, to save this one—to cross the gulf that separated an Irish cop from a Chicano street fighter. Bob Grant wouldn't leave Rich Calderon alone.

He concentrated on his hunch that this big rowdy punk would make a hell of a wrestler. It gave the two of them something to work on together—a means of connection for Grant and a nod to the machismo in Rich, an alternative to the parties and the street fights that nobody could construe as chicken shit.

The hunch was correct, paying off beyond Grant's wildest imaginings. It brought Rich Calderon a state championship his senior year at Overfelt High. It brought him a silver medal in the Pan-American Games in 1974. It won him a spot on the 1976 U.S. Olympic team.

In 1978, Rich told Bob Grant something else that he'd never imagined possible. He said he was applying to the Police Academy.

Fifteen years later, Rich was still surprised that he pulled it off. "My family and friends thought I was nuts. Police were not the people you wanted to become if you were Mexican. The idea was 'Cops don't like us,' and 'We don't like them.' That was that."

But somehow he sold it to them. And in 1982, Officer Richard Calderon was assigned to the Street Crimes Detail in downtown San Jose. Pretty soon, he noticed that he was irrelevant.

Whatever suspicions a Mexican-American family in East San Jose had of cops, they were mild by comparison with the views Vietnamese brought with them to the United States. The views that were deeply imbedded in *nho nha*.

In Saigon, the cops were literally criminals. South Vietnam's two largest law enforcement agencies, the Security Police and the Municipal Police, were both openly controlled by the Binh Xuyen, a racketeering outfit that held a monopoly on gambling, opium trafficking, and prostitution and exacted bribes on the import and sale of rice, fish, and pork.

Ten years after the first Southeast Asian refugees moved into rotting apartment buildings in central San Jose, five years after their numbers had soared to seventy-five thousand in the city and their hard work had built a prosperous Little Saigon downtown, the Vietnamese still never talked to cops. Not just about *nho nha:* If there were robberies, stick-ups, assaults, extortions in Little Saigon that were the sad commonplaces of American life and unrelated to the parallel world, the San Jose Police Department didn't know about them either, not officially. They knew only of the occasional rumor, the whispered murmurings.

Nobody called the station house. Nobody paid attention to Richard Calderon.

He told me about it over a coffee in the Dac Phuc, a joint on Santa Clara Street where Vietnamese journalists hang out. He hadn't been enthusiastic about taking a reporter around—it was the department's idea; Chief MacNamara had this thing about press relations— and I suspected he hoped one of the journalists in the Dac Phuc would join us and shift my attention to a different kind of story. But that didn't happen, and with time he got used to the fact that I'd be around awhile.

A flush rose in his face when he spoke about the frustration he had felt at the beginning. Rich Calderon wasn't used to losing.

"I thought about it all the time that first year, when I would spend a whole week on the beat without anybody so much as looking at me. I thought: I changed my own family's ideas about cops. Why can't I do it for the Vietnamese, too? Why?"

There was no answer until Roger Phong taught Rich to say hello. Phong was a restaurateur in San Jose, dishing out big bowls of *pho,* the beef noodle soup that Vietnamese eat for breakfast and lunch. He had a modest shop on Santa Clara Street, one of the few places downtown where a cop could expect more than dead silence with his lunch. No one knew what Phong's life had been in Vietnam, but it was clearly not *pho.* He was an immensely cultivated man who read scholarly works on Asian and European history. Rich Calderon had never met anyone quite like him.

"He could speak French, Spanish, and Cantonese, as well as Vietnamese and English. Meanwhile, I couldn't say a thing, not even hello, in the language of the people I was supposed to be protecting. That's crazy. So one morning, I decided it was time to do something about it. I asked Mr. Phong how to greet him in Vietnamese."

Phong looked Rich in the eye, and saw whatever it was that Bob Grant had seen. He decided to educate Officer Richard Calderon.

Soon the cop was toting around a notebook in the pocket above his police revolver, jotting down useful words, checking translations and pronunciations with Phong, and gradually making every Vietnamese merchant on his downtown beat into an ad hoc professor. The notebook was succeeded by a second, then a third and a fourth. Rich Calderon took his homework with him everywhere he went. He'd chat in Vietnamese with his Anglo and Chicano buddies at the station house, just for the practice of forming the sounds, then provide English and Spanish translations. A tape recorder always sat on the front seat of his unmarked police Buick, enunciating stock phrases and sentences:

"*Giup do nguoi nao*"—"to come to someone's aid."

"*Troi het tanh mua*"—"The rain has stopped falling."

"*Toi nhan thay rang toi da lam*"—"I find that I was mistaken."

The complex tones and semantic back alleys of Vietnamese make it one of the most difficult languages in the world. Depending on its spoken inflection, the monosyllable *bo* may mean a bundle or an ox, an old servant or a medicinal restorative, to sweep away, spit, place, crawl, or strike, to appoint or name, a pretension or a collection, a government ministry, large or profitable, crumbling or worthwhile, border or shore, father, abandonment, friend, or chamber pot. Rich Calderon learned, through painful experience, that *cu,* the word for "uncle," which is respectfully used as a salutation for older men, translates as "penis" if it is mispronounced. That *choi* can mean "entertain" or "get laid." That *de* is both "easy" and "horny."

In the beginning, when Rich tried out his phrases on people in the streets or on merchants in the noodle parlors and video shops of downtown San Jose, they just turned away, often with a muffled laugh. But he kept at it. It was like wrestling practice, like the early times with Bob Grant. That was the most important lesson Grant had taught him, not to give up.

Eventually, people stopped laughing when Rich made outrageous mistakes. They'd correct him. Then one day they started responding to his questions, answering him in Vietnamese, patiently, so he would understand and learn more. And the police department started receiving calls, very slowly at first, about problems. About the *bui doi* and their stickups. Even, sometimes, about the paramilitary groups and the fund-raising rackets.

The callers always asked for Cao Van Duc, "Mr. Virtue." It was the name Roger Phong gave Rich when he reached a certain plateau that more than satisfied his teacher, when he began to understand meanings beyond what the words said. Getting the name, Rich thought, was like making the Olympic team.

The pool halls and noodle joints of Little Saigon, the runaways and graffiti: They became a kind of code for Cao Van Duc, a measure of the distance he'd traveled since Roger Phong taught him to say hello. Slowly, painstakingly, he was beginning to read it. He was after the subtext, the one that would move him past the easy stuff—Sonny Minh, dodging through the warrens off First Street, was easy, a conventional dope dealer—and into the world below.

That kid back in the Thanh Hung: He could be headed for the motel archipelago, following the road that carried Nam Tran to prison. He could be floating.

The graffiti in the restaurant: One day it might lead Rich somewhere, bring him a level deeper into the secret of *nho nha*.

It would be better—even Rich said this—if the San Jose police could recruit Vietnamese and Cambodians for the force. But the moment hadn't come yet; the willingness to talk to Cao Van Duc was the thinnest of wedges in a thick emotional wall. Maybe the opening would be large enough to convince Southeast Asians to become policemen in a couple of years. Or maybe ten. Or maybe never.

There is a numbing, dispiriting flatness to the landscape of San Jose. The city doesn't have the dramatic hills of San Francisco or a respectable river like Saigon's. It sprawls over the southern mudflats of the bay in an endless blanket of single-story, look-alike subdivisions. But it draws people. It has factories and jobs. It is a big place and growing, big enough to hold a panoply of dreams and the usual urban terrors. San Jose doesn't look like a major city, but it *is* one, full of codes and confusions. A Babel. In one small corner of it, one cop wanted to make sense of what he heard, partly because another cop, twenty years ago, had done the same thing.

It was 3:30 P.M., more than ten hours after Rich Calderon had shown up at the station house to answer an emergency call in Little Saigon—a call, like so many, that no one else was equipped to handle. He was tired, he said, but he still had a few shops to visit, a few questions to ask, when a white teenager crossed Sixth Street in front of us. His scalp was shaved clean, except for a ring of light fuzz on the rear of his head that encircled a tattoo of an iron cross. The fierce heat notwithstanding, he wore high black boots, black corduroy slacks, a black vest over a thermal undershirt. The fingers of his right hand were also tattooed, sequentially, with the letters N-A-Z-I. He fit the rough description of a skinhead who had beaten up an elderly Vietnamese man nearby a few days before. Rich flashed his badge, said he wanted to call in an identity check, explained why. They talked.

"So, this tattoo," Rich said. "Does it mean you're a real Nazi, or just aspiring? I don't know too much about you guys—what are the goals of your group?"

The initial answer was "aspiring," period. But the teenager, who said his name was James, became more voluble as he realized he was not about to be summarily arrested.

"I mean, I don't do what skinheads usually do, like cutting down anybody who is not white, like a gook or something. But I still think of myself as a skinhead, because I feel we have to put the Aryans, meaning us whites, back on top."

Rich listened politely, waiting for a reply on his radio.

"You know," James continued, "we got to deal with the problem that us whites are outnumbered by these other races in our own country. But I don't believe in just bashing them anymore either."

The radio squawked back a negative on the identity check. Although there were no grounds on which to hold James any longer, Rich clearly regarded him as trouble waiting to happen.

"Do you mind if I take your picture for our files? I've got a Polaroid in my car. It'll take me just a minute to go get it."

"Sure, man. I got nothing to hide."

The scene hangs in the memory: Rich Calderon peering intently through the camera. James, half-scowling, half-smiling, leaning against the fence of a used car lot. Two baffled Vietnamese grannies watching from the sidewalk.

EPILOGUE:
THE LAST OF THE HMONG

Xong Vang was six years old when the Hmong began their journey out of the Laotian highlands, about to spend the next four years in the Ban Vinai refugee camp on the west bank of the Mekong. She was one of those children pictured in the tribal embroideries—"story cloths," they call them—endlessly fleeing an endless war.

Today she is an animated study in mascara and permed hair, wearing large round earrings and a necklace of gold hearts over a striped pullover with just the right amount of fashionable droop. "C'mon in, you guys," she says at the door of her family's home in Fresno, California. "Take a seat."

Xong has perfected the full repertoire of speech affectations favored by girls her age from Miami to Anchorage: sentences opened with "like," an exaggerated fondness for the phrases "I mean" and "you know." She is sweet sixteen, Miss American Teen. Of her first ten years—the war in Indochina, the escape from Laos, the crossing of the Mekong, the Thai camp—"I don't remember anything at all," she says.

This is what virtually every Hmong teenager insists. The slate is a blank before their arrival in the United States. They remember nothing.

"We left Laos in 1976, I think," says Xong's cousin Teng Lee, who has just turned eighteen. "I read a book about what happened there."

His brother Ka, a lanky sixteen-year-old in running shorts and a Fresno High T-shirt, shrugs his shoulders when asked about his arrival in the San Joaquin Valley. "I dunno," he answers, "That was a long time ago."

The Lees moved to Fresno four years ago.

"My friends and I, we don't ever talk about these things, you know," says Xong. "I mean, we usually talk about our boyfriends. Like how hard it is breaking up, and whether it's better to let him go or should you try to hold on to him."

"What does Laos mean to you?" I ask.

She pauses for several minutes before answering. "When I think of Laos," she finally says, "it is a lot of trees. It's not like America. No TV, no buildings, an old place."

She pauses again. "My mother and father pray and pray to go back."

In a photograph, the Vang family stands before the Fresno house where we meet: Xong at center left next to her sister Kia, parents to the rear, several more siblings to the right. The house is a classic San Joaquin Valley frame bungalow fronted by a picket fence. Xong's mother wears a plaid oxford shirt. Her father, smiling, waves jauntily at the camera. Out of context, this single portrait speaks of the familiar, the normal—a whole family as thoroughly Americanized as Xong. In fact, there is as little of America on the slate of Kuo Pao Vang as there is of Laos on his daughter's.

"My parents don't speak much English," says Xong. "Just 'yes' and 'no,' 'me' and 'you.' My mom tried to learn. You know, she took these adult classes. But the lights in the classroom made her dizzy, and one day she threw up. So she stopped going. My dad, he says that there must be something wrong with his brain. He says it isn't able to learn anything anymore."

Kuo Pao Vang sits quietly on the couch as we talk, getting up every now and then to walk to the kitchen or bathroom. He never says a word.

In the wedding portrait atop their television set, Bee Xiong is the thin, introspective eighteen-year-old groom. Yer Vang, then seventeen, is his bride, smiling fiercely into the camera lens. They are two years older when I visit them in San Jose. Bee is employed as a sander in a furniture factory. They have an eleven-month-old daughter. Her name is Julia.

Their home is a small, sparsely furnished apartment just west of the Golden State Freeway near downtown. The building hasn't seen paint or even perfunctory maintenance in a very long time.

What was once a lawn is a garden of weeds and windblown newspapers. The walls of the foyer are smeared with graffiti: FUCK OFF! JOE BOYS. PUTA.

The rent is $575 a month, more than half of Bee's gross pay before taxes. There's almost nothing left after food and utility bills. To make ends meet, Bee and Yer have taken in a boarder, Nia Her, twenty, another Hmong, whose bed occupies a corner of the living room.

The fathers of Bee and Yer are dead; their mothers remain in Laos. Nia lost touch with his family in 1977, when he was sent away from the Plain of Jars for his own safety. After months in the jungle, Nia, Bee, Yer, and a few of their siblings turned up in the refugee camps, alone. Alone, they had swum across the Mekong, clutching lashings of bamboo to stay afloat. They were not yet ten years old.

In the apartment kitchen, Yer is stirring a pot of tomato sauce. "Bee loves pizza and spaghetti," she says.

Outside, on a trash-strewn street where two junked cars rust in abandonment, the eccentric, surrealistic drama of American immigration plays on. Four Buddhist nuns, heads shaved and limbs garbed in loose white gowns, walk past. On a balcony, several Gujuratis chat over tea. A Salvadoran boy runs up the apartment staircase and down again. There are also Cambodian, ethnic Lao and Vietnamese refugees on the block, says Yer. Yet it is as if they were all impelled here by utterly personal impulses, rather than by any shared calamity; no one ever mentions Indochina, the war. American-style privacy is the rule.

There is *nho nha* here, the silent refusal to forget, the intention to preserve a separate world. But there is a paradox, too: the inevitable loss of memory.

They came to San Jose from the San Joaquin Valley, Bee succinctly explains, "because there is work."

He is a reticent conversationalist. "Basically I like the job," he says. "It's a small company with not so many workers: Filipinos, blacks, whites. We get along pretty well."

After a great deal of prodding by Yer, he adds that, yes, sanding can be hard, dirty work. That he wishes the pay were a bit higher. That their rent could be lower. That there is too much traffic in San Jose. These may seem the gentlest of complaints, but they represent an enormous stride forward; slowly, Bee Xiong is developing a taste for Yankee skepticism.

Yer is already there. "Those problems in Fresno, in the valley: the men sitting around all day with nothing to do. Maybe it's because there are just too many Hmong out there. "Maybe it's better to go out on your own."

In Fresno, where Yer met Bee, more than 80 percent of Hmong adult males are still on public assistance, marooned in a world that speaks a language they can't understand. These are the very men who fought a twenty-year secret war, who led their families down from Phou Bia Mountain, across the Mekong and the Pacific, and then across the American continent. Many have become de facto hermits, refusing to leave their apartments for weeks at a time. The children do the translating at supermarkets, find the jobs at McDonald's that buy the family cars, take the driver's license exams and read the welfare department notices.

"If you live among other people," Yer says, "you have no choice but to learn English, to learn how to do things for yourself. In Fresno, you can get by just being with other Hmong all the time. But what happens if you get sick? You can't even go to a hospital without help. I don't want that. I don't want it for my daughter or for us."

Bee listens until she has finished. "I think many more Hmong will be coming to San Jose," he says.

Half a generation has passed since the first of the Hmong arrived in America. Half a generation ago, a man named Moua Dang led the first of their junkyard caravans west, searching—as the tribe had always searched—for a new beginning that would leave them whole. A people. The *hmong*: "free men."

They had come to be emblematic for me in their fierce insistence that the past and the future could be reconciled. I wanted to believe that a slender strand of continuity could be preserved somehow. That history didn't have to be a constant process of stark divorces between beginnings and ends. For myself as much as for them, I wanted the Hmong to prove it.

That's why I've driven out to the valley on an August morning when the air hangs listlessly over Route 99—the same road that carried Moua Dang and Palee to the migrant workers' camps in 1976—and I am reminded of so many other sweltering days on the distant margins of the South China Sea. Heat and humidity will always do that to me after a dozen years on the road in Asia.

Moua had disappeared back in the mid-1980s, after the great Hmong exodus to California. It was unexpected, a short resignation letter sent to the Lao Family Community, the tribal social agency he himself had founded in 1982, and then a gap that took many months to fill. Moua had been the man with answers. The man who was waiting in the Central Valley when the Hmong U-Hauls and over-loaded Buicks pulled in from the East Coast. The man who figured out how to feed and clothe a population that at some points was growing by more than five thousand a month. There are people in his tribe who will never understand Moua Dang's decision.

There's the natural compulsion to wonder what happened to him, to wonder why he suddenly quit. But more than that is behind my return to the valley, although I know I won't be able to explain it to Moua. It's that need for reassurance, some sense of connection between beginnings and ends. I hadn't mentioned it on the phone. I don't mention it now, as we talk in the midafternoon, leaning against a cyclone fence.

Moau's face is creased and weathered from the dry heat of the San Joaquin summer. At 5:00 A.M. he had risen to feed 650 animals while Palee made breakfast for the children, who now number five, and headed to her current job as a nutritional aide at the Merced Family Health Center. He shakes his head, wipes the bill of a cap reading JOHN DEERE across his brow. He's heavier now, a little paunchy around the middle, but his shoulders are still blocky and powerful. The presence is still there. Lines fan out from his eyes, crinkle as he speaks.

"My wife and I hardly see each other anymore. There's always something to do. The hogs are experts at breaking troughs and pipes, so I have to be expert at fixing them. When the sows are ready, they all seem to foal at once. Some days last forty-eight hours."

Moua Dang is now a farmer. Not the Hmong kind of farmer, working common fields with other members of his clan, but an American farmer, struggling alone. An individualist. An entrepreneur, a long way from the tribal society of the Plain of Jars.

This is not the dream that seized Moua in Richmond, Virginia, in the dark winter of 1976, the dream that drove the Hmong on one unimaginable exodus through the Laotian jungle and a second over the plains and mountains of America. This is not the re-creation of an ancient tribal world in a new land. Moua's dream, the dream of a new future for the Hmong—as a people, a tribe—failed. He knew that in 1985, when he set out on a very different path.

It has been nip and tuck, running the piggery, overseeing two Merced grocery stores he has an interest in, paying off a welter of small loans from relatives and friends that finance his operation.

"I've got to make good," Moua says.

"You have to understand: I didn't resign because I wanted to end my duty to my people. But I got tired of fighting for charity every year. If you don't have your own job and money in America, people don't take you seriously. They won't even talk to you. If I couldn't sell myself—couldn't prove that I could be a success—the county and the state would never take any of the Hmong seriously.

"I tell everyone: We have to build for the next decade, the next generation."

Moua is pensive. In the distance a neighbor's irrigation pumps beat out a regular rhythm, filling the ditches around peach trees that hang heavy with the August crop. The air is full of the sweet, powerful smell of ripe fruit. The pumps echo like a pounding heart against the barn. They throb ceaselessly, like the drums at Ban Vinai.

"I walked out of Laos," Moua says, breaking his silence. "But when I go back it will be on a Boeing jet."

ACKNOWLEDGMENTS

I've been far luckier than many reporters in Asia when it comes to editors. Three, in particular, stand out: Dan Rosenheim of the *San Francisco Chronicle*, Sandy Close of Pacific News Service and Jeffrey Klein of the *San Jose Mercury News*. Without them, quite simply, there would have been no dispatches from the Pacific Century.

Sharon Silva was my companion and accomplice on many of the journeys described here. No words can do justice to the role she played in the materialization of this book.

I also owe a considerable debt to William German, Matt Wilson, Betty Kirkendall and Jack Breibart of the *Chronicle*; Franz Schurmann, Jon Stewart, and Peter Solomon of Pacific News Service; Margaret Scott and Ian Buruma at the *Far Eastern Economic Review*; Susan Brenneman and David Talbot of the *San Francisco Examiner*; Mark Powelson and Amy Rennert of *San Francisco Focus*; and Leonora Weiner of *Parenting* magazine. Much of *Dispatches from the Pacific Century* draws on my reporting for their publications over the past twelve years.

Erica Marcus, Lisa Chung, Matilda Young, Wigbert Figueras, Frank Browning, Kimun Lee, Maggie Gin and Bud McLeod contributed timely advice. Susan Johnson, a reporter who crossed the divide between newspaper journalism and books several years before I mustered the courage to do so, helped me to understand the changes in pace and concentration necessary to make such a leap.

In Bonnie Nadell, I have been blessed with America's hardest-working and toughest agent. She forced me to go back to the typewriter again and again, until there was no doubt in her mind that the proposal behind the book was sound. Then she sold it to an editor in three weeks.

That editor, to my great good fortune, was Elizabeth Perle of Addison-Wesley, who proved even tougher than Bonnie and every bit as supportive. Her staff, most notably production coordinator

Tiffany Cobb and copy editor Rachel Parks, smoothed out countless rough spots in the manuscript.

Finally, there are the sources of my dispatches, the men and women who are the editors in the drama of the Pacific Century's birth. In much of Asia, the phenomenal economic boom of the past twenty years has been built on a triumph of the Western-style free market that has not been accompanied by the extension of Western-style civil liberties. China is the most obvious example, but even in Asian societies that seem, on the surface, as democratic as those of America or Europe, citizens who attempt to speak freely often face dire consequences. For that reason, the names and identities of several characters in *Dispatches from the Pacific Century* have been altered.